D0992059

The Art of Being Free

CONTESTATIONS

A series edited by

WILLIAM E. CONNOLLY

A complete list of titles in the series appears at the end of the book.

The Art of Being Free

Taking Liberties with
Tocqueville, Marx, and Arendt

Mark Reinhardt

Cornell University Press

Ithaca and London

Copyright © 1997 by Cornell University

All rights reserved. Except for brief quotations in a review, this book, or parts
thereof, must not be reproduced in any form without permission in writing
from the publisher. For information, address Cornell University Press,
Sage House, 512 East State Street, Ithaca, New York 14850.

First published 1997 by Cornell University Press

Printed in the United States of America

⊚ The paper in this book meets the minimum requirements
of the American National Standard for Information Sciences —
Permanence of Paper for Printed Library Materials, ANSI Z39.48-1984.

Library of Congress Cataloging-in-Publication Data
Reinhardt, Mark.
The art of being free : taking liberties with Tocqueville, Marx, and Arendt / Mark Reinhardt.
    p.   cm. — (Contestations)
Includes bibliographical references and index.
ISBN 0-8014-3137-9 (cloth : alk. paper)
    1. Liberty.   2. Democracy.   3. Tocqueville, Alexis de, 1805-1859—Contributions in political
science.   4. Marx, Karl, 1818-1883—Contributions in political science.   5. Arendt,
Hannah—Contributions in political science.   I. Title.   II. Series.
JC585.R445   1997
323.44—dc21   96-46294

Cloth printing   10   9   8   7   6   5   4   3   2   1

For Molly

Nothing is more fertile in marvels than the art of being free, but nothing is harder than freedom's apprenticeship.

—Alexis de Tocqueville

Liberty is a practice.

—Michel Foucault

The Street finds its own uses for things—uses the manufacturers never imagined.

—William Gibson

Contents

Preface:
The Art of Being Free

Reading frees itself from the soil that determined it. . . . Emancipated from places, the reading body is freer in its movements. It thus transcribes in its attitudes every subject's ability to convert the text through reading and "run it" the way one runs traffic lights.

—Michel de Certeau

The way of theorizing pursued in these pages is informed by my work as a teacher. Since I began that work, much of my time has been given to teaching multiple versions of an introductory course in political theory. The course examines some of the concerns at the center of this book— freedom and equality, democracy and subjection, individuality and differ- ence, the places and practices of politics. I try to show why these topics matter, arguing that the American polity confronts them all the time, if not always in the most self-conscious, satisfying, or generous of ways. The course works, and I come to feel I am pursuing a calling as well as punch- ing a clock, only when this attempt to bring the world into the classroom succeeds. Political theory becomes worth doing when theories from the past speak to the present. Perhaps this is obvious. But it is a lesson I had to learn on the job. I learned it from the students in my very first class, and their instruction changed my way of both teaching and reading "ca- nonical" texts. This book bears the stamp of that instruction.

The lesson was burned into my memory in the fall of 1989. That season was remarkable for the political struggles that transformed the nations of Eastern and Central Europe, but I (also) recall it for my utter failure to engage students with the thought of Karl Marx. My course focused on a handful of "epic" theorists, taking them in chronological succession. It was late in the semester and well into those world-changing popular rebellions by the time we got to the works of the renowned theorist of revolution. My students were underwhelmed by the encounter. Their responses ranged from blank indifference to irritation. After all, wasn't every morning's headline a reminder that Marx's moment had passed, that his ideas had failed the test of time and experience? Why labor to make sense of such difficult writings? I responded to these questions like a scholar: I contextualized. Situating Marx in his time and place, reading him with and against the philosophical traditions he came out of, I tried to show what he had accomplished relative to his contemporaries and predecessors. As a pedagogical tactic, contextualization failed. Why *should* it have worked? The students were looking for someone relevant to their concerns. I eventually came to believe they were right.

Of course, one of the marks of a great text is that it can challenge readers' sense of what is relevant, unsettling certainties not only about prevailing answers but about what questions are worth asking. Powerful theories of the past instruct us by leading us out of the present. The most powerful of all, however, also lead us back to it. As they distance us from the positions offered in contemporary debates, they help us to scrutinize the very framework of agreement within which these debates take place. Their challenge to contemporary priorities begins from and, in the end, returns to questions that matter now. Or so I concluded in thinking about my time with those disgruntled students. Now, in my classes, texts from different eras and genres jostle against each other, arguing over questions and answers, problems and their definitions. Malcolm X questions Socrates. Aristotle meets Catharine MacKinnon. Tocqueville struggles with Foucault over problems of political subjectivity, while Marx interrogates the construction and elision of class identities in contemporary talk about "the economy," and Arendt converses with Toni Morrison about American narratives of belonging and freedom. Students still respond sometimes with puzzlement and irritation (as Socrates might ask, what worthwhile political pedagogy never irritates?). But they are rarely indifferent. The work they do in response to these staged encounters is often imperfect—which keeps me usefully employed—yet it brings me satisfaction by offering engaged thinking that is at once theoretical and political.

Usually, this thinking ignores certain scholarly proprieties. The theorists brought into dialogue are frequently people who could never have met. They would have found it difficult to talk to each other. They differ in conclusions and assumptions, in standards of argument and evidence, in the epistemic or ontological structures within which their claims are articulated. Bringing their works together, and bringing them to bear on the present, requires one to slip through these barriers to exchange: the nuances of context are forsaken in the attempt to pursue problems that matter. And so I encourage students to exercise a certain freedom in reading. In making use of the texts, they run a few traffic lights. Running lights is a dangerous business, of course; there are reasons for the rules of the road. I try to make students aware of the dangers and reasons, but I also let them know that there is both pleasure and opportunity in taking certain risks, at least if these are taken skillfully. As Certeau puts it, in words that helped inspire these reflections, "reading . . . introduces an 'art' which is anything but passive." [1] For those who are artful, there is room to move.

Tocqueville suggests that there is an "art of being free": freedom is a practice that requires study and skill. His analyses of political life look at the ways states and societies leave space or block opportunities for the exercise of this art. Can texts also foreclose or open such spaces? Might the arts of freedom and reading be connected? I believe they are. Democratizing textual authority is crucial to democratizing political authority, for effective political agency depends on the ability to interpret the signs that direct traffic through the polity and to inscribe one's signature upon the world. The connection is easiest to see in the classroom. There, to change reading practices is to change relations among students, relations that—in a limited way and in a special environment, to be sure—are necessarily political. Who talks, how they talk, and what they are willing and able to talk about are fundamentally shaped by a course's types and ways of reading. Encouraging the reading body to be freer in its movements promotes the kinds of relationships and conversations that make teaching worthwhile. Cultivating the art that Certeau calls "reading as poaching" makes it easier to learn something about the other arts of politics: this way of reading opens up questions about the practice of freedom even as it enables readers to experience that practice.

Thanks, in part, to the instruction provided by resistant students, this approach has filtered into my writing as well. I seek freedom in these pages, and the search is conducted in similar ways: there is much poaching in the chapters that follow, and they at times show a studied disregard for the red lights of scholarly caution. My themes are pursued through extended encounters with Tocqueville, Marx, and Arendt. The reasons for this selection will be explored more fully in Chapter 1. Let it suffice now to say that their rich works—which reveal much about the authority of texts and the textualization of authority—instruct us through their insights into the art of being free and their efforts to evade certain political questions. To get the most of my encounters with them, I try to extend the insights and expose the evasions through my own art of reading freely.

Although this book proceeds through a few intensive readings, its purpose is to address present predicaments in the theory and practice of freedom and democracy. The authors engaged speak powerfully and provocatively to us, across those barriers of time, beyond their immediate concerns, even against their own most explicit purposes and conclusions. To make the most of what they have to say, it is sometimes useful to emancipate the texts from their original places (it is not only the reading body that moves: as Edward Said reminds us, theory also travels).[2] At a time when—as we will see—the very notion of place is increasingly problematic, when the locations of politics are multiplying and the politics of location are unusually complex, confusing, and contested, this emancipation is called for as never before. Ours is a moment in which the best way to pay tribute to one's source of intellectual inspiration is, as Foucault once remarked of his own appropriation of Nietzsche's work, "to use it, deform it, make it groan and protest": in seeking to expand the contemporary practice of liberty, it is necessary to take liberties with the theories handed down from previous ages.[3]

This literary tactic of taking liberties is enabled by an approach that could be called "serious irony."[4] Though serious about the texts' achievements and limitations, it is ironic in its refusal to be governed entirely by them. While written under the tutelage of these authors and allied to some of their basic insights and commitments, it deploys them in arguments that differ willfully and at times perversely from the originals. There *is* an underlying faithfulness in my readings but they are, to borrow from Donna Haraway's discussion of irony, "perhaps more faithful as blasphemy is faithful, than as reverent worship and identification."[5] Irony is not a science or a method. In interpretation, as in politics, being free with others is—to say it again—a matter of art. That art is open, partial, for "nothing that is complete breathes."[6] If there is a "methodological" principle guiding this work, it is the deliberate avoidance of interpretive and theoretical systems. The chapters that follow are a series of exercises in thought, textual skirmishes in which the goal is the emancipation of particular insights that can be bent toward contemporary purposes. But if serious irony requires one to read against the grain, it is not ventriloquism: this approach neither presupposes nor sustains the conviction that any text always means anything one says it does. If that were true, there would be nothing to learn, no reason to undertake the patient and difficult work of reading, to engage the thought of *these* thinkers rather than others. I turn to Tocqueville, Marx, and Arendt because they have something important to teach (though the lessons we need from them now are not always the ones most valued by the authors or their previous readers), and that conviction is what sustains the interplay of criticism, approbation, and appropriation that is the main substance of the pages that follow. Those pages conduct a search for scraps—not whole cloth but fragments that, from book to book and theorist to theorist, can be stitched together into something different from what was intended by the original makers. As any number of writers have remarked since Lévi-Strauss made bricolage a celebrated trope, and as the great collective project of quilting to re-member lives lost to AIDS has shown with particular poignancy in recent years, finding a past that can speak to our time is work for political bricoleurs.[7] If, as Arendt argued some years ago, the threads tying us to "the Great Tradition" of political thought have long been irreparably broken, then we have nothing to lose by taking up the impure work of sampling: the bits and pieces from which we can invent a usable past will otherwise go to waste, or will get reified, fetishized, made the basis of nostalgic and ultimately doomed attempts to recover worlds gone by.[8] Why sanctify what is lost to us? Scholars of political thought have worshipped long enough; perhaps a bit of interpretive blasphemy can aid the work of freedom. After all, there are liberties to be taken.

MARK REINHARDT

Williamstown, Massachusetts

Acknowledgments

This book would not have been written if so many people had not given so much, so generously. A few years ago, Roger Haydon of Cornell University Press was gracious enough to sustain my confidence in my ability to write the book I wanted to write while telling me that the dissertation that I had submitted to him was far from that book. My dissertation committee members, Peter Euben, Bob Meister, Hanna Pitkin, and Jack Schaar—extraordinary readers and teachers, all—were all essential to the realization of this project, even as it grew into something that gives each of them grounds for quarrel and skepticism. I particularly thank Schaar for voicing the skepticism in his inimitable way, Pitkin for detailed written comments, and Euben for many hours of transcontinental conversations about each of the book's several stages. My debt to these teachers is beyond repayment. The same applies to my good friend and colleague Paige Baty, for without our years of conversation about the vocation of theory and the writing life—not to mention her encouragement and good, practical suggestions about particulars—this book would never have been completed. Williams College's Center for the Humanities and Social Sciences provided a congenial setting for a year of writing. All of my colleagues there also provided encouragement and stimulating conversations, but that and more were offered by Shawn Rosenheim and David Edwards, my informal but essential assistant professor, first-book support group. In the final year of this project, I was often sustained by the faith in my scholarship shown by my exemplary departmental colleagues, Raymond Baker, Sam Crane, Jim Mahon, and Alex Willingham.

On two crucial occasions, Allan and Judy Sher kindly provided a tranquil place to work with an ocean view. Jem Axelrod and Eric Zimmerman served as my transcontinental, on-line quote finders. Vicki Hsueh assisted ably and efficiently in proofreading and formatting the manuscript. Terry McKiernan ably demonstrated the editorial uses of the proverbial fine-tooth comb. Lisa Turner was a discriminating copy editor with a fine ear for prose. Linda Shearer and Stefanie Jandl were terrific guides to both the art of painting and the art of getting things for free. Tony Siracusa lent his ears at key moments and offered sage advice.

Particular chapters or aspects of the manuscript benefited from the responses of Stuart Clarke, Jeff Isaac, Michael MacDonald, Sandy Petrey, Jana Sawicki, Michael Shapiro, and Stephen Tifft. I'm at least equally obliged to my several years of conversations with my friends and fellow political theorists John Ely, Mehta Mendel-Reyes, Sophia Mihic, Melissa Orlie, and George Shulman (who commented astutely on Chapters 2 and 3). With interlocutors like these, a hotel crawling with political scientists becomes worth enduring for a few days every year.

Chris Rocco read every word of every draft of every chapter, and his enthusiasm and willingness to tell me what I needed to do were matched only by his eagerness for me to do the same for his book. I responded in kind and I suppose that makes us even, but I remain grateful. A late assessment of the whole manuscript by Bill Chaloupka was just what the doctor ordered. Earlier, Tom Dumm provided the best kind of reader's report—generous in its vision of my project and exacting in its assessment of how that vision was realized. I thank him for the ensuing intellectual exchanges it has enabled; the book, and my view of the field, are much the better for that. I do not know how to begin to thank William Connolly, whose editorial support and critical acumen have been simply extraordinary. His early interest in the project was sustained over more time and through more travails than he could possibly have bargained for. I'm glad he's thought so much about Job, since waiting for the manuscript's completion required something of that character's patience.

The various members of my family have had to do their share of forbearing, too. Thanks to Mary and Stan Lelewer and to Ramona Ripston and Stephen Reinhardt for providing essential hospitality in the final months of revision. Special thanks to my mother Mary Lelewer and my father Stephen Reinhardt for all of their kindnesses and tact. My in-laws, Jim and Robin Magavern endured much too, always with good cheer; they were often a great help. My grandfather, Gottfried Reinhardt, gave some crucial advice from his own writing experiences; I am grateful that he lived to see the book accepted for publication. I'm grateful, too, that the book's many intrusions into the life of my sons Simon and Max did not keep them from being inexhaustible (though sometimes exhausting) sources of wonder and joy. But the person who has most borne this book's disruptive effects is my wife, Molly Magavern. These she has endured with more grace than I deserve. I dedicate this work to her for that, for helping me to see that a book's only a book when it comes to an end, and for all that she brings to my life, week in and week out, year after year.

M. R.

The Art of Being Free

CHAPTER ONE

Introduction:
Making Space for Politics

There is not going to be the space to continue as we are or as we were.
— Bernice Johnson Reagon

When we discover in this world no earth or rock to stand or walk upon but only shifting sea and sky and wind, the mature response is not to lament the loss of fixity but to learn to sail.
— James Boyd White

Political Beginnings, Late-Modern States

This book begins from two perplexing ironies, and it is shaped by my understanding of the connections between them. The first irony is distinctive to the present. Democracy and freedom have attained an unprecedented global appeal as political ideals, yet their ability to encompass contemporary political experience grows increasingly uncertain: it is no longer clear that the institutional forms conventionally believed to embody these ideals are willing or able to perform the tasks expected of them, and the forms are often strained or distorted by the very forces that have aided the spread and legitimation of the ideals. I argue that this odd contemporary condition requires fresh reflection on the meaning and requirements of freedom and democracy, and my reflections lead me to advocate ways of opening new public spaces and cultivating practices of politicization. This argument leads into the terrain of the second irony, which is perennial: political theories designed to promote free public spaces and democratic political practices persistently undercut them as well. The tendency to subvert or flee from the very political goods being pursued can be found in the works of Alexis de Tocqueville, Karl

Marx, and Hannah Arendt, the theorists to whom I turn for assistance in thinking through the tasks of contemporary politicization. Although it appears to be narrower in scope and less significant in its consequences, the second irony illuminates the first. Tracing the ways in which theorists both foster and undercut projects of politicization helps us to understand the problems and opportunities peculiar to politics in the present, and to overcome some of the commitments and convictions that constrain democratic possibility today. The chapters that follow are thus largely given over to explorations of textual twistings and turnings, but the explorations take their bearings from my concern with much broader institutional and cultural dilemmas. Before proceeding to the works of the three theorists, then, it seems important to say a few words about the transformations and dislocations that mark the late-modern political condition.[1]

Consider some of the difficulties these changes pose to the theory and practice of democracy. As an aspiration or attribute of states, democracy is a modern invention. From its beginnings as a scandalous, subversive, even revolutionary idea, through the present moment of ostensible global appeal, the relationship between aspiration and attribution has been murky, marred by imperfections. Democracy has traditionally (if, as we will see, problematically) been theorized largely in terms of self-government: a democratic polity is one in which "the people" rule themselves. As skeptics have long enjoyed pointing out, and some American political scientists make careers demonstrating, it has never been very clear what it would mean for the people to rule in a large, complex, modern, nation-state or how that rule could be institutionalized in a fully satisfactory way: that popular self-government is a vexing and, at best, imperfectly realized idea is hardly news.[2] Yet under late-modern conditions, certain problems of self-government have, at the very least, intensified. While more people than ever pay lip service to the importance of citizen control of states through regular, contested elections, parliamentary governance, and the like, traditional notions of citizenship and governance seem increasingly ill-equipped to respond to the changes wrought by the economic, cultural, demographic, and technological flows of globalization.

Nowhere is this clearer than in the case of the state, which, in late-modernity, is caught up in a distinctive dialectic of power and powerlessness. Exercising unprecedented influence over the manner of birth and death and the quality of health and welfare, managing vast integrated "systems" of production and exchange, commanding complex networks of surveillance, information, and employees, extending inquiries and property into the nether regions of the solar system, and stockpiling weapons that can destroy the species, the contemporary state confronts the individual citizen as a force of staggering proportions and complexity: here is power as it has never been wielded before. Yet, at the same time, even the largest and wealthiest states often seem incapable of exercising the powers traditionally assigned to them by democratic theories. It is not just that the scale and scope of state institutions greatly exceed the limits that, according to classical democratic doctrine, must be observed if the citizenry is to exercise control, but that contemporary global conditions fundamentally constrain the ability of those institutions themselves to determine the national destiny.[3] This combination of power and powerlessness is easy to see; that the two ostensibly opposing conditions mutually reinforce each other is perhaps less evident.

To begin with one side of this dialectic of reinforcement, consider some of the forces that pose problems to the conventional understandings of the sovereign, democratic state. States today are confronted not only by economic institutions that transcend their borders and at times match or exceed their scale, but also by the unusual mobility and mutability of power itself. As Sheldon Wolin writes, the application of scientific knowledge and technological innovation has made late-modern power, at least in principle, "endlessly reproducible and . . . increasingly independent of civic virtue." Thus, with "a few oil wells, a few investors, a few technicians, it is possible to construct a nuclear device or finance revolution. . . . [This form of] imperialism tends to be nonterritorial, degrounded, projecting its influence throughout the world."[4] Nor are capital and technologically intensified power the only forces that scramble conventional notions of civic virtue and sovereign control as they cross territorial borders. As images, products, entertainment, and bodies migrate with increasing rapidity, identities—ethnic, national, civic—collide and mutate as well. Such circulation, too, is not altogether new, as this nation of immigrants presumably knows well. But both the character and effects of this circulation have changed as the relationships between state and nation, collective identity and geographic proximity have become more tenuous, and as those between originary homeland and current residence have grown more complex, entangled: as Arjun Appadurai writes of the ways in which the movement of peoples and cultures has changed the United States and its place in the global order in recent years, there is a "difference between being a land of immigrants and being one node in a postnational network of diasporas."[5]

What kind of sovereignty is exercised by a diasporic nodal point? Dense and elaborate global networks of finance and exchange, mobile and potent technologized powers, migrant populations and cultural formations, mutating identities—these significant features of late-modern life can confound and contain the state's capacities to exercise control. Yet it is often precisely in its responses to such global dislocations that states develop those powers that make them so formidable from the standpoint of specific populations. Many of states' harshest measures flow from their increasingly central role as institutions for the application of international economic pressures to domestic bodies politic; and attempts to secure control, stabilize boundaries, and regulate the character of population in a world of such profound flux fuel late-modern efforts to develop political technologies of surveillance and discipline. As Wolin suggests—analyzing a development that we can read as a response to globalizing pressures on both economic security and the integrity of territorially based sovereignty—contemporary welfare states increasingly come to *need* malleable "marginal" populations: "Marginalization is . . . a way of introducing variability: the marginalized groups become the 'stuff' of a form of state power that . . . finds itself increasingly deprived of flexibility by its own structure. . . . Welfare recipients signify a distinct category, the virtueless citizen. The virtueless citizen has no a priori claim not to be shaped in accordance with the rational requirements of state power."[6] At this pivotal moment in the political career of American welfarism, it is important to note that marginal populations can be made through both the extension and the retraction of state services. Either way, such calculated acts of making marginality involve the intensification of internal disciplines and the local application of systemic economic pressures, and these, in turn, set in motion the migrations and mutations that then limit the efficacy of states and confound conventional notions of citizenship.

Imagine the following scenario, for instance. Under the tutelage of the IMF and the pressures of international competition, Central American governments cut spending in the state sector and the support offered to the poorest segments of their populations. This spurs further emigration to the United States. As additional thousands arrive on the segregated and video-monitored streets of Los Angeles, that vast, diasporic megalopolis's Latino/a population, long a source of white anxiety and resentment, becomes a charged object in the rhetorical contests of gubernatorial candidates. Courting suburban white (and, to a degree, urban black) voters who have themselves suffered from economic dislocations originating in the global movement of money and production, and who seek specific bodies who can be held responsible for the attendant stresses and strains, the politicians compete to provide the most convincing proposals for fortifying borders, halting the flow of immigration, tracking down "illegal aliens," and ensuring that only those with the requisite credentials receive employment or social services. Even the half-hearted attempt to carry out these policies will require refinements of the apparatuses of surveillance and monitoring, further entanglements between the paths of individual lives and the powers and procedures of state.[7] And, no doubt, further shifts in population and money, and further challenges to sovereign power, result from these developments.

So things stand shortly after the "triumph" of "liberal, pluralist, capitalist, democracy" that has been trumpeted so widely since the end of the cold war.[8] Exerting immense disciplinary pressures on their citizenries, yet themselves pushed and pulled by forces substantially beyond their control, the institutions of the late-modern state raise unusually difficult questions about what democratic governance, at least that governance lodged in those state institutions, can mean. The late-modern conditions of which these institutions are one part also raise questions about the locations of politics, both because the loci of sovereign control in the contemporary global (dis)order are by no means unitary or easy to identify, and because the intrusions of disciplinary powers into the everyday life of individuals challenge the easy identification of the problem of democracy with the question of who is sovereign.[9] If democracy also means sharing in the production and exercise of power, then the scope for democratic inquiry and action extends well beyond the problem of electoral rule, and the questions of where, how, and when to practice democracy are in need of rethinking. At the very least, an inquiry into democracy sensitive to the transformations and interactions sketched above must pursue several further questions: What spaces are available for and appropriate to the exercise of democracy under late-modern conditions? What kinds of interactions and relationships mark that exercise? What kinds of civic identity and public life best serve democracy in a culturally complex, heterogeneous polity? Indeed, to return to the perplexity with which I began this chapter, what shall democracy and freedom *mean* under such conditions? In the following chapters, I will pursue these questions at length. Here, I suggest simply that none of the easy, ready-made answers offered by prevailing political theoretical traditions are adequate or satisfying, and no response is less useful than the triumphal assertion of certainties about "the West." Perhaps the least helpful of all such thoughtless certainties is the very conceit from which the triumphalist narrative begins—that "we" know what politics is and where it takes place. It is to resist this certainty, above all, that I turn to the work of Tocqueville, Marx, and Arendt.

Dangerous Ground: Thinking the Political

At a time when state institutions exercise uncertain and imperfect sovereign control while wielding formidable powers against individuals, sites for the direct practice of politics could not be more important. If we are witnessing both a contraction of officially sanctioned spaces for citizen action and an intensification of the forms of marginalizing and subjugating discipline, then it is crucial to identify ways of resisting disciplines and opening new spaces in both "legitimate" and hitherto forbidden locations. Tocqueville, Marx, and Arendt are not the only theorists who help us to think about these tasks, but they are exemplary sources for such thinking.[10] One reason they are particularly useful for my purposes is that their accounts of free political action and democratic practice do not limit us to state institutions. Taken together, their works push beyond state-centered frameworks through a twofold displacement of the conventional problematic of sovereignty. The first displacement, common to each thinker, is the identification of forms of rule that originate or operate outside of state channels, an identification that indicates that the struggle for self-government must be pursued along a far wider set of social, cultural, and economic pathways than are mapped by most theories of sovereign power. The second, and perhaps still more important, displacement occurs through the complex criticism of the paradigm of governance or rule itself. This displacement occurs most productively when the works are read in conversation with each other. From Marx, who repeatedly equates politics with class rule, through Tocqueville, who occupies an ambiguous and equivocal position, to Arendt, who often denies that rule has any part to play in genuine politics, these thinkers cover a broad spectrum of opinion on the centrality of the sovereignty problematic to thinking about the political. None of these thinkers handles the problem in a wholly satisfactory way, but if we draw upon the insights of all of them, and force them to interrogate each other across their contending positons, they help us to weaken and attenuate—without altogether breaking—the conceptual linkages through which the modern imagination has so often tied questions of sovereignty to those of freedom and democracy. The conversation among them enables us to see that either the simple reduction of the latter two terms to the first or the refusal to acknowledge the political centrality of the imperatives of rule makes it impossible adequately to rethink political prospects today.[11] By helping us both to understand and resist these conflations of state and politics, democracy and sovereignty, the theorists illuminate, in different ways, the multiple spaces and practices in and through which individuals and groups can help to constitute their lives, their selves, their worlds. They instruct us about where and how those spaces can be brought into being, and they help us to understand acts of making space as some of the prime moments of politics.

Because they facilitate our understanding of the spaces in which politics happens, Tocqueville, Marx, and Arendt can also be read in ways that help us resist what I take to be the other main barrier to an adequate contemporary theoretical engagement with democracy, the conflation of politics and community. Each of the thinkers is necessarily concerned with problems of political community, but none of them simply reduces the spaces of politics to those of community. While portions of their work—particularly in the case of Tocqueville and Marx—do conflate the terms, the works also offer much material that facilitates the struggle against this move. Of course, we must approach these writings warily even when they avoid the communitarian reduction of politics: the shifting forms and character of contemporary power, and the migrations and mutations that accompany the processes of globalization have brought the American polity (among others) a diversity that is not easily negotiated within the kinds of spaces envisioned by *any* work in the political theoretical canon. The attempt to limit politics to the sites established by earlier times or thinkers is at best unwise and at worst punitive, repressive. If the idea of political space is to be employed at all under contemporary conditions, spaces can no longer be understood as singular or unified, permanent or pure, as governed by unproblematic or incontestable codes of speech and action, admission and exclusion.[12] In the following chapters I show both where the spaces presented in the theorists' works fail to depart from those understandings, and how the texts enable us, if we are free with them, to conceive of such spaces in more imaginative and useful ways. Although none of the theorists, not even our near-contemporary Arendt, confronted the full challenge of late-modern dislocations, the differences between their concern and mine open an avenue for critical appropriations.

The most generative source of my appropriations, and thus my most fundamental reason for turning to these particular figures, is the complex and contradictory relationship to politics enacted in their works. Despite the fundamental differences among them, Tocqueville, Marx, and Arendt are all what (deliberately misusing a term of Richard Rorty's) might be called strong poets of the political: they valorize the places and practices of politicization, doing so not only through explicit commitments and arguments but through their way of writing theory. Their works are centrally preoccupied with exposing the common desire to abandon the dangerous—but also fertile and exhilarating—ground of politics: much of their writing shows how prevailing forms of thought and practice mask or evade political processes and possibilities, and each thinker presents these evasive tendencies as among the modern era's central threats to human freedom. But as I indicated above in sketching the ironies that prompt and preoccupy this book, Tocqueville, Marx, and Arendt also yield, at pivotal moments in their thinking, to this desire to evade the terrain of politics, and each yields precisely in order to establish the conceptions of political freedom or democracy he or she values. Tocqueville's commitment to preserving diverse forms of human being by cultivating the arts of politics leads him to depoliticize the moral and cultural foundations of democratic life in a way that ultimately homogenizes human relations. Marx's critique of exploitation and domination under liberalism and capitalism prompts his theorization of revolutionary struggles for emancipation, but his theories anchor revolution in structures of class and forces of history often presented as existing prior to political articulation, and he reads the liberating human relations constructed through political struggle as pointers toward a future free of struggle, politics, and—thus—much that he prizes most highly. In seeking to recuperate political space and action in an age she presents as hostile to them, Arendt purges them of much of their content, thereby removing some of the most important contemporary forms of power and conditions of experience from the reach of political criticism or negotiation.

My substantive chapters take up the question of why thinkers who have so much to say about the spaces and practices of politicization would depoliticize in the name of . . . politics. Although such paradoxes are common in political theory, it is crucial to my investigations that they mark the thought of even these strong poets of the political. The central object of each of my readings is thus to probe the relationship between the moments of politicization and those of flight, and to use this understanding to uncover insights that can be employed without thereby retaining the textual or conceptual strategies of evasion. Read artfully and with a will to use them for one's own purposes, the works of Tocqueville, Marx, and Arendt offer not only rich resources for reflection but also some of the tools necessary for taking apart their own specific forms of depoliticization: if the texts are not exactly self-deconstructing artifacts, they at least facilitate their own interrogation and transformation. By taking liberties, one can turn Tocqueville's accounts of the art of being free and tutelary power against his insistence on fissureless cultural foundations for democracy, Marx's remarkable rhetorical performances against his formal theoretical pronouncements about history and revolutionary agency, and Arendt's understanding of the mobility of political spaces and the agonistic character of action, and her critique of normalization against her tendency to empty politics of its content and fix the world through reifying dichotomies.

Each chapter focuses on specific writings that will facilitate such an ironic approach, employing whatever objects of analysis and ways of reading best suit the thinker in question: Chapters 2 and 3 explore the uses and limits of a single text, Tocqueville's *Democracy in America*, reading it in response to the gaps between the America he described and the America of the present; Chapter 4 takes up a handful of Marx's works, playing with the tensions between and within them in order to assess his writing (about) freedom; Chapter 5 confronts themes that run throughout Arendt's major writings, using the confrontation to find non-Arendtian uses and locations for spaces of—more or less—Arendtian politics. The last of these chapters concludes with a brief analysis of the unusually practical theory and inventively theoretical practice of the AIDS activist group, ACT UP. I read ACT UP as illustrative of an ironically Arendtian approach to political space and, indeed, as emblematic of political possibilities for which I argue in my treatment of each thinker. This final analysis is not a grand "synthesis" of all that precedes it (just as, for reasons I elaborate in Chapter 5, Arendt is not this book's "culminating" thinker in any sense that implies privilege or completion), but I end by engaging ACT UP because the engagement clarifies and exemplifies some of my most important claims about overcoming evasion and making space for politics.

Resisting the means by which the theoretical texts foreclose politics does not entail simply dismissing either these means or the concerns behind them. They are worth understanding because comparable techniques and concerns are at work in the world today, shaping many anxious cultural and institutional responses to the fraught ways in which diverse modes of life encounter each other within and across the boundaries of the democratic state. Furthermore, the theorists' concerns repay careful attention because of their intellectual seriousness: they are deeply considered responses to the dangers of political life, and any effort to invent and extend politicizing practices is strengthened by passing through such considerations. Attending respectfully to each thinker's depoliticizing moves expands the possibilities for learning from the conversation among the works. One valuable way to read Tocqueville's account of association against his attempt to secure democracy's foundations is to link that account to Marx's way of narrating political struggle. The politics recorded and enabled by Marx's narrative forms can, in turn, more effectively be used to overcome the limits of his explicit theorization of struggle if these forms are read with an eye toward Arendt's understanding of "enacted stories" of political identity and the spaces in which these performances appear. And Arendt's efforts to sustain political enactment are more easily protected from her purification of politics if they are approached with an appreciation for what Marx reveals about the ineliminable role of force in political contestation and what Tocqueville has to say about the more quotidian dimensions of democracy in action. Read with and against each other—and, at their best moments, taken individually as well—the works of these thinkers register tensions that enliven political theory and practice, tensions that call not for transcendence but for creative negotiation and an ability to live with contradiction. Thinking through these tensions, then, helps make space for politics by loosening the hold of traditional conceptual straitjackets, showing why the attempt to instantiate wholly conventional notions of freedom and democracy in this perplexing, late-modern time can only be disabling.

Political evasions, political tensions, political perplexities: the attentive reader will have noticed that "politics" has served as the central term in my discussion of these thinkers without yet receiving much clarification. Perhaps a few introductory words would be helpful. I think it crucial that an approach to politics highlight both the constitution, structuring, and exercise of power, and the making and hearing of claims about responsibility for such structures, powers, and actions. The former allows us—indeed requires us—to find politics in its diverse late-modern locations, which is often to say, as I have already argued, outside of the formal governing and electoral institutions that remain at the center of most political science. The latter enables us to understand that while politics can be anywhere, it is not necessarily being practiced everywhere at every moment. We can, then, recognize the blurriness and contestability of the boundaries of politics without insisting, categorically, that such boundaries are never possible or desirable. Out of this approach to the articulation of power and the contestability of boundaries, I treat politics as a shifting constellation involving, in various precarious balances and in complex relations of mutual constitution, the clash of contending interests, the pursuit of fundamental principles, and the creation of identities and differences. Each of these senses of the term is common in political theory, but they are often pursued exclusively. My readings of the three theorists show why it is often tempting to single out one or another of these meanings and how wholly excluding any of them necessarily closes important spaces of freedom and constrains democratic possibility. When I speak of "evasion," I refer to the effort to deny the connections among the terms or to hide the workings of at least one of these dimensions of a practice, relationship, or institution.

That is my point of departure, but it is not, of course, anything like a definition. It might seem only reasonable that a work of reflection on the production and evasion of the political begin with a simple, comprehensive, and declarative sentence about what politics "is," founding all subsequent work on that declaration. But though the following chapters explore the interrelations among "politics," "democracy," and "freedom," I do not think that a more methodical laying out of terms now will advance my task. The political is best thought as an activity, not as an object that can be fixed and put on display, once and for all. Only through their complex and heterogeneous uses in texts and struggles are the basic terms of political discourse — "politics" no less than others — brought into existence and given a meaning: as James Boyd White observes, it is the work of political rhetoric to "create the objects of its persuasion." [13] I have chosen my texts and my way of approaching them in order to explore the processes of creation. The *activity* of thinking the political is central to the writings of Tocqueville, Marx, and Arendt, and it is by following the unfolding of this activity — thereby noting its insights and blindness, confrontations and evasions, coherence and incoherences — and by putting my central terms to work that I hope to produce, through my own activities of inquiry and tactical appropriation, a richer vision of politics.

A richer vision: my goal is neither more nor less than this. Though this book is motivated by the global perplexities with which I began, it is not, by any means, an *answer* to them, a "solution" to our political riddles. To a large degree, the problems are practical and can only be confronted through political action: we can only find our way, haltingly, through trial and error, struggle and reconciliation. No work of theory can decisively resolve such worldly problems in a way that avoids the hard practical work. To think otherwise is to try to escape the dangerous ground of politics. But there is still work for theory to do, because the contemporary problems of freedom and equality, difference and commonality, public spaces and their disciplinary closure, are rooted in political imaginaries in need of enrichment. Even from the most narrowly practical standpoint, how we think and talk about these problems — how we frame or identify them — *matters.* Struggle over the shape of the political imaginary is among the key activities of democratic politics. [14] My goal in the textual exercises that follow is to push at the edges of prevailing imaginations, to expand and complicate what we take democracy and freedom to mean in ways that are responsive to the institutional transformations of late-modernity.

There's No Place Like Home: "Community" and the Politics of Nostalgia

To respond to these transformations is not necessarily to resent them or wish them away. One need not believe that we live at the end of history, or that history is simply the forward march of progress, to conclude that there is no going back. The sad and intimidating truth is that there is no golden age for which late-modern democrats can yearn. History offers us rich resources for reflection but little direct guidance: the past may serve as a storehouse of provocative examples, a repository of "thought fragments" that can be wrested "into the world of the living,"[15] but it is not our destination or even an accurate road-map. Without relentless attention to the inability of past spaces to encompass the contemporary dilemmas of democratizing difference, the return to the three theorists is likely to be an exercise in nostalgia. In order to avoid undertaking such an exercise, I conclude this introduction with a broad engagement with the discourse of "communitarianism."

Over the past two decades or so, this discourse has provided the most prominent political theoretical idiom for articulating the call to rethink public life and the demands of freedom. Communitarian literature is instructive because it reveals what it would mean to embrace the most evasive moments in the work of Tocqueville, Marx, and Arendt. It is not that Tocqueville, Marx, and Arendt are always the inspirations for such depoliticizing moves—though communitarian writers do at times invoke the authority of one or another of these authors, particularly Tocqueville—but that the most problematical evasions I find in the texts of the three theorists recur repeatedly in this pervasive contemporary response to our condition. Communitarianism thus offers an ideal introduction to pitfalls that my readings expose and avoid in the chapters that follow, while serving as a reminder that these pitfalls lie in wait not just in this or that academic text but in the polity's broader discourses of program and policy.[16]

By "communitarians," I mean such writers as Charles Taylor, Michael Sandel, Alasdair MacIntyre, Robert Bellah and his colleagues, and the writers gathered around Amitai Etzioni's journal *The Responsive Community*.[17] Like any theoretical school, these thinkers are a diverse lot; they differ over a number of important issues of politics and theory.[18] Some of these authors, particularly Taylor, have produced work of great subtlety and power. My brief characterization will necessarily smooth over the differences and ignore the subtle depths. Creating a broad and composite portrait, I run the risk of misrepresentation. But the point here is not to offer a decisive refutation of the communitarian *oeuvre*, just to use a few general critical remarks to sketch the kinds of argumentative moves that will be interrogated and resisted in my subsequent chapters. My comments are less a position within the "liberal-communitarian debate" that has consumed so much of Anglo-American academic political theory since the mid-1970s than an introduction to my subsequent attempt to avoid the debate's problems. I doubt there is much more to be said within its terms, which have by now hardened into slogans and which, all along, have tended to pit reified and overly abstract notions of community and individuality against each other.[19] In criticizing communitarianism, I am thus not casting this book as a "liberal" answer, and nor am I seeking some kind of middle ground between the poles. Despite the intensity of the disputes, the contending positions are as problematic for what they share as for what distinguishes them. In the following chapters, I attempt to offer a political alternative, moving through (some of) the same terrain while following a different course. As a first intimation of that direction, though, let us take a closer look at the communitarian route that has been so well-traveled in recent years.

The central claim of communitarian thinkers is that the contemporary "advanced" nations in general, and American society in particular, are plagued by the loss of community. As Amitai Etzioni puts it in his recent manifesto for the official communitarian movement, "Our society is suffering from a severe case of deficient we-ness and the values that only communities can properly uphold."[20] In most portraits of this communal deficit, the loss appears to be both experiential and intellectual. What too many Americans experience, on the communitarian account, is a fragmented and alienated world in which social ties are loose, the sense of belonging is severely attenuated, and individuals are too given over to the desperate and ultimately unfulfilling pursuit of private self-interest. As a result, the individual self is now more isolated, impoverished, and weak than it was at other moments, under other social conditions. But few communitarian writings represent American life as a uniform experience of quiet desperation or mindless striving for gain. In general, they tend to find many shards or pockets of community across the cultural landscape and along the life-paths of most citizens. Here is where communitarians point to our intellectual deficit, arguing that our actual experiences of genuine community are obscured or misrepresented by our inherited, liberal-individualist ways of thinking and talking about self and society. Because the individual is seen simply as a self-sufficient, self-maximizing, rights-bearing creature, we too often deny the important sustenance that community, in fact, offers all of us. The result is both a general withering of responsibility and a failure to think about how our remnants of community could be knitted together into a tighter, more healing and coherent whole.

In sum, the communitarian reading of the late-modern political condition is (sometimes frankly) nostalgic: it plots American or Western history as a story of loss, a loss of commonality, a loss of immediacy, a loss of harmony, all of which add up to a loss of belonging and home. This invocation of home and wholeness rests upon or deploys two noteworthy conceptual moves. The most important is essentially ontological: communitarian thought, whether it acknowledges it or not, is a teleological approach to human being.[21] Communitarian argument starts with the incontestable observation that all individuals are products of—are given form by and build relationships within—communities, and proceeds to the highly problematic conviction that it is possible to create social forms in which all individual selves are fundamentally whole and attuned. The forging of greater social solidarity, the revival of a shared notion of the common good, is presented as the remedy for individual wounds and disaffections. Making society whole again will fill the painful holes in individual existence.

The second, explanatory, move follows from the first. Since human communities can offer wholeness and integration, there must be a factor or factors that account for our actual experience of alienation. Our failure to live up to our ontologically given possibilities for togetherness is not only explicable but correctable. The explanations can be materialist or intellectualist, though the latter tend to be more developed and insistent. The materialist explanation blames the structural and institutional transformations of modern society for destroying the fabric of commonality. The idealist explanation treats liberal and Enlightenment thought, and American individualist ideology, as causal agents of decline.[22] Communitarians argue among themselves about the relationship between these two explanations—is late-modern institutional life the product of bad individualist ideology, or does the ideology simply sanctify underlying institutional changes?—but the underlying premise is the same: we suffer from *surplus diversity.* Whatever its source, the proliferation of differences has blinded us to the need for and possibilities of an overarching common good.[23]

The diagnosis suggests the cure: only by rediscovering a language of commonality and the good can we redress our problems of alienation and fragmentation. It is here that the idealist element predominates, for communitarian suggestions about how to counteract the fragmenting drift of late modernity tend to stay in the realm of exhortation. What is needed is what Etzioni and *The Responsive Community* repeatedly characterize as a "moral revival," a return to an understanding of our foundational values and our common fate. If we would simply agree to seek the common good together, the first and most important step in the restoration of belonging will have been taken.

Although this broad sketch may not do justice to either the philosophical rigor of the best communitarian arguments or the range of differences among them, it is sufficient for my purpose of marking the problems that a late-modern democratic appropriation of earlier thinkers must strive to understand and avoid. The first such problem is what might be called the teleological homogenization of moral space. The certainty that fragmentation is our problem leads to an argument about the "common good" in which each of the two terms is handled with dangerous simplicity. The forging of the "common" is treated as if it were without cost, and the idea that political contests must be over the good is assumed to be unproblematic. The ultimate culprit here is the assumption that individual selves will be most fully developed through their harmonious assimilation into a comprehensive and integrated moral order. The dissonances and disciplines which this integration entails (e.g., the—inequitably distributed— costs exacted when political desires and discourses must be channeled through a rhetoric of the common or the good) are passed over in silence or dismissed as minor troubles.

This moralized homogeneity thereby produces an evasion of politics that is, secondly, fortified by using the language of wholeness and belonging to obscure the question of power. The masking of power is subtle: after all, most communitarian writers insist that communities must now be more egalitarian than the hierarchies of old, that belonging should not mean subordination. But the focus on "community," as such, tends to displace the issue of political space and political practice. Or, more subtly still, those communitarians (Taylor and Sandel, for example) who *do* call for a revival of democratic political spaces, patrol the borders of those spaces in such a way as to remove the most crucial and explosive questions about political identity and agency. By presupposing that the end is the creation of a common culture in which all are formed, by characterizing a contest over the common good in which all must participate, they obscure the politics of hegemony, the play of powers in which interests, identities, and differences are not simply hierarchically structured but *produced*. How selves are to be formed, which forms of selfhood are to be privileged, what cultural foundations produce which patterns of subjugation—these central problems of late-modern democratic politics are systematically elided in the communitarian vision. Communitarianism thus serves as a kind of lens for filtering out precisely those matters that call for rethinking. Like those who have sighted the end of history in the passing of the cold war, the communitarians essentially think that the past has already answered our problems. While mournful communitarian stories of loss seem diametrically opposed to the triumphalist celebrations, and while the best of the former are considerably more theoretically sophisticated and politically generous than any of the latter, both camps are united in their flight from the present.

It can be misleading, however, to characterize communitarianism as an "evasion" of politics. There is never really the kind of escape that this term may imply. As I show in my examination of the works of Tocqueville, Marx, and Arendt, moments of political evasion are also moments in which politics is carried on by other means, under other names—which is to say that they are the most insidious of all political moves. The communitarian refusal to think through all of the complexities and perplexities of constructing a commons and debating a good fosters a reactionary politics of inequitable exclusion and disciplinary inclusion. Because our heterogeneity is cast as surplus difference, because the lack of a unified moral language is portrayed as a correctable deficit, communitarian arguments necessarily portray the citizenry as in need of improvement and reformation. The communitarian argument is thus—despite the celebrations of the virtues of daily community life that are common in this literature—necessarily hostile to the texture of everyday moral and political experience in the contemporary world, and incapable of acknowledging the politics of its own positioning and production of subjects.

Even the most elegant and philosophical works, such as Taylor's, display a disdain for the structures of contemporary subjectivity—for it is these structures that are partly responsible for our plight, and it is these structures that must be refashioned if we are to be whole again.[24] But this resentful politics, and its costs—and, hence, the connection between my book's two motivating ironies—come out most clearly in the less philosophical, more popular, policy-oriented communitarian texts. *The Responsive Community* is filled with angry denunciations of the excessively libertine character of contemporary citizens, laws, and arguments. Teenage pregnancy, AIDS, and abortion rates, for example, are all seen as symptoms of the moral failure to imagine community in a sufficiently harmonious and responsible way. The journal recommends various disciplinary policies—for instance, drug testing and constraints on divorce—to restore the needed sense of obligation and belonging.[25] Responsibility must be assumed by those recalcitrant individuals and social groups who currently refuse to accept it; and if they will not do so voluntarily, they will be gently, or not so gently, drawn back into the fold. The work of community-building is endless, and it seems to allow little scope for democratizing the experience of power amidst the changes which occasion so much communitarian resentment.

The impulses at work in these policies—the attempt to overcome individual alienation through the construction of an integrative harmony, the underwriting of such attempts through the employment of moralized teleologies, and the denial of the political play of power or force that attends such impositions—course through the writings of Tocqueville, Marx, and Arendt as well. The writings are shaped by strong countervailing impulses, too, but the possibility of falling into nostalgia or obscuring the workings of contemporary discipline confronts any attempt to read them for affirmative instruction. My readings identify and try to avoid these traps, and my argument is that the traps *are* avoidable. As the richest reflections of Tocqueville, Marx, and Arendt show, the search for practices and spaces of politicization need not rest on the communitarian foundations described above and should not be construed as authorizing a project of combating "excessive" individuality and difference. I read their works for ways of understanding that the cultivation of such practices and spaces is, indeed, one crucial strategy for sustaining resilient selfhood and allowing differences to proliferate—and my concluding examination of ACT UP exemplifies this point. ACT UP used many of the very contemporary forces lamented by communitarian thinkers (for instance the communications technologies and discursive codes of commercialized mass media) to introduce alternative forms and places of publicity, and one of the central projects thereby carried out was the disruption of homogenizing notions of the nation's imagined community and "the general public."[26] An encounter with ACT UP sheds an illuminating critical light on laments about "our" deficit of "we-ness." This encounter is, then, the final moment in my argument about how to resist the techniques and institutions that have undermined both common action *and* resistance to the common. The contemporary multiplication and intensification of disciplines has made it more difficult for citizens to engage in the activities that develop the skills needed for confident challenges or the articulation of alternative forms of life. Along with some communitarian critics, I will talk about how these skills can be cultivated by all of us and distributed more evenly across the population. But to argue that the art of being free needs greater attention in our time is neither to bemoan the loss of a more adequate community nor to set up some prior moment as a lost golden age.

Though I read each theorist against the nostalgic search for unproblematic moral foundations, my aim is *not* to peel away layers of communitarian misinterpretation in order to produce a more authentic account. Authenticity—if such a thing were possible—would not be adequate to my task. Because my readings appropriate usable thoughts and expose paradigmatic limitations, my purposes in each chapter ultimately diverge from those of the theorist in question: it is out of the desire to think the contemporary problems of politics and freedom that I have turned to the tactic of taking liberties. A thoroughly serious irony can wrest insights from texts that otherwise might fuel communitarian resentment. Even this way of reading has its risks, but there are still compelling reasons to undertake a knowingly inauthentic salvage operation. Though this time is not the end of history, it has seen the unraveling of political and theoretical traditions, and so—to reiterate—late-moderns have no single, coherent, stable, inherited way of making adequate sense of our dilemmas of democracy and public life. Under such conditions, it is better to appropriate scraps than to try to restore the systems and contexts of a vanished world, and better, too, to recombine valuable fragments than simply to turn one's back on *all* the resources of the past.

When all that is said, however, an important question lingers on: is it even *possible*, anymore, to speak of democratic public spaces without invoking a past imagined not only as more secure and stable, but also as more "truly" political and free? It may be that the very language of freedom and democracy, politicization and depoliticization, space and publicity, contains an irreducible element of nostalgia today. Even if that were so, of course, one might wonder whether that is really something to be feared. After all, at its root, "nostalgia" simply means a longing for home.[27] Surely that is a longing most of us feel, at least some of the time. And why not? Who could deny that, for all too many people, late-modern life provides far too little in the way of comfort, security, or sense of place? In such a moment, what could be wrong with the wish to be at home in the world?

Could it be that, in this sense of the word, nostalgia is not only an un-avoidable sentiment but a salutary one? Perhaps. But all too often, as the communitarians' writings show, nostalgic theories of belonging demand severe sacrifices in exchange for the comforts of home: the ties of community that are prescribed as a remedy for the problems of fragmentation and rootlessness are too constricting for the conditions in which we must now live. While these theories offer warmth and shelter to some bodies, others are cast outside into the cold of night. Even inside, by the fire, the proprieties and propinquities of home exact psychic and political costs; outside very different and more obviously destructive fires rage. Ours is, as Homi Bhabha writes (invoking Arendt even as he resists and rewrites her), a time of "unhomeliness," of "displacement," an "in-between moment" in which "the borders between home and world become confused and, uncannily, the private and the public become part of each other, forcing upon us a vision that is as divided as it is disorienting."[28] In the era of displacement, the cultivation of (less pure, more heterogeneous, and widely scattered) political spaces is not a nostalgic goal but a vital part of the struggle for a free and democratic future. Unhomeliness is a dangerous condition, but it is the unavoidable predicament of all present and (currently foreseeable) future politics—and, anyway, as Foucault once remarked, "everything is dangerous."

Everything is dangerous: that thought should hover, in all its somber intensity, over any reflection on the extension of democracy and the proliferation of political spaces. As I argue in subsequent chapters, even the most radically democratic transformation of political power and practices necessarily exacts costs and produces subjugation. The desire to evade or deny these costs, perhaps the most insidious form of nostalgia, is a constant temptation for democratic thinking. But to note the inevitable persistence of this temptation is not to say that the pursuit of democracy must necessarily give in to the yearning to relive an imagined past or to construct a homogeneous moral landscape. Nor should awareness of the inevitable risks of thought and struggle disable the democratic enterprise: as Foucault himself insisted, if everything is dangerous then there is certainly no point in fleeing the dangerous ground of politics.[29] There is no safe place to go.

CHAPTER TWO

Disturbing *Democracy:* Reading (in) the Gaps between Tocqueville's America and Ours

By the enjoyment of a dangerous liberty, the Americans learn the art of rendering the dangers of freedom less formidable.

I admit that I saw in America more than America; it was the shape of democracy itself which I sought, its inclinations, character, prejudices and passions; I wanted to understand it so as at least to know what we have to fear or hope therefrom.

—Alexis de Tocqueville

Disturbing *Democracy*

Some books are known too well. Widely cited, often discussed, they disappear behind a wall of commentary. The more that is written about them, the less they seem to offer. As interpretations settle into well-worn grooves, reading such a book becomes almost unnecessary: its power to provoke is lost because we have already encountered its "message" over and over again. *Democracy in America* may be one of these books. The serious student of politics can scarcely avoid crossing its path, for it has been a staple of scholarly discussion in this country for generations. Through its repeated appearances in academic and journalistic examinations of American institutions and culture, it has been granted an authority matched by few other commentaries. Tocqueville's work has thus acquired all the comforts of familiarity. Though accounts of his teachings vary widely, they tend to rest easily within the political categories of the day. Whether offered as celebrations of the status quo or in the service of political critique, whether viewing Tocqueville as an optimist or a pessimist, whether classifying him as an aristocratic conservative, a paradigmatic nineteenth-century liberal, or a republican alternative to liberalism, these readings leave established ways of understanding the identity of America and the meaning of freedom and democracy largely undisturbed. In these accounts, Tocqueville emerges as an historically significant thinker who can—possibly—still inform political observations, but not as one who undermines established certainties about what politics is and where it takes place.[1]

How could it be otherwise, now? What could we who live at the edge of the twenty-first century and in the twilight of modernity still learn from Tocqueville's discussion of an America that seems ever more remote from ours? How could that discussion prompt fresh thought about our time, our world, our own political dilemmas? At this late date, the reassuring but unchallenging familiarity of Tocqueville's work, the sense that it tells us what we already know, can seem inevitable. But it may be possible to escape the familiar pattern, to turn the work toward other ends: perhaps *Democracy in America* can continue to provoke those open to provocation. Perhaps this text is more powerful when given less authority. That is the possibility the following two chapters pursue. They attempt, in passing, to unsettle familiar readings of Tocqueville and, more directly, to read him as an unsettling thinker. In short, they aim to disturb. A disturbing reading of *Democracy in America* might put uncomfortable questions to established interpretations of contemporary American democracy.[2]

Such a reading must begin with the recognition that democracy itself is disturbing.[3] To disturb means, among other things, "to break up the quiet or settled order of" and "to make uneasy."[4] Democracy's distinctive and potentially powerful ways of breaking up order can make people—whether they are its participants or observers, friends or foes—uneasy. As it circulates through theories of democracy, this unease prompts the development of strategies for containing or channeling the democratic impulse, for ensuring that "settled order" is not disturbed *too* much. Of course, any polity needs a great deal of order, but against that need sympathetic theories of democracy must weigh the need for creative disturbance: they must articulate distinctively *democratic* forms of (dis)order. Democratic theorists tend to respond to this task, one of the most fundamental challenges of modern politics, with ambivalence. In their works, both order and disturbance become complex objects of attraction and repulsion, longing and fear.

Tocqueville was certainly ambivalent in his thinking about the kind of order democracy requires, and one might say that *Democracy* responds to that ambivalence by institutionalizing disturbance. To institutionalize means means both to establish and to confine. *Democracy* employs each form of institutionalization at different moments (when it does not make use of both at once).[5] This internal conflict is part of a broader pattern, for *Democracy* is a profoundly ambivalent book. It is ambivalent about the consequences of democratization. It is ambivalent, and hence ambiguous, about what "democracy" is, about what phenomena or conditions the term should designate. It is ambivalent about America, modernity, equality, the state—perhaps all of its central subjects, including even freedom. Riven with competing impulses, *Democracy* is a work of many moods, by turns dire, somber, hopeful, celebratory. Often, it hovers anxiously between these extremes, seeing contradictory possibilities, sensing both limitations and virtues in nearly every condition it considers.

This ambivalence—this disturbed quality—could be taken as a mark of *Democracy*'s failure to achieve coherence or closure. I will treat it as an important resource, an enabling condition of disturbing readings. *Democracy*'s fissures and fractures provide an opening for hermeneutic poachers, a point of entry for those willing to take liberties with the text. Open a crack, apply leverage, and an argument can be dislodged from its place and put to different, more contemporary purposes. Turn a portion of the argument against the whole, and *Democracy* provides a critique of itself. Read *Democracy* against itself, and it becomes possible to read it against the settled order of received interpretation: dissident voices (to switch metaphors) can thus be amplified and made to speak against the comforting and stabilizing roles Tocqueville so often plays for us.

But isn't this is the oldest trick (played) on the book? American readers have *always* tried to make *Democracy* speak to the present, to incorporate it into their own projects. Roger Boesche opens his recent monograph on Tocqueville with an indictment of this very tendency: "Too many people," he complains, "call Tocqueville's ideas their own."[6] Because Tocqueville "straddled political categories and hence embraced ideas found in almost all of them," readers find it easy to fortify their own arguments with selective citations from his texts. The persistent tendency to "claim him as an ally" does violence to the difference between Tocqueville's conceptual framework and those of later times. Read anachronistically, Tocqueville is misunderstood and thereby diminished: the only way to cut through the distortions and recognize the nuances of Tocqueville's thought is to "immerse ourselves in *his* century."[7]

Boesche's warning about the danger of denying Tocqueville's breadth and complexity is important, and historical research is one way of diminishing that danger. Yet historicism is hardly the *only* way to wring complex meanings from a text. Anachronism need not bring amnesia, and to focus on disturbing democracy is not to make Tocqueville himself a partisan in today's struggles. If the aim is to avoid assimilating *Democracy* into comforting political categories, irony offers protections of its own. Refuse to be limited to the search for the true author, the authentic intention, and there is no need to construct a monolithic Tocqueville who stands solidly in your camp. It becomes possible to appropriate and extend his analyses while explicitly struggling against some of his deepest commitments. In my reading, *Democracy*'s internal tensions are more than tools for lifting the useful quote, the friendly argument (though they are that, too): tension is territory for exploration, ambivalence an avenue to insight. Nothing about *Democracy* is as instructive as its way of alternating between the containment, evasion, and promotion of democratic disturbance. I will chart these alternations and seek their sources, using the search both as a way of establishing my own distance from Tocqueville's commitments and as an opportunity to take liberties with particular arguments. This way of being free with Tocqueville might scandalize the historicist, but it nonetheless differs from the type of interpretation criticized by Boesche. The differences, and their political stakes, can be clarified further by pausing briefly on some of the more striking features of *Democracy*'s map of American conditions.

Reading the Maps, Reading (in) the Gaps

Democracy's map? Where can it be found? Not on any single page, for the book contains no charts or graphs, no tables or sketches—no illustrations at all. But a written text can itself be a kind of map, and *Democracy* is such a text. Its theoretical enterprise is essentially cartographic: Tocqueville's intention is to orient his readers, to guide them through unfamiliar conditions, and *Democracy* has always been read for its ability to find order in and avenues through the confusing terrain of American political life. The language of cartography draws attention to that original intention and subsequent interpretive tradition, but speaking of maps also emphasizes Tocqueville's acts of world-making, his (con)figuring of America and democracy. The nation and political formation he investigates are not simply found objects, but things he helps to constitute. (*Democracy* is thus a constitutional text in more than one sense.) Maps orient their users for particular reasons and view their territories from particular perspectives, constructing landscapes even as they describe them. These constructions are intrinsically political artifacts: cartography is never aimless or innocent.[8]

Tocqueville's cartography is an attempt to comprehend a world in transition. If democracy is remaking the modern social, cultural, and political landscape, *Democracy* will chart those changes. The book scans the social and political topography of America in order to reveal processes that are also—though more slowly, less visibly, and in different ways—changing the contours of European nations. The most significant feature, the most profound force of change, is singled out in the first sentence: "No novelty in the United States struck me more vividly during my stay there than the equality of conditions."[9] Tocqueville goes on to map a world in which the broadening and deepening of equality is the fundamental movement of modernity. The United States is figured as the forward point of that movement and hence a privileged site for the rethinking of politics that the new era requires.[10] Two brief references are enough to sketch some of the map's main outlines:

> It is hard to explain the place filled by political concerns in the life of an American. To take a hand in the government of society and to talk about it is his most important business and, so to say, the only pleasure he knows. . . . If an American should be reduced to occupying himself with his own affairs, at that moment half his existence would be snatched away from him; he would feel it as a vast void in his life and become incredibly unhappy.[11]

> In the United States there is no religious hatred because religion is universally respected and no sect is predominant; there is no class hatred because the people is everything and nobody dares to struggle against it; and finally, there is no public distress to exploit because the physical state of the country offers such an immense scope to industry that man has only to be left to himself to work marvels.[12]

The pervasiveness of political commitment and the gentleness of social antagonisms are points to which *Democracy* returns repeatedly. Each return sharpens the contrast between the Old and New worlds: compared to European societies, America is a land of harmonious, egalitarian activity. Lacking an entrenched aristocracy, Americans have been spared the difficult and dangerous problem of dismantling age-old structures of privilege and deprivation. While substantial social differences persist, they are shifting and surpassable: there is always room to move or a chance to change one's fortunes. Where cultural cleavages continue, they rest on a solid bedrock of agreement. Historically free from both permanent inequalities and unbridgeable differences, the new nation has been able to become the land of dynamic democratic citizenship. Americans have developed unparalleled spaces for the acquisition of political skills and the exercise of self-government; citizens can thus share in political life to an extent and with an enthusiasm unmatched anywhere else.

This quick sketch of Tocqueville's complex account borders on caricature, exaggerating obvious features while failing to reproduce the nuances and shadows that are so much a part of his work. Yet, as is sometimes the case with caricatures, these exaggerated strokes reveal something important about the character of their subject. Though the idealization of the egalitarian and democratic dimensions of American life is only one tendency within an ambivalent text, it has been a profoundly influential tendency. Emphasizing that tendency magnifies the differences between Tocqueville's America and ours, thereby, and perhaps paradoxically, highlighting the very qualities that have proved important to many subsequent cartographers: the absence of entrenched hierarchy and the breadth of participation have served as primary interpretive axes, providing the main coordinates for much Tocquevillian thinking about later Americas.

These coordinates establish a field of navigations, of possible interpretive strategies. Within this field, there is room for substantial political differences. For example, to concentrate largely on the absence of entrenched feudal hierarchy, as have historians in the school of "American exceptionalism," establishes political concerns different from those that emerge from a focus on the institutions and activities of early American self-government.[13] Within each of these orientations, there can be further differences of principle and commitment. Rather than surveying this entire political field, I will turn briefly to the approach most relevant to my own argument, to work that uses Tocqueville's map to orient fundamental criticism of the condition of democracy in our own time. A number of recent and contemporary democratic theorists have developed criticism of this sort, using Tocqueville himself, or Tocquevillian coordinates, to argue that this century has been marked by the weakening of democratic practices and the at least partial disappearance of democratic public spaces. The best of these works offer powerful ideals and indictments, and much of that power comes from their appeals to a time when democracy was more vibrant, more meaningful.[14] These appeals show how Tocqueville's map, and particularly its participatory axis, remains politically useful even though—or because—it charts a world so different from ours. But arguments based on evocations of democracy's allegedly happier past also reveal the pitfalls that typically lie in wait for those seeking solace and guidance from *Democracy*. These pitfalls are most evident in a work of criticism with particularly strong and explicit debts to Tocqueville, Robert Bellah et al.'s *Habits of the Heart*. With this work, we see how the general problems of communitarian nostalgia are given a specifically Tocquevillian inflection and authorization.

A best-selling sociological analysis of "Individualism and Commitment in American Life," *Habits* argues that this country now suffers from both a decline of democratic institutions and the loss of a common moral vocabulary, a shared political language. Taking Tocqueville's America as the standard of civic health, the authors present the subsequent transformation of the polity as a fall story. That narrative allows them to acquire critical distance on present institutions, thereby authorizing a call for political renewal and the construction of a more active civic life, but it also enacts a politics of resentment and exclusion. Despite periodic acknowledgements that the enforced cultural and moral homogeneity of an earlier era cannot serve the cause of democracy in today's heterogeneous nation, *Habits* imposes a tight, oppressive grid on the contemporary cultural landscape: the profiles of American lives are drawn from a narrow (white and middle class) spectrum, and the range of lives and political subjectivities that the authors deem legitimate or desirable is far narrower still. Though the authors understand themselves to be offering an invitation to collaborative action for affirmative ends, a disapproving moral teleology inheres in the text's rhetoric, in the type of tale it tells. The story demands a redemptive return to older ways, a replication of Tocqueville's America, and this demand can only be a met by violently denying how we now live — or, more accurately, by constructing an American "we" that necessarily subordinates or disciplines large sections of the populace. As Michael Shapiro observes of the interviews and profiles that run throughout the book, "no voices contend in *Habits*. Each individual voice is cast as if it were groping within its discursive inadequacies toward a communitarian destiny that it would realize if it were to recognize the more transcendent political discourse of the authors existing deep within itself."[15] To depart from the authors' demanding teleology, to fail to adopt their particular vocabulary of common purpose and civic virtue, is to be deficient and in need of correction. And as most citizens are found to be both deficient and resistant to correction, *Habits* seethes with resentment against the choices, judgments, and ethical frameworks that structure ordinary life today.[16]

Habits, then, can only articulate its call for democratization by simultaneously invoking the cultural coherence of an earlier America. That older landscape is presented as democracy's native soil, the condition of its healthy growth: a return of consensus on the common good is *necessary* to the recreation of self-governance. The book thus advocates a popular "empowerment" that could only be achieved by first undertaking a severe remaking of the populace. The Tocquevillean motivations for this move provoke a question about the plausibility of turning Tocqueville's idealization of American democracy toward radical ends today: must any appropriation of *Democracy* share *Habits'* project of disciplinary moral return? Certainly not on all counts. Other Tocquevillian democratic theorists have sought to learn from earlier democratic practices while refusing to lament the loss of harmony. Sheldon Wolin's work, for example, elaborates a critique of contemporary modes of discipline which takes its bearings from his concern with the complex problems of difference in American political life; his handling of those problems cannot be assessed adequately through a brief against *Habits'* simpler, more reductive analysis.[17] In its simplicity, however, *Habits* provides a salutary warning that must be heeded by any democratic encounter with Tocqueville today. Most obviously, the warning is about the abuse of history, the difficulties of using an imagined, homogeneous past to navigate the undeniably heterogeneous present. But there is another, perhaps more important, lesson as well: in its insistence on linking the reinvigoration of democracy to a project of moral return, *Habits* serves as a reminder of the troubling politics of Tocqueville's original map, of the problems of difference and commonality that attended the construction of *his* America.

At times, *Democracy* imposes a homogeneity of its own: as several scholars have argued in recent years, the book's emphasis on the lack of fundamental divisions and disparities flattens the terrain of Jacksonian America.[18] Even aside from the genocidal displacement of the indigenous population and the contention over slavery (topics *Democracy* does treat at length, albeit problematically), the Jacksonian moment was one of profound struggle, of battles over wealth and power, belief and belonging, sexuality and identity—indeed, as one historian put it, over "the first principles of democracy itself."[19] In *Democracy*, such struggles are often masked or muted and are sometimes rendered altogether invisible. To erase these struggles is to evade some of the most fundamental problems of democratic politics.

Though basic familiarity with the Jacksonian context makes it easier to note this evasion, the matter is not one that needs to be left to historians or contextualists: the most important questions raised by Tocqueville's erasures are political and theoretical, not empirical, and these can be explored fruitfully by paying careful attention to *Democracy*'s internal tensions and textual operations. Ambivalent text that it is, *Democracy* contains counter-tendencies, alternative approaches and commitments, which make the evasions more visible and offer resources for thinking about them. *Democracy* can provide techniques and tactics for combatting its evasions, for extending its democratic impulse to the profoundly political clashes it often ignores. Yet the problem is still more complicated, for some strands in the text suggest that "evasion" is not always a fitting term for Tocqueville's response to cultural struggle. At times, like *Habits*, *Democracy* explicitly sanctions the suppression of difference, linking the vitality of democratic self-government to the production and maintenance of American homogeneity and hegemony; it is here that disturbance is "institutionalized" in the most confining sense of that term.[20] To break out of this confinement and bring the disturbing radicalism of democracy to bear on questions of social power and cultural difference, as I will below, is to push against some of the most important elements in Tocqueville's thinking. To disturb *Democracy*, and thus American democracy, it is necessary to be aware not only of the difficulties of using Tocqueville's map now but of the politics encoded in its original cartography.

Reading to disturb does not mean simply concentrating on the differences between that cartography and those of contemporary historians, or the distance between past and present. If too simple and sympathetic a return to *Democracy* leads to a politics of nostalgia and resentment, overemphasizing our distance turns the book into a historical curio, depriving Tocqueville's words of their power to interrogate the present and engage our democratic questions. Both sympathy and disengagement carry dangers, then, and these are not easy to avoid. In constructing this typology of errors, I have located the temptations traversed by my own trail through *Democracy*. No doubt each of them still lies waiting—camouflaged—in some of the pages that follow. But if the temptations cannot be banished altogether, they can be transformed by combining and supplementing them. I call this response, my own way of navigating the Tocquevillian terrain, reading (in) the gaps between his America and ours.

To read the gaps is to mark and reflect on the dislocations that come from taking *Democracy* as a contemporary guide. This way of reading notes the discipline and denial such guidance can produce, using these to ask what forms of discipline and denial inhere in the Tocquevillian understanding of democracy and politics. To read *in* the gaps is to use distance and dislocation for more affirmative lessons, to find room for criticism and reconceptualizations of democracy in the space between that earlier America and ours. This requires taking liberties, acting, for a time, as if

Democracy issues a challenge to our own conditions of unfreedom and the imperfections in our democratic theories and practices. Reading (in) the gaps is scavenging *Democracy* for useful tools, tricks, and tropes, while remembering that too literal a return can only be a trap.

I shall attempt such a reading in two stages. The remainder of this chapter will approach *Democracy* affirmatively, first reading it for its most democratic impulses, its most ambitious commitments to both the pluralization of power and the preservation of individuality and diversity, and then using these for critical purchase on contemporary American thought and practice. Chapter 3 will take up the costs of that affirmation by identifying the evasions of politics and the containment of difference that lie beneath the sometimes radical pluralism of *Democracy* (thereby returning to features that my own sympathetic first reading deliberately evades). By tracking that logic of containment and exclusion, by entering more deeply into the problems posed by Tocqueville's ambivalence, it is possible to use *Democracy* to frame the challenges facing contemporary democratic thought and to ask how far that book enables us to go in meeting them.

The Subject of Freedom

The most useful point of entry is the fundamental challenge Tocqueville faced in his work. As noted earlier, he wanted to observe and understand the basic shaping forces of modernity, to explore the most advanced position of the movement toward equality. Though that movement had been underway for centuries, it had recently accelerated so forcefully that the old ways of making sense of politics were no longer useful. Tocqueville was serious when, in introducing the first volume of *Democracy*, he proclaimed, "A new political science is needed for a world itself quite new."[21] This often quoted remark reveals both the scope of the book and the theoretical ambition of the author. While that ambition does not seem to be peculiar to Tocqueville—he is hardly the only modern theorist to present a new science of politics—he gave these familiar words a distinctive spin. His "science" was not to be a precise method or a system that would reveal the laws of social motion.[22] In part, he was evoking an *attitude*, a way of responding to time and change. Tocqueville wished to purge (his) political thinking of nostalgia, to prevent attachments to the past from obscuring the workings of the present world and the political possibilities for action in the future. But there was more to the call for new thinking than this rejection of backward-looking sentimentality. Tocqueville sought a certain kind of political knowledge: he wanted to comprehend the forms—and the fate—of freedom under the new dispensation. His new political science was an attempt to understand how the practice of liberty could be reinvented in and for egalitarian democracies, and to illuminate the modes of subjugation that would take hold if that reinvention did not succeed. These explorations were practical in intent, for Tocqueville's aim was to help expand the scope of free action and foster resistance to new forms of despotism.[23]

This characterization, of course, raises more questions than it answers. "Freedom" is a protean and slippery word, and this elusiveness certainly marks its appearances in Tocqueville's work. Though he repeatedly insists that it is the principle to which he is most deeply attached, he never gives freedom a precise and thorough definition: *liberté* is a floating, polysemic term throughout *Democracy*, and Tocqueville neither acknowledges this nor offers any guidance through his maze of meanings. He was not, after all, a systematic or particularly "philosophical" writer. His bold books are hardly mere empiricist collections of facts, but their conceptual investigations are always embedded in analyses of mores, institutions, events. Since that is their virtue, the source of their richness, there is little to gain from constructing too formal an edifice on the foundation of his highly contextual analyses. Still, the more significant features of *Democracy*'s approach to freedom deserve a few words of explanation.

The most significant features of all are signaled in the line that provided my title and has already served as a recurring figure for my way of reading: "nothing is more fertile in marvels than the art of being free, but nothing is harder than freedom's apprenticeship."[24] What does it mean to say that being free is a matter of art and that this art requires a demanding apprenticeship? Most obviously, this suggests that freedom is not only a status but an activity—something that involves *doing* as well as *having*. The activity can be pursued well or badly, with varying degrees of skill. Freedom is something that can be learned, something we must work on to learn well: like any art, being free takes practice. And, like other arts, it is sustained by *practices* (patterns of activity, organized ways of being-in-the-world). For Tocqueville, this particular art exists largely in being practiced, in its exercise. Being free is, in this respect, a *performing* art.[25] Adept performers are able to act well, both with and against others: they are artful in the collective pursuit of common tasks and shared ends, but also in resisting the grand and petty tyrannies of collective life; they are adept at pursuing their self-interest, but they are also interested in elaborating their selfhood, in giving shape to their lives rather than simply adhering to a preexisting pattern. The art of being free transforms both its practitioners and the stage on which they act: experience in the ways of freedom makes individuals more resilient and institutions more open to human initiative and diversity. And it is because his ultimate concern is with the strength of individuality and the preservation of human diversity that Tocqueville valorizes the practice of freedom.

Where are we and what are we doing when we practice this art? Employed both with and against others, transforming both self and world, Tocqueville's art moves across some of the conceptual boundaries common to theoretical discussions of freedom, thereby bringing together concerns that are often viewed as separate or even incompatible. Consider, to take the most important case, the way this approach leads Tocqueville to straddle a familiar, if problematic, distinction between "private" and "public" liberty.[26] Private liberty concerns the socially or legally guaranteed sphere within which action can be autonomous: it is the ability of individuals, as individuals, to do as they like without interference from the state, the community, or other individuals. Theories of private liberty thus tend to identify the places or activities in which we are *rightfully* beyond control or regulation. Public liberty, in contrast, refers not to barriers against interference, but to our ability to share, as citizens or members of institutions, in the shaping of a common political life. While theorists of private liberty insist that the question of freedom is fundamentally separate from the question of democracy, conceptions of public liberty directly link these questions. Theories of public liberty tend to identify the sites and pursuits that should be subject to broad participation or collective self-government.[27]

Democracy combines and, in doing so, subtly changes these concerns. Like the theorists of private liberty, Tocqueville seeks to defend individuals from encroachments by others: he presents freedom as, in part, a matter of being unobstructed or left alone. He believes in robust and widely applied individual rights (the right to think and speak freely, to associate, etc.). He worries, repeatedly and urgently, about the power of the modern state, its potential to constrain bodies and minds. He stresses the ways that majorities can endanger minorities. He fears that the forms of individuality unleashed by modernity, forms that seem bold and adventurous, may prove very fragile, may bend under the force of public opinion or break beneath the weight of bureaucratic institutions. But Tocqueville's commitment to individuality and spaces free from interference is joined and advanced by a commitment to spaces for common action, to broad participation in public affairs. Like the theorists of public liberty, Tocqueville sees political activity as a primary form of freedom in its own right:

the democratic extension of participation is also the expansion of (a certain kind of) freedom. And creating institutions that facilitate the popular exercise of this freedom can, potentially, strengthen those forms of right and selfhood that the modern state might otherwise constrain.

Clearly, then, *Democracy* uses *liberté* to refer, at different moments, to the "private" and the "public" forms of freedom: Tocqueville's freedom is a matter both of protections against intrusion and of sharing in political power. It is tempting to summarize this approach, to bring the different uses of *liberté* into alignment, by saying that the two forms of freedom are seen as mutually reinforcing: private liberties allow public liberty to be preserved, for they allow it to be exercised without oppressive, self-destructive excesses, and public liberties create citizens empowered to preserve private liberties and the institutions that sustain them. Yet this tidy formulation, which captures something important in *Democracy*'s argument, does not do justice to the text's dissonant complexity. It implies too much harmony, for, as the first epigraph to this chapter suggests, the forms of freedom are not always aligned. They *can* be reinforcing, but they are also "dangerous"—and not least to each other. Tocqueville returns to these dangers, anxiously and endlessly, pitting the forms of freedom against each other and privileging each one at different places in his argument. He suggests that the balance of freedoms is a crucial problem in the patterning of cultures and political institutions, a problem that admits responses of varying degrees of success. But *Democracy* neither seeks nor offers a stable "solution" to the problem, a secure resting place beyond danger to structures of self and society.

For Tocqueville, the dangers of politics must be negotiated by art. *Democracy* argues that the public dimensions of freedom can strengthen selves and even aid the protection of private liberties, but it does not suggest that living under conditions of public freedom can make the self fully attuned to or realized by the world around it. At his most nuanced moments, at least, Tocqueville does not drive dissonance from political order or political subjectivity.[28] He shows that even free and just political orders can exact profound costs from individual subjects, for there are always problems of "fit," and any socially sanctioned or privileged way of being necessarily drives other ways (and hence other selves, other parts of the self) underground or out of existence. And, again, it is the fate—the resilience or vulnerability, creativity or constraint, diversity or homogeneity—of human selves that is his ultimate concern when he writes about freedom. Tocqueville's worries about the balance of freedoms are over how that balance will affect individuals' ability to act and to withstand action. That is why he also sees benefits in the tension between forms of freedom, valuing these forms for the ways they push against each other. Both kinds of liberties are resources for artful subjects who may be called upon, at different moments (or simultaneously within a complex moment), to undertake common business or to break free from the constraints of common opinion, to use their freedom to get something done or to preserve their freedom by keeping something from being done to them. The most important of freedom's "marvels" are to be found not in any one location (in private or public) or in any one institution (though institutions play a crucial role in preventing or promoting the taking of liberties) but in this very resourcefulness, in the way art expands the scope for action and protects individuality and difference by enabling individuals to participate in the construction and contestation of political order.

At its most optimistic moments, *Democracy* concludes that Americans have become an artful political people. By democratizing the art of being free, by extending its scope and passing it (on) through democratic culture and institutions, they have fostered resilient forms of selfhood and left space for diverse ways of living and being. But even these celebratory moments (which are of course balanced by far darker conclusions) are subtended by a deep anxiety. The source of the anxiety is modernity itself: Tocqueville is so attentive to matters of political art because he sees it as a necessary response to the dangerous consequences of modern, egalitarian social transformations. It is to his account of those transformations, another necessary preface to Tocqueville's America, that we turn now.

From Aristocracy to Democracy: The Self Unbound

Democracy describes the growth of equality as more than a consequence or fact of modernity. As Robert Nisbet writes, equality is "conceived as a historical process rather than a simple condition."[29] It is the engine of modern change, the central character in the grand historical narrative that Tocqueville uses to frame his analyses of American conditions. The central categories, the stages of this narrative, are aristocracy and democracy: the rise of equality turns an aristocratic world into a democratic one.[30] In modernity, equality and democracy march forward together, for "there is hardly an important event in the last seven hundred years which has not turned out to be advantageous for equality," and "everywhere the diverse happenings in the lives of peoples have turned to democracy's profit."[31] Beneficiary of the egalitarian dismantling of aristocracy, democracy is the destiny of modern nations.

Democracy's approach to democracy is fully intelligible only against the background of its sketch of that older, aristocratic world (a sketch that Tocqueville would redraw in more detail in his *Ancien Regime*). This picture calls our attention to the power of custom and connection. Tocqueville renders aristocracies as tightly knit orders in which individuals (if that word is even appropriate to his account of the time) can understand themselves only in terms of their ties to others, their place in an elaborately articulated social structure: life is lived and interpreted within an intricate network of affiliations and dependencies. These networks are of course formidably hierarchical, but the hierarchies generate and sustain obligations to public service. Even when the many have neither the space nor the skills to act, the great are expected—and often able—to do so. It does not take unusual art to join actors and audience, for the bonds of hierarchy are themselves enough: "In aristocratic societies men have no need to unite for action since they are held firmly together."[32]

Tocqueville's anxiety, his ambivalence about modernity, flows from his understanding of what happens when the egalitarian movement from aristocracy to democracy sunders these ties. On the one hand, there is liberation: people are delivered out of bondage. It is not only that individuals are emancipated from their subordination to those above them in a fixed hierarchy (though they are, and that is important), but also that individuality is itself unfettered. The self becomes mobile, plastic; cut loose from its traditional moorings, it is (potentially) launched on a journey of discovery and invention.[33] But this journey is perilous, and foremost among the perils is the possibility that the self will, in the end, be diminished. Unlike many Enlightenment champions of modernity, Tocqueville cannot view the dissolution of the old order as wholly or unambiguously liberating. On his account, bonds not only restrain activity but make it possible. The decline of aristocratic ties thus poses a deep problem: democratic dissolution places individuals in a peculiar double condition in which they are at once "independent" (their shackles have fallen away) and "weak" (they do not necessarily have anyone to lean on).[34] The politically appropriate response to this condition is the establishment of more deliberate, egalitarian, and freely chosen links between people.

The point is not that society becomes a mere artifact of the contractual transactions of preexisting selves, but that individuals need new kinds of empowering social practices. Democratic citizens "would all . . . find themselves helpless if they did not learn to help each other voluntarily."[35] And the result of that helplessness would not be chaos—anarchy is not Tocqueville's real fear—but more oppressive forms of order.[36] While aristocratic societies had many "natural" centers of power that could prevent despotic uniformity, the unbound citizens of democracy can be preyed upon by centralizing and bureaucratizing powers. If independence does produce weakness, if individuals do lose power and become more vulnerable to pressures from society and state, it is independence that will ultimately suffer: the result will be a culture of conformity populated by subservient selves. Democracies need political art to keep the newly liberated self from being crushed by forces too powerful to resist, to stave off rule by demagogues and functionaries and to combat the potential for oppression within the *demos* itself.

Tocqueville's sketch of the aristocratic world, a world of warm belonging and virtuous leaders, is clearly another idealization, one that is of dubious value to contemporary democrats. That *Democracy* sometimes takes that stylized portrait too literally, thereby falling prey to nostalgia for a more stable and connected world, is hard to dispute (there is a textual basis for conservative, anti-modern appropriations of the work).[37] But the main thrust of *Democracy* is against that nostalgia, promoting neither a restoration nor a continuation of aristocratic political and social forms. For one thing, democracy is presented as a global inevitability: there can be no turning back.[38] For another, the advance of democracy is described as a deepening and extension of *justice*, even if that advance is not without its costs.[39] Perhaps most important, *Democracy*'s account of democracy's dangers sometimes underwrites an argument for further democratization, and does so in the name of *freedom;* as we will see, the book suggests democratic cures for democratic ills. However reluctantly, Tocqueville is led to embrace democracy's distinctive opportunities, and his assessment of democracy's perils and modernity's costs lends his account of those opportunities a distinctive and fruitful complexity. Taking certain liberties, I shall propose that contemporary circumstances allow *Democracy* to lead us much farther down that path of opportunity than its author ever intended. The best place to start an account of Tocqueville's anxious pursuit of democracy and the path it opens to contemporary readers is his account of the institutions of American self-government. It is thus necessary to go back to the American democracy that he discovered—and, of course, invented—in the 1830s, following him as he probes the shape of its institutions and the character of its culture.

American Self-Government and the Practice of Freedom

If *Democracy* strikes different tones at different moments, if both its projections and its arguments vary substantially over the course of the book, it begins on a very hopeful note. Though Tocqueville has worries—

moral, political, aesthetic—about America and its democratic condition, his discussion of local self-government is marked by respect, even wonder. America, the land of equality, is also teeming with local forms of public freedom: "With much care and skill, power has been broken into fragments in the American township, so the maximum number of people have some concern with public affairs."[40] The structure of the township ensures that there are multiple sites for freedom to be practiced, multiple opportunities for the acquisition of experience in governance and the making of political decisions.

This fragmentation of power does not produce dissipation, for the towns and villages exercise significant control over their own destinies: in local politics the stakes are substantial and the opportunities are real. For Tocqueville, that is a crucial fact. Only when participatory institutions are independent and powerful can there be genuine "citizens" and not just "docile subjects."[41] In a democracy, citizens need the opportunity to act *as* citizens; they need experience in the constitution and exercise of power. The participatory character of America's local, democratic institutions sustains robust political agency, making actors competent and resilient. Citizens really do learn how to shape the common fate and pursue their own purposes as well. These opportunities to share in the exercise of power and to advance one's interests work to draw a broad range of people into political life. The member of a township comes to view it as "a free, strong corporation of which he is a part and which is worth the trouble trying to direct."[42] And so the American citizenry has developed its singular passion for politics, a passion pursued more widely than anywhere else.[43]

We see, already, how *Democracy* brings freedom and democracy together, for Tocqueville uses the language of freedom to talk about the American township's democratic governance. The local institutions of democratic participation are crucial to the dissemination of the art of being free: "Local institutions are to liberty what primary schools are to science; they put it within the people's reach; they teach people to appreciate its peaceful enjoyment and accustom them to make use of it."[44] What could be described as one of the most radical features of American democracy, the putting of public business into the people's hands, is here admired for its effects on the populace. The township institutionalizes (promotes and sustains) democratic disturbance, and thus empowers the citizenry.[45] Local governance provides an important structural support for the creation and preservation of those democratic ties that are necessary to protect modern selfhood, to allow modern individuals to both exercise and preserve their freedoms. The admiring report on the township is thus an important moment in *Democracy*'s assessment of the American version of modernity. Yet—and this is the source of Tocqueville's wonder about America—local liberty is not common in the modern world. "Local freedom," *Democracy* argues, "is a rare and fragile thing. . . . Of all forms of liberty . . . [it] is the most prone to the encroachments of authority." Modern nations exert enormous centripetal force. The more "advanced" a political order, the more likely it is to be intolerant of local autonomy. To survive the modern drift toward centralization, local freedom must have deep roots: before it "has become a part of mores it can easily be destroyed, and it cannot enter into mores without a long-recognized legal existence."[46]

Mores presuppose laws, but the laws themselves presumably required a foundation in mores: this remark leaves one wondering how Americans possibly *could* have developed this local freedom. *Democracy* here seems ready to founder on what William Connolly has identified as a recurring paradox in democratic theory, in which the establishment of a democratic community in a manifestly undemocratic world seems to require that "effect . . . become cause and cause . . . become effect."[47] This paradox is usually resolved, Connolly reminds us, by violence, by acts of founding that suppress or reconstruct those refractory features of political society and subjectivity that seem to stand in the way of (the theorist's vision of) democracy. But *Democracy* immediately works to dissolve the sense of paradox, to ease our perplexity, by claiming that American local liberty has a long and rich history that cannot be reduced to a moment of founding or to any originating act of conscious intention. Local freedom is something that "almost in secret," fortuitously, in response to time and circumstance, custom and law, "springs up of its own accord."[48] So it is, Tocqueville proclaims, with the American case. True, the American act of founding has helped matters, for the federal system has protected local power. But the origins of that power, and the liberty that makes it possible, go back well before the Constitution and the Revolution. Tocqueville suggests that the prerevolutionary towns, which he compares to Athens in their active political life and their participatory institutions, benefited from both the history of English liberties and the fortunate circumstances of the colonists.[49] That history means that the mores necessary to sustain the life of freedom were present in America from the beginning, and the earliest legal structures sustained these mores. Inheritors and cultivators of the "spirit of freedom," architects of a national structure that preserves local power, Americans have been able to forge and maintain distinctly modern versions of those local institutions of governance that enable citizens to practice the art of being free.[50]

These remarks suggest, then, that the art of freedom is much more than a matter of governance, and is not only to be exercised in the official institutions of the township. If those institutions draw strength from and help sustain the "spirit of freedom," that spirit must also be embodied elsewhere. If municipal institutions multiply the sites of politics and expand the opportunities for exercising freedom, they do not, alone, provide *enough* sites and opportunities. Free municipal institutions require the existence of other places for the practice of political art, and these forms have purposes that extend beyond those of the township. The art of being free must touch national as well as local life, and must be exercised in society as well as the state. Citizens need not only stable, already-institutionalized spaces for the exercise of freedom, but also skill in *creating* those spaces themselves. These skills are learned and employed, and the most important additional political spaces are constructed, through what Tocqueville calls "association."

Most simply put, associations are groups of people organized for an explicit purpose: "An association unites the energies of divergent minds and directs them toward a clearly indicated goal."[51] They are instruments of both creation and struggle, aimed at bringing new things into the world or confronting existing institutions, practices, laws. Tocqueville endows all such organizations with a potential political significance, for all draw individuals into the give and take of collective life, but he also distinguishes between "civil" and more strictly "political" associations. The latter, which range from small and transient public assemblies to the major political parties, are particularly important in disseminating political skill and, of course, in facilitating democratic contests over law and policy. Civil associations alone are not sufficient to sustain a democratic life, for they do not necessarily offer enough space for politics. But much of the success of the directly political associations comes from their being embedded within a much larger network of civil associations; it is this larger context that supports popular aptitude in and understanding of political association. *Democracy* describes America as a nation in which associations are more numerous, less regulated, and more skillfully used, than anywhere else.[52] Indeed, Americans are "forever forming associations," and doing so for "a thousand different" purposes:

> Americans combine to give fetes, found seminaries, build churches, distribute books, and send missionaries to the antipodes. Hospitals, prisons, and schools take shape this way. Finally, if they want to proclaim a

great truth or propagate some feeling by the encouragement of a great example, they form an association. In every case, at the head of any new undertaking, where in France you would find the government or in England some territorial magnate, in the United States you are sure to find an association.⁵³

Associations, then, are among the most distinguishing features of Tocqueville's America. They are crucial to the structure and culture of the polity, occupying positions that are filled by very different institutions and habits in other nations. But Tocqueville's primary interest is not in the fact that associations are peculiarly American but in the political and theoretical implications they have for his underlying anxieties about modern forms of order, freedom, and individuality. He investigates associations in order to assess their successes and limitations in responding to those egalitarian transformations that produce the post-aristocratic, unbound self. Associations are presented as offering (at least potentially) a uniquely democratic way of constructing that form of political (dis)order that strengthens selves and sustains action.

The active sense that Tocqueville gives to the term is the key to its importance in his analysis. As Roger Boesche has argued, Tocqueville differs from the familiar mainstream American political science literature on "interest groups" in using "association" not only as a noun but as a verb, one that conveys both a sense of energy and the ability to transcend isolation.⁵⁴ Association is a practice of relating to others; it provides a kind of grammar for conduct, a set of rules that structure and make possible the actions of subjects. For Tocqueville, there is an art of *associating*, an art of vital importance to the art of being free. This art is learned through regular exercise. Political associations, in particular, are "great free schools to which all citizens come to be taught the general theory of association."⁵⁵ That "theory" is necessary for there to be a free, democratic life: the skills of association are an integral part of the enjoyment and protection of public freedom and private liberty. In democracies, "knowledge of how to combine is the mother of all other forms of knowledge."⁵⁶ This knowledge is crucial to the making of artful citizens, for when we know how to combine our political horizons can expand almost without limit: "There is no end which the human will despairs of attaining by the *free action of the collective power of individuals*."⁵⁷

It is worth lingering over this remark. Here, Tocqueville again connects freedom with democracy, while also locating the practices of democracy on the terrain of a certain kind of power relationship. Perhaps it would be better to say that *Democracy* suggests that democracy *means* that individuals can take part in the constitution of a certain kind of power, for association allows people to share in the production and exercise of a power that changes the constitutive features of a common world. The practice of association is thus a crucial linkage in Tocqueville's connection between American freedom and American democracy. But how does the link work? What is this form of power, this democratic way of relating to others, this free bond fit for the social conditions of egalitarian modernity? The power produced and channeled through the practice of association aims at both discord and concord, challenge and affirmation, using each of these ends to inform or modify the other: exercised by and against citizens who are understood to be free, this power resists existing and attempted tyrannies while refusing to let the act of resistance occasion tyrannies of its own. Association is thus a practice that *democratizes struggle*. It is a practice of struggle because groups may confront each other or the state over the most fundamental political differences of will, interest, and opinion, and the point of the confrontation is often to achieve a decisive victory. But association democratizes that confrontation by setting certain limits on the forms of antagonism, on the way victory is achieved and defined. American associations seek victory through the constitution of moral authority and the search for persuasive arguments; and this search means that it is always possible for there to be more contestation. On Tocqueville's account, this is important not only for the way it affects hostile encounters but for its influence on the internal dynamics of organizations as well: in their intragroup life, democratic associations allow for "individual independence," for "will and reason." They do not demand or foster servility, but strengthen their members.[58] Those practiced in the art of associating know not only how to collaborate for group ends but how to assert themselves and their opinions within the group.

For these reasons, Tocqueville's conclusions about association parallel those about the organs of municipal participation: the more widely these democratic forms are spread, the more actively they are used, the freer the polity and more empowered the citizenry. Traversed by innumerable associations and teeming with small, accessible, and politically significant municipal institutions, Tocqueville's America is a polity rich in political spaces. *Democracy* would seem to be a very reassuring exercise in cartography. If America is the advance guard of political modernity, it has responded to its situation by developing forms of political life that capitalize on modern opportunities while easing modern dangers. From the standpoint of Tocqueville's anxious concern with the strength and resilience of individual subjectivity, his conclusions here suggest an unambivalent endorsement of American democracy, implying that the more radical the democracy—the more broadly power is disseminated, the more numerous the spaces of action and contestation, the more refined citizens' skills in disturbing settled orders—the more satisfactory it will be. Or so the discussion so far would seem to indicate.

 This discussion has been one-sided, however, and—taken alone—fundamentally misleading. *Democracy* is anything but unambivalent. Even when the goal is an ironic radicalization of Tocqueville's thought, it is necessary to come to terms with the complexity of *Democracy*'s impulses and judgments, to see the currents that must be resisted as well as those that can carry us forward in pursuit of democracy. If I have so far emphasized Tocqueville's commitment to broad and energetic political activity, it is also important to acknowledge his doubts about direct political participation and perhaps about democracy itself. For all of its admiration, *Democracy* expresses deep fears about the American political condition. It is time to confront them.

Against "Excess"

In its anxious worrying over the status of freedom under the modern, egalitarian dispensation, *Democracy* circles around the problem of democratic excess. This problem looms particularly large in Volume One, where the primary fear seems to be that America's egalitarian popular politics will be carried too far. The nation's culture and institutions may not offer enough barriers to the exercise of popular will; the masses may overrun private rights and liberties; American democracy may disturb settled order too much. These fears can be seen in Tocqueville's admiring commentary on the Constitution. His consideration of the formal structure of the American national government closely follows *The Federalist*, a work that obviously influenced both his understanding of the mechanics of the American state and his judgments about its successes and failures.[59]

 If Tocqueville is an advocate of vigorous local self-government and of universal knowledge of the art of association, his discussion of the American Constitution shows him to prefer national government by a virtuous elite of representatives. Here, the *demos* are figured as undisciplined, wild, constitutionally (in all senses) unsuited for having a direct role in the most momentous political decisions. Tocqueville thus asks how a society can guard itself against the extremes of democratic enthusiasm while preserving democratic rule. In this discussion, the central task of modern, national democratic governance seems to be to insulate representatives from popular passion while tying them to popular interests. Good representatives are responsible, in the double sense that they are both accountable to others and possessed of unusual prudence and devotion to duty. This ideal of elite representation is most powerfully articulated in Tocqueville's discussion of the Senate. He finds the Senate to be an important counterweight to the "vulgar demeanor" of the House: the popular will is "refined" when it is mediated by indirect election. The senators represent the "lofty thoughts" and "generous instincts" of the majority, but not its "petty passions" and "vices."[60]

The extent of Tocqueville's support for national government by an enlightened, responsive elite should not be underestimated. In fact, he was suspicious even of the degree of insulation achieved by the Senate. Throughout his life, he retained a belief in the virtues of enlightened, constitutional monarchy.[61] On the other hand, even when Tocqueville gives his most sympathetic and aristocratic gloss on the Federalist interpretation of the American state, he retains his admiration for participatory localism and its democratic construction of political relationships. He seems to believe both that local affairs are the rightful business of local citizens and that a locally active—and thus politically educated—citizenry will be the most enlightened constituency for the governors of national affairs. If his comments about the state show his fear of populist democracy, they also show his optimism: he thinks the federal system is doing its job, safeguarding liberty. But we cannot stop at that optimistic assessment, for we have not yet engaged his deepest fears about the threat of modern equality to liberty: engaging them provides resources crucial to the democratic reappropriation of *Democracy*.

Individualism, Conformity, Despotism

We begin to see the depth of Tocqueville's fears in his discussion of resentment, with his suggestion that a deadly dialectic of envy may inhere in the unfolding of modern democracy. He proposes that the advance of democratic and egalitarian conditions only fans the desire for more equality; it makes complete equality of power and circumstances seem to be a very real and appealing possibility, and turns those who stand above the mean into objects of mass resentment. But the goal of complete equality always recedes from those who pursue it; the means offered by egalitarian social orders fail to do the work that resentful subjects ask of them: "Democratic institutions awaken and flatter the passion for equality without ever being able to satisfy it entirely."[62] In one of his darkest moments, Tocqueville concludes that the resulting form of envy is dangerously corrosive: it ultimately destroys not only individual dignity but democratic political structures themselves, for this envy produces a "debased taste for equality" which "leads the weak to want to drag the strong down to their level and which induces men to prefer equality in servitude to inequality in freedom."[63]

Tocqueville is by no means sure, however, that egalitarian servitude is the American future. Though sensitive to the politics of resentment, he questions the conclusion that the dialectic of envy will prove fatal. There are countervailing sentiments at work in the very logic of equality. Perhaps most important among them is that "legitimate passion for equality" which arouses in all men a desire to be strong and respected," a desire that "tends to elevate the little man to the ranks of the great."[64] That more elevated ambition, which may be democracy's greatest hope, is one possible outcome of the modern, egalitarian unfettering of individuality. But modern individuality still remains the source of Tocqueville's most anguished fears; and before pursuing his democratic hopes, we need to follow the fears, step by step, to the end. The next step is *Democracy*'s discussion of majority tyranny.

Majority tyranny is among *Democracy*'s most complex theoretical constructions, a many-sided object of analysis and concern. The distinctiveness of Tocqueville's concern is hard to see, because the object seems so familiar: "the tyranny of the majority" is a stock phrase of contemporary American political discourse. At the level of high-minded principle, at least, Americans all know that the rights of "the individual" are not secure unless there are rigorous safeguards against the imposition of majority will. The pervasive sense that this common knowledge is a defining part of the American political heritage enables "majority tyranny" to function as a powerful tool in political struggles: sometimes merely invoking the concept is enough to beat back a proposal, policy, or law. But if the tool can be put to effective (perhaps even liberating) uses, it has grown dull with age. Through repeated use in a wide variety of contexts, the idea of majority tyranny has acquired a banality that blocks critical inquiry and argument. Even the manifold and at times brutal oppressions that minorities (gays and lesbians, people of color, Muslims, countless individuals who in one way or another "deviate" from norms or prevailing standards) continue to suffer are often taken to confirm the theoretical soundness of the received understanding of majority tyranny as a more or less straightforward infringement of fundamental rights. Tocqueville is a crucial figure in the genealogy of that understanding, but his work subjects that understanding to unsettling questions, for his fears extend well beyond those most commonly expressed today.[65]

The point is not that Tocqueville rejects the concern with minority rights—as we saw in considering his fear of democratic excess, that concern animates his argument—but that this commitment is yoked to a series of broader worries and analyses. These transfigure the terms of inquiry and debate, and so it may prove fruitful to reconstruct *Democracy*'s approach as a series of increasingly provocative variations on an all-too-familiar theme. The first move beyond the question of rights and their formal infringement is Tocqueville's attention to the problem of the inhibition of thought, the social constraint of subjectivity. In democracies, he argues, "public opinion" can become "more and more the mistress of the world." Where it rules, where it is (at least in principle) the most important source of authority, and where the checks against it are few, public opinion can overwhelm individuals, making them feel "isolated and defenseless," insignificant. Popular attitudes can reach into the most inward recesses of mind and spirit. Originality, independent thinking, and the willingness to resist prevailing judgments will be severely restricted—if not curtailed altogether.[66] Democracy is a threat.

Though more nuanced and challenging than arguments that focus exclusively on the status of formal rights, these reflections are still, of course, familiar. The story of the dissolution of individuality into the mass has been a staple of American liberal social criticism in this century, and was famously placed at the center of the liberal theory of liberty by John Stuart Mill. But if both Mill and any number of American critics of mass society owe (and acknowledge) fundamental debts to Tocqueville, the latter gives the story of individuality and mass a rather different moral. While Tocqueville has a fundamental commitment to diversity and individual development, he turns the familiar liberal analyses upside down by arguing that the concern with individual autonomy—or, rather, that a certain way of understanding and pursuing autonomy—can lead to the worst kind of homogeneity and the worst kind of majoritarian tyranny. Through the social creation of a certain form of individuality, the form he calls "individualism," novel and particularly pernicious forms of despotism can arise; if it feeds the advance of despotism, individualism ultimately erodes both individuality and difference. It is here that the reflections on tyranny take a more striking turn.

The analysis of individualism, elaborated in the second volume of *Democracy*, is the culmination of Tocqueville's ambivalent reflections on the unfettering of the modern self. The analysis presents individualism as something new in the world, a distinctive cultural form, a way of scripting the self that emerged from the egalitarian restructuring of social relations. As equality of material condition increases, as old hierarchies are dismantled, individuals increasingly come to see themselves as entirely able to "look after their own needs." But individualism is not a merely healthy independence, the self-assertiveness of those who do not have to bow and scrape before superiors. Nor is this "calm and considered" response to the social conditions of egalitarian democracy the same as ordinary selfishness or "egoism," a passion which, Tocqueville suggests, has always been found among human beings. In contrast to that driving passion, individualism is a "misguided judgment" about the relationship between the individual and the broader structures of society, the larger questions of politics, the fundamental conditions of power. Individualism leads people to "form the habit of thinking of themselves in isolation and imagine their whole destiny is in their hands." Thinking of themselves as fundamentally unattached and self-sufficient, individualists choose to "isolate" themselves, to "withdraw into the circle of family and friends."[67]

This withdrawal is a trap: individualism leads people to ignore the outside world, but the world is often less willing to ignore them. The kind of autonomy presumed by withdrawal is a disastrous fiction, a denial of the elaborate and potentially dangerous structures and relations within which individuals are inevitably enmeshed. As a result, the privatized subject produced by individualism is in jeopardy of falling under the worst forms of tyranny. That people's interests will not necessarily be well served by a political system that they ignore is the very least of the dangers. Individuals who have withdrawn completely into a narrowly private world are unlikely to learn or retain competence in the art of being free; they will often lack the skills of both political collaboration and resistance. This leaves them vulnerable to the social pressures of (potentially) intolerant majorities, makes public opinion tower over figures who have no experience in pushing back and few resources for doing so. Lacking political experience and resources, the privatized individualist subject is still more vulnerable to the state, to the centralizing political forces of etatism: "Despotism, by its very nature suspicious, sees the isolation of men as the best guarantee of its own permanence."[68] Isolation is not only the enabling condition but the defining consequence of despotism, for despotism is a regime that deliberately works to substitute its own powers of regulation, coordination, and initiative for the independent political practices of citizens. Thus despotism and the isolation that can come from equality "fatally complete and support each other."[69] As despotism succeeds in extinguishing political space, it makes resistance more difficult.

This analysis already take us us a substantial step away from the parallel one made by thinkers such as Mill, but a still more substantial difference comes when Tocqueville suggests a particular kind of egalitarian remedy for this problematic result of modern egalitarianism. While theorists such as Mill argue that the preservation of liberty requires us to draw a protective circle around each individual, Tocqueville suggests that drawing the circle in the wrong way will bring about everything Millians and many other liberals fear. For Tocqueville, the individualist threat to liberty can only be counteracted by promoting a fundamental equality in public freedom, in the wielding of political power and in access to political spaces. Tocqueville turns to democratic politics to ensure that certain ties will bind modern individuals and to remind those individuals that the ties are there. In democratic political activity, we cannot pretend that we are solitary, wholly self-present and self-sufficient creatures. But the point is *not* simply to anchor the self in relations with others: driven by fears of tyranny and conformity, Tocqueville seeks political forms that offer individuals strength and skill in resisting the pressures of collective life. By avoiding the pitfalls of isolation, by entering into more active political relations with others, individuals can become more empowered, more capable of genuine independence and struggle. Once again, citizens need access to the experience and education of being free.

A certain form of collective life, then, turns out to be the condition of preserving not only democracy but space for the protection of individuality and difference. Does this perspective not place us within that communitarian discourse that has circulated so mournfully through the theoretical academy and the American polity in recent years? There are certainly communitarian moments in Tocqueville's discussion, which sounds some of the very themes picked up by *Habits* and other laments about the unraveling of America's moral fabric in our time. For some years now, we have been warned by cultural critics that the turning away from common bonds and tasks is placing the polity and the self in danger. But it is important to emphasize the significance of *Democracy*'s emphasis on *politics*, and the way that term is inflected in Tocqueville's work. He does not simply try to draw us into the warmth of "community" and belonging, and he does not presuppose that the solution to the ills of individualism is a univocal, "shared language of the good" that will bring all selves and values into harmony.[70] There is warmth in community but also the potential for suffocation and subjection; while Tocquevillean politics operates within community, it also pushes against communal suffocations.

In its emphasis on politics, *Democracy*'s analysis of individualism and despotism is also more than a mere call for "mediating institutions" that can serve as buffers between citizen and state. The point is not only political incorporation but political contestation. Democratic ties are necessary and enabling, but they, too, can be constricting. Public freedom is an invaluable antidote to the corrosions of individualism but it is not without problems of its own. Citizenship is a crucial role, and citizen a crucial identity, but this role/identity can also drive others out of existence. Even amidst his analyses of the uses of politics in the struggle against individualism, Tocqueville remains wary of democratic excess.[71] Once again, there are no clear escapes from danger, no guarantees, no fully settled order that will solve the complex public and private problems of freedom and despotism, individuality and community. *Democracy* presents democratic politicization as the *best* (which is not to say unproblematic) response precisely because it leaves scope for both stable connections, common ties, and for disturbance. And it is common—that is to say democratic—opinion that sometimes most needs to be disturbed. This is where the pluralism of Tocqueville's politics, the multiplicity and heterogeneity of his political sites, is of paramount importance: on his account, a polity rich in spaces for action and the skills of acting is one in which individuals will have the best chances of negotiating the dangers, resisting the incursions of despotic institutions *and* pushing back against the potential tyrannies of the common. Tocqueville feels that it is necessary to draw citizens into a common life but also necessary to fortify them against that life's costs and demands.

That Tocqueville's worries about despotism modify (without abolishing) Volume One's fear of democratic excess should now be clear. As *Democracy*'s second volume takes up the problem of individualism, the foremost evil becomes not too much participation but too little; the greatest (but not the only) potential source of oppression becomes depoliticization.[72] What is perhaps less clear, but also important, is that this analysis speaks to Tocqueville's anxieties about equality as well. It sharpens the conclusion already implicit in Volume One's discussion of municipal freedom: only an egalitarian deepening of political democracy can counter the dangers of social equality (and this complicates Tocqueville's commitment to a distanced federal elite, providing even Tocquevillian reasons for pushing against that commitment). In a rare—and perhaps unearned—moment of unqualified optimism, Tocqueville concludes that the American case decisively confirms this lesson: "The Americans have used freedom to combat the individualism born of equality, and they have won."[73]

Now I referred to an "egalitarian" response to equality's problems, but Tocqueville here speaks simply of freedom as an antidote to the problems caused by equality. It may seem that my harmonious phrasing camouflages one of the central conflicts that troubles him. Is he not, like many contemporary conservatives, warning us about the inherent and fundamental clash between freedom and equality? I believe not. While his work often centers on the potential *tensions* between freedom and equality, and while he does not imagine that they are easily transcended, he does believe these tensions can be transformed and eased. It is possible to reduce the modern threat to freedom by fusing freedom and equality in a particular way: democratic public freedom, the freedom to act with and against others in public space, is precisely that form of freedom which depends upon a basic equality of persons. By giving all a role in the constitution and contestation of collective power, this freedom offers a democratic response to the perils of modernity. In characterizing such a fusion of equality and freedom, Tocqueville writes, "Let us suppose that all the citizens take part in the government and that each of them has an equal right to do so. Then, no man is different from his fellows and nobody can wield tyrannical power; men will be perfectly free because they are entirely equal, and they will be perfectly equal because they are entirely free. Democratic peoples are tending toward that ideal."[74] Tocqueville goes on to qualify these remarks, for actual nations diverge from the ideal in "a thousand" ways. Furthermore, the taste for freedom is not the same as the taste for equality—and it is the latter taste that predominates in "democratic ages." The latter taste comes, as it were, naturally, while the former often requires careful cultivation.[75]

Tocqueville's qualifications are appropriate. Looking at America, he can see that it is no land of perfect freedom and equality. He is too shrewd and worldly to believe that any society will reach perfection, or to feel that aspirations toward perfection are an entirely benign force in political life. I think, however, that these remarks from Volume Two nevertheless express one of *Democracy*'s fundamental insights: under conditions of modernity, freedom and equality must be pursued together or neither will be achieved adequately. Equality without freedom is not worth having, and, without equality, the kinds of freedoms Tocqueville values will not endure. If no society needs to or should try to implement an order in which all are "entirely equal," if that totalizing aspiration would threaten the human diversity that Tocqueville cherishes, the ideal of *egalitarian* liberty can still serve as a modern society's goal. "Egalitarian," here, means that citizens all need access to political space and political power—and for this access to be meaningful, for that power to be exercised democratically, no citizen can have the ability to dictate the terms of another's life. "Political" freedom thus has "social" prerequisites, and requires the absence of fundamental social structures of command and rule. The goal for a modern, democratic society, then, is the creation of an equality that elevates the citizenry, that raises ordinary people to dignity, authority, and power.[76] And for this elevation to be fully successful, on *Democracy*'s account, all members of the polity must become adept practitioners of the art of being free.

When Tocqueville viewed America from the standpoint of that ideal, it looked pretty good to him, despite his significant criticisms and his deep fears. But contemporary America clearly bears little resemblance to this sunny picture of egalitarian public freedom. The question we must ask is whether Tocqueville helps or hinders our ability to talk about how, where, and why the structure of the American polity departs from that ideal.

That Was Then, This Is Now

The foregoing construction of Tocqueville's reasoning and conclusions is not intended to drive the ambivalence from his thought, to deny the anxieties about equality and democracy that remain in *Democracy* from beginning to end. But, for a time, I want to shove those anxieties aside, to pass over the problem of their relationship to the egalitarian sentiments in the text, in order to ask a different kind of question: Can those voices in *Democracy* that call out most loudly for the empowerment of the democratic citizenry, and those that express the deepest fears of despotism, be drawn into the service of a critical reading of contemporary American democracy? Might taking certain liberties with the text aid our understanding of the status of American liberties? Can *Democracy* still be disturbing—can it inform fundamental political criticism without thereby sanctioning a nostalgic project of restoration?

Reading *Democracy* today, it is hard to overlook a great irony: Tocqueville tried to find in America the general features of the modern democratic condition, but what he saw as the portent of a new age now looks like the final moment of a vanished world. The America of *Democracy* is largely agrarian, and almost exclusively middle class (middle, in the sense that most citizens have "a comfortable existence equally far from wealth and poverty").[77] No wealthy class rules the poorer classes or controls the institutions of state. Most commerce and industry are carried on by people not above "the common level" of their employees. Workers can easily unite and gain fair wages, for capital is weak and labor is strong.[78] Under these conditions, everyone has a stake and a place in the existing order. So, while some individuals are certainly richer than others, social inequality is not great enough to undermine a fundamental political equality—the equality of citizens who all deserve public respect and access to public space, and who are therefore able to collaborate in the exercise of power.[79] In this egalitarian America, public freedom is nourished by practices of democratic association and secured by independent and powerful municipal institutions.

Yet one "great and unfortunate exception" looms, like a menacing cloud, over this inviting, pastoral landscape. In a well-known chapter, Tocqueville observes that a new and singularly exploitative "aristocracy" may be created by "industry." The industrial economy can create a "vicious circle" in which workers become poorer, more vulnerable, "easier to oppress."[80] Under such conditions a new, predatory class of immense wealth may emerge. Industrialism is thus the one potential avenue through which the democratic movement of modernity can be reversed, through which "permanent inequality" can return to the world. But Tocqueville does not imagine that this return is very likely. Though he despises the potential despotism he sees in industrial hierarchy, he does not fear it very much. Industrialism is atypical, "a monstrosity within the general social condition," and great hierarchies are unlikely to cast their shadows over much of American democracy's vast terrain.[81]

Today, of course, Americans occupy very different ground. Tocqueville's pastoral landscape is barely recognizable to those who live amidst late-modern forms of bureaucratic-capitalist order. That dislocation is of tremendous significance: because he believed that social relations of command and obedience were vanishing and would continue to do so, Tocqueville's thinking about freedom and democracy was spared some of the most difficult dilemmas. We cannot expect the currents of modern social development to carry us toward ever greater equality. Tocqueville missed some of our most fundamental problems because his discussion of industrialism was an aside. As Jack Lively puts it, Tocqueville "wrote in parentheses what was to be the bold type of the next century's history."[82]

While he worried about despotisms born of equality, the despotisms of the present day are fundamentally inegalitarian. We work, play, go to school, and carry out the daily business of living amidst complex hierarchies of prestige, privilege, and power. How should this contemporary experience shape the reading of *Democracy?*

One could rate Tocqueville on some kind of prognosticator's scorecard, showing how badly he failed on this point. Recognizing that failure is indeed important if one is to navigate successfully between Tocqueville's America and ours, but I do not wish my own journey simply to demonstrate the limits of Tocqueville's predictive skills. What if, instead of turning the difference between his map and our world into a critique of *Democracy*, we paused for a while to read in the gaps between them? What happens, in other words, if we read our own hierarchies, our late-modern singularities, through the perspective provided by Tocqueville's account? What would we see if we anachronistically employed some of *Democracy*'s categories as if they were designed to encompass present circumstances? Perhaps the contours of our own despotisms and our distinctive democratic possibilities would be thrown into sharper relief.

Tutelary Power, Tocquevillian Politics

The closing pages of *Democracy* are haunted by the specter of despotism. "Despotism," at least, is what Tocqueville *calls* the evil that stalks his nightmares about the future—but he also suggests that the word he settles for is, in some important and revealing way, inadequate. "Such old words as 'despotism' and 'tyranny' do not fit," because the new threat is unprecedented, exceeds the ordinary referents of those familiar terms.[83] Unable to create a term adequate to the subjugations that concern him, Tocqueville presses "despotism" into service, stretching an old word to fit new conditions but signaling that these conditions push at the boundaries of the traditional political imagination. The fear that strains Tocqueville's inherited political vocabulary, is of a "brand of orderly, gentle, peaceful, slavery." This form of despotism confronts its subjects as,

an immense, tutelary power which is alone responsible for securing their enjoyment and watching over their fate. That power is absolute, thoughtful of detail, orderly, provident, and gentle. It likes to see the citizens enjoy themselves, provided they think of nothing but enjoyment. . . . It provides for their security, forsees and supplies their necessities, facilitates their pleasures, manages their principal concerns, directs their industry, makes rules for their testaments, divides their inheritances. . . . It covers the whole of social life with a network of petty, complicated rules that are both minute and uniform. . . . It does not break men's will but softens, bends, and guides it."[84]

What makes this gentle despotism new, above all, is that it can be "democratic." It is capable of hiding "under the shadow of the sovereignty of the people" and being "combined . . . with some of the external forms of freedom."[85]

These passages attempt to trace the outlines of a new form of state power that may mark modern democracies: the agent wielding tutelary power is government. By speaking of this power as a potentially "democratic" phenomenon, *Democracy* suggests several possibilities. The most obvious, which extends the earlier discussion of individualism, is that formal democracy can be accompanied by substantive disenfranchisement. In this script, the state stages a kind of phantom national politics, giving the regime a semblance of legitimacy while giving the people a semblance of power. Despite their carefully engineered "consent" and their ritualized forms of participation, the citizens do not take part in the most important of political decisions. Many lack political education or capacity, because their own participatory political life has been smothered. Municipal institutions have withered or become hollowed out forms. The art of association is spread quite unevenly through the population. Power and independence are not the common citizen's lot. The fictions of popular rule draw attention away from the sorry condition of the practices and places in which citizenship can be exercised.

Is this nightmare so hard for us to recognize? Tocqueville may here be prescient enough for our needs: his sketch of a possible future captures some of the crucial features of the contemporary American experience of politics. But which features does it capture? It would be too limiting to stop with this most familiar rendition of Tocqueville's fears. We know much about substantive disengagement amidst the rituals of electoral sovereignty, but *Democracy*'s descriptions of the new despotism are not only, or most interestingly, about disenfranchisement and the withering of civic spirit. They are also about the invention or intensification of a particular kind of *power*. The diagnosis of tutelary power is an attempt to capture a distinctive modern social logic, a fundamental way of organizing human experience. This way—which aims to create a particular kind of pliable, vulnerable political subject—proceeds through the production of both of uniformity and uniqueness, combination and separation. Despotic power separates, in that it works to isolate individuals, breaking or preventing self-generated, lateral, practices of sociality and solidarity. It individualizes, in that the subject of tutelage is classified and evaluated by measuring his or her qualities against a series of increasingly codified norms. Yet this codification also results, at the same time, in a certain kind of homogenization, a proliferation of rules. And disciplinary rule becomes the means of binding isolated subjects together. The dream of despotism is of a world in which all ties are those of the state or of "privacy," and in which all decisions can be reached through appeals to technique and code. Tocqueville presents this dream as a nightmare not only because it is contrary to his own aspirations but because he fears that tutelary power is incorrigibly expansionary, that it always seeks to draw more and more power to itself, to colonize more and more of the social world. In principle, the aim of maximizing the "security" of the population and managing "enjoyment" through tutelary intervention has no limit. In practice, the proliferation of despotic institutions erodes other forms of power and thus requires . . . still more despotism.

Here *Democracy* has something to say to late-moderns—and what it tells us concerns more than the state. Though the state is identified by Tocqueville as the agent exercising tutelary power, his analysis becomes more useful and disturbing when we shift our attention from the question of agency to that of technique or form. If we detach the analysis from Tocqueville's own circumstances and conclusions, it is easy to see that tutelary power—a set of techniques or forms of governing, a way of constructing relationships—is by no means limited to formal institutions of political rule.[86] Recognizing this (re-cognizing Tocqueville's map) expands the field of political analysis, relocating the crucial sites of power and struggle. Consider, for example, how such an appropriation of *Democracy* might lead us to redescribe those features of the late-modern political economy that Tocqueville largely failed to anticipate.

If we take our bearings from Tocqueville's sketch of the new *forms* of power, and ignore his own acts of locating politics and ascribing agency, the institutions of corporate organization can themselves be analyzed as apparatuses of governance. The problem is not simply the creation of that aristocracy that he feared only parenthetically, as it were, but the growth and intensification of those forms of power that were the main subjects of his anxious reflections on the state. The governing structures of the capitalist workplace embody the very social logic that Tocqueville feared: like his new despotism, they have colonized more and more of the political world, displacing other modes of organization, other forms of power. As these forms of governance expand across the terrain of political life, the public spaces Tocqueville valued implode and disappear. Institutions for the exercise of local self-governance, the forms of local action, are swept away. Many of the most fundamental of political questions are removed from any direct, civic control. The power to make significant decisions gravitates from the locality to the national stage, and beyond.

The problems with the tutelary forms of corporate power are not, however, confined to the matter of imperialism or external conquest; they are "domestic" as well. In their internal aims and practices, these governments are essentially despotic regimes, structures of command and obedience. They will not tolerate citizens (even if citizenship is understood in terms less exacting than Tocqueville's); they demand subjects. They therefore work to isolate individuals, to prevent the development of the practices of self-government and to destroy these practices where they exist (except for those sporadic moments when these practices are seen as necessary to the increase of productivity). Nor is hierarchy the only problem, here; modes of corporate governance are also about subjectivity. Ever "thoughtful of detail," they proliferate rules, manage "enjoyment," produce norms, mold subjectivities, engage in surveillance in the name of "security." No doubt, there is scope for resistance and struggle, and no doubt some are skilled in the arts of operating on this terrain. But there is very little of the democratic space Tocqueville described and very little scope for the full range of practices that make up his art of being free. Both the "internal" and "external" structures of corporate command and obedience, then, are fundamental abridgements of democracy; they look far more like his nervous speculations on despotism.[87]

Described in this way, our political economy appears as a fundamental obstacle to our freedom, and this problem seems to point toward only one solution: to replace the forms of corporate despotism, we would have to reclaim power from these private governments and dismantle their elaborate chains of command. We would need to return meaningful control to those directly political institutions in which we exercise our citizenship, and we would need to transform the internal empires of work. Read with a certain liberty, at least, *Democracy* would seem to tell us—despite Tocqueville's own notorious hostility to it—that democracy today can only be realized through socialism.

This blasphemous suggestion is at most half serious, however, and not only because of the ironies and tragedies that have followed the socialist project—and perhaps undone it—as this most violent century comes to a close. Though I am serious in claiming that *Democracy*'s account of despotism and democracy can be pressed into useful service in the critique of prevailing forms of corporate power, it would be a mistake to dismiss what Tocqueville has to say about the tutelary state. We should not restrict ourselves to his attributions of agency and his location of politics, but we should not simply dispense with them either. Our "public" institutions of governance can, of course, be described justly with the terms employed in the foregoing analysis of corporate rule. That the state looms large in the popular imagination of unfreedom, that it is so powerful a magnet for political resentment in our times, is no accident. But though the rhetoric of our political campaigns often portrays state and "the private sector" as enemies locked in a battle for supremacy, though the main rhetorical clash is between those who advocate the triumph of the latter and those who talk of a more productive truce, I want to use *Democracy* to suggest that the two combatants are better thought of as Siamese twins. And this is not only because each is arranged in such a way as to violate traditional democratic notions of what popular rule entails: the problem extends beyond that of sovereignty to that of modalities of power. The institutions and practices of tutelary power, of Tocqueville's new despotism, are to be found on both sides of the divide between state and society—indeed, they change the very nature of that divide, blurring the distinction between the two terms, providing modes of governance that reach into all walks of life, all domains of experience. The crucial issue in late-modern polities, then, is not a simple one of whether to locate power in society or the state; as we are faced with interlocking forms of tutelary power, at every level of organization, we cannot use one level to "conquer" another. The project of extending and invigorating democracy requires not merely the creation of institutions more responsive to popular will, but interventions into the forms and practices through which power, and indeed "the people," are constituted.[88]

The retaking of private power by the national, "democratic" state is not, therefore, a fully satisfactory reponse, does not resolve the problems in question. In part, the trouble is that state institutions are bound up with the same modalities of power that are targeted by the democratic critique of capitalism. The state is too big for the job. But in our time, our world, it is also too small: as we have seen, the forces and flows of globalization, the structures and circulation of capital and technology, have clearly exceeded the control of any sovereign, national entity. Under contemporary global conditions, as Connolly puts it, there is "a widening gap between the power of the most powerful states and the power they would require to be self-governing and self-determining."[89] There is much the state *cannot* conquer; it cannot seek the power to be fully "self-determining" without exacerbating the very undemocratic (tutelary and despotic) features that Tocqueville helps us to see.

Where does this conclusion leave us? If Tocqueville aids our critical reading of contemporary powers and problems, the path through them, the route toward a more democratic America, is less clear. Shall we evade the problems and limits of the statist program by returning to localism? Must we recreate that older America in which towns were largely sovereign over their destinies and the assembled citizens were sovereign over the towns? We cannot. The globalizing forces of late-modernity leave local institutions far less sovereign than states, far less in control than ever before. There has not only been a loss of local power but a change in the very shape, the very meaning, of locality. As Michael Sorkin puts it, with thought provoking exaggeration, "Main St. is now the space between airports, the fiber-optic cables linking the fax machines of the multi-national corporations' far-flung offices, an invisible world-wide skein of economic relations."[90] The forces of globalization will not be undone—not by theoretical criticism, not even by careful and concerted political action. Tocqueville's America is not only long gone; it is irrecoverable. When we deny this, reading in the gaps between that America and ours becomes nostalgia for a lost identity, and the critical use of *Democracy* gives way to the desire to impose discipline, to the enactment of cultural violence in the doomed quest for a more familiar form of politics.[91]

Furthermore, if Tocqueville can only suggest a return to older forms of localism, then it is not possible to read him in a genuinely disturbing way. If the story of modernity's destruction of democratic locality is a sad one, if it offers a bleak account of contemporary politics, it is neither new nor especially unsettling. When it does not underwrite the drive for a disciplinary settling of social order, it can only produce a very familiar resignation. Indeed, resignation has accompanied this modern story from the beginning: at least since Rousseau, there has been a powerful tendency to portray the conditions of democratic community as always already lost. For *Democracy* to disturb, it must sustain a reading that neither falls silent on the contemporary politics of bureaucratic discipline and the globalizing dislocations of democracy, nor retells the despairing story of the impossibility of democracy in world that is too large, complex, and interconnected to fit inside the four walls of the town hall. Neither complacency nor nostalgia will do. Can Tocqueville offer anything else?

I believe he can, at least if we are willing to borrow from his insights while refusing to remain bound by his intentions. While my initial formulation will be preliminary, I believe it is possible to uncouple Tocqueville's account of political art, and his critical reflections on despotism, from both the institutional conditions of his America and the wary elitism of his own political vision. The lesson I draw from *Democracy* is that, for democracy to be meaningful, it must be radically plural: it must enable heterogeneous actors to share, in many ways and many places, in exercising and challenging the power that shapes their lives, their selves. In the America of *Democracy*, this meant, above all, a certain kind of localism in government. The arts of being free, the acts of common purpose and resistances to the tyranny of the common, were often performed in particular state institutions. If many of those institutions have fallen into impotence or irrelevance, or out of existence altogether, if the corporation, the nation, and the global political economy have changed the scale, form, and locations of politics, one of the central insights of *Democracy*'s analysis of municipal institutions remains instructive: the spaces and places of politics are not simply the enabling conditions but also the *products* of action. In Tocqueville's America, the citizenry was not only adept at using the institutions of the township, but at constituting the arenas of politics through the exercise of political art. Perhaps an ironically Tocquevillian pursuit of late-modern democracy could begin from the conviction that the spaces of politics need not map precisely onto the terrain of state.

Democracy suggests that democratic institutions can be created by democratic actors, and it shows how and why the failure to construct and make use of multiple sites for politicization, for collaboration and resistance, can foster insidious forms of despotism. It does this while refusing to identify politics with "community" as such, warning us against the dangers as well as the necessity and beauty of common ties. Just as tutelary power moves across and confounds tidy distinctions between state and society, so too can this rich, protean sense of democratic politicization. Under the conditions of late-modernity, we should read *Democracy* as a challenge to create spaces and practices of democracy wherever we are. This means being mindful of the most specific, intimate, and thus local features of political power, but it does not require stubbornly hanging on to *Democracy*'s particular form of localism despite all that has changed. The challenge is not to recreate the township, to reconnect democracy to the self-governing municipality, but to reconstruct democratic practices even when and where that connection has been broken. This means seeking democracy fragmentarily, partially, within our various institutions and against them. It means being willing, at times, to challenge and move outside of formal political institutions and the the channels of rule.

Of course, this first formulation does not suggest (and nor will my subsequent elaborations) that *Democracy* offers us anything like a "solution" to the late-modern dilemmas of democracy. No book, old or new, could do that, for these dilemmas—which are to a significant extent structural— are unlikely to be resolved any time soon. There is not at the moment (and certainly not in Tocqueville's work) anything like an institutional design that will restore full sovereignty to the assembled *demos*—wherever that assembly is located and however "the people" are conceived. Nor, at least on the reading of *Democracy* I have proposed, is the problem of democracy *ever* of a kind that admits of "solutions." To reiterate: there is no escape from the dangerous ground of politics, no political form or culture that obviates the need for struggle, contestation, artfulness. This is not to belittle questions of rule and institutional design, to dismiss them as irrelevant. These questions matter. But if we are looking to open avenues for democratic thought and action, some of the most promising and interesting paths lie elsewhere, and Tocqueville helps point the way for such an intellectual and political redirection. Because his understanding of democracy calls our attention to the practices of politicization, of solidarity and resistance, because he makes the resilience of individuals integral to the democratic condition, he invites us to pursue a reconstructive democratic politics that works not only against but also (partly) outside of the tutelary regimes of modern governance.

What would such a politics look like? What can the call for it mean now? These questions demand a more substantial engagement with a democracy mobile and flexible enough for the formidable obstacle course of late-modern institutional life. But the most appropriate first response is to ask yet another question: what is *left out* of this appeal for a "post-localist," Tocquevillian reimagination of democracy? As I noted at the beginning of this chapter, and hinted at various moments since then, my appropriation of *Democracy*, here, relies on my tactical repression of some of Tocqueville's most fundamental and problematic commitments. Though it enables political criticism and insight, this way of reading also has its costs. It is time for an accounting: the return of the repressed can no longer be avoided, not so much because of the imperatives of scholarly fidelity but because it is crucial, *politically*, to see whether and how the missing elements in *Democracy* prompt a reassessment of the tasks confronting democracy today.

CHAPTER THREE

(Con)Founding Democracy:
Containment, Evasion, Appropriation

Despotism may be able to do without faith, but freedom cannot. . . . How could society escape destruction if, when political ties are relaxed, moral ties are not tightened? And what can be done with a people master of itself if it is not subject to God?

—Alexis de Tocqueville

To live in this pluralistic world means to experience freedom as a continual oscillation between belonging and disorientation.

—Gianni Vattimo

Making America Safe for Democracy

The title of this chapter is more than a pun, for my claim is that Tocqueville can teach us something important about the ways in which foundings, the acts through which democracy is established or secured, inevitably confound some of the democratic impulses that inspired them. The teaching is immanent in the way his study of America proceeds: *Democracy* places fundamental limits on democracy's scope and substance, yet it does so with the intention of putting democracy on a more secure moral and cultural foundation. Tocqueville does not say this as explicitly or reflectively as he might, and his effort to secure democracy is marked by unacknowledged impasses and troubling silences. Partly for that reason, his constraints on democratic possibility are severe, indeed excessive. While these limitations are among *Democracy*'s most notable and edifying features, that does not reduce the work to an "instructive failure," an object lesson about what moves democrats must avoid. Tocqueville's particular way of confounding democracy should be contested, but simply abandoning the moral and cultural problems with which he wrestles is neither easy nor desirable. These problems are, as I shall show, integral to democracy's practice; and when democratic theory evades them, the confounding only gets worse. My aim is thus to take Tocqueville's concerns and inquiries seriously while resisting his conclusions. Through an interrogation of his attempt to place certain forms of authority beneath the reach of democratic inquiry or criticism, I elaborate a contemporary argument for the radical democratization of cultural power, once again drawing on Tocquevillian insights as I do so. This argument extends and refines the account of democratic politicization offered in the previous chapter.

It is not possible to make sense of Tocqueville's way of confounding democracy, however, without acknowledging the major strands in his thinking that I avoided in Chapter 2. My reading has sought to turn his most expansive democratic insights against late-modern forms of discipline, but Tocqueville weaves disciplinary imperatives into the fabric of democracy itself. I have proposed bringing a post-localist politics inspired by him to bear on power's multiple and heterogeneous contemporary sites, but his work essentially declares many of these sites to be out of bounds. Though I have no qualms about stepping over the boundaries authors construct, even the freest of readings must be wary of the traps and obstacles a text strews across the path of interpretation. In this case, the textual fortifications are formidable: *Democracy* seeks to forge indissoluble analytical links between those politicizing arguments I have employed and the calculated depoliticizations I would challenge, repelling such democratic challenges by construing them as necessarily self-defeating. Tocqueville's ultimate claim is not simply that a contestable moral order is undesirable but that only with certain restrictions on contestation can political democracy flourish or even endure: he would have us conclude that his (con)founding provides the most sustainable form of democratic life, and the one most conducive to the preservation of freedom. This is the central claim that I wish both to interrogate and to resist, beginning with a sustained assessment of its theoretical and political costs. These costs are evident in many places, but perhaps nowhere more obviously than in *Democracy*'s map of America.

Consider, again, the gaps in Tocqueville's cartography, the missing people and relationships, the ways in which—as historians and critics have been noting for some years—his survey of a nation without class and without fundamental antagonisms greatly exaggerates the degree of material equality and cultural consensus.[1] Tocqueville placed too many free Americans among the comfortable middle classes: his rich are not rich enough and his undercounted poor are not poor enough. His America is too free not only of disparities of wealth and power but also of barriers to mobility. Through differences of skill and the vagaries of fortune, Tocqueville's enterprising, self-made citizens rise and fall in a social order without fixed positions or sharp cleavages. This curious plotting of social coordinates of course affects the author's survey of political life: once differences of means and opportunity are camouflaged, it becomes possible to evade the struggles these differences provoke. Thus Tocqueville's map reveals nothing of the fractious politics of organized class interest or ethnic conflict. There is little on the political institutions and struggles of the urban areas in this pastoral representation, but then there are no angry farmers and no agitation for land reform, either. As for religion, Christian faith is nearly universal among Tocqueville's Americans, and the range and relations of different denominations do not seem to be sources of fundamental tension. Evangelicalism is not bound up with the pursuit of power and control, is not linked to contests over workplace discipline, the morals of laborers, and the prerogatives of capital. (How could the link be made when those contests, too, are largely missing from this account?) Like much else that matters, then, the political complexities and contradictions of religion in the Jacksonian age remain uncharted by this rendering of American life. There are gaps aplenty: Tocqueville draws a curious map indeed.

These gaps should not be reduced to errors of method or problems in the author's approach to fact. Though one could catalog shortcomings of that kind—casting a critical glance at the limited social circles within which the French aristocrat moved during his journey, or examining his way of interpreting "data"—such an approach would not reach the heart of the matter: it would not take us to the core of Tocqueville's politics or to the ways *Democracy* pushes hardest against radical appropriations. To get there, we must turn away from the language of fact and error and instead examine *Democracy*'s conceptual imperatives and textual strategies. As both Stephen Schneck and William Connolly have argued, the homogenization of American cultural geography is driven by pressures that flow from deep within *Democracy*'s political imagination.[2] In Schneck's words, "The rhetorical idea of [Tocqueville's] America requires such homogeneity."[3] But this "rhetorical idea," and the map that it produces, are in turn required by Tocqueville's idea of democracy itself. The gaps can be read only through a reexamination of that ambivalent idea, for only by recalling its tensions do we see why this particular America is necessary to the security of Tocquevillian democracy.

Tocqueville's ambivalence toward democracy is bound up with another, at least equally deep and significant, ambivalence over the problem of modern (dis)order. In Chapter 2, I argued that *Democracy*'s greatest worry seems to be that order will be too extreme, too severe. Democracy, understood as social leveling and its attendant individualism, may ultimately promote the excess of order that Tocqueville, for want of a better word, calls "despotism." Out of this fear of democracy, Tocqueville turns to a democratic remedy, arguing that citizens who share in the exercise of political power will provide the most effective resistance to the encroachments of the tutelary state. Such sharing promotes cooperation and solidarity, and thus alternative forms of order, but it also fosters resistance and disorder as well. Modern democratic societies must institutionalize— promote sites and practices of—disturbance. If disturbance is dangerous (after all, Tocqueville fears popular excess, too), it is a necessary danger: the exercise and preservation of freedom require space for contestation, openness to challenge. When I showed this earlier, however, I refused to ask, or at least pursue vigorously, a critical question: how much space, how much openness? Taking up that question, we must now confront the ways in which *Democracy* counters its own impulse to sanction disorder. By placing certain moral convictions and cultural formations outside the bounds of criticism, the text confines disturbance even as it promotes it. Tocqueville's enthusiasm for democratic politicization extends only so far.

If his enthusiasm were less restrained, he would be capable of recognizing and representing the less equal, more culturally contested, America that we see when looking back at the Jacksonian age. He could more fully appreciate the democratic character of that age's struggles against prevailing patterns of wealth and power, and the democratic significance of contests over the meaning of America. How else, he might ask, would inequalities be confronted but through the political arts of acting with and against others? How could a democracy avoid the conflictual negotiation of differences? But this is not his response. Tocqueville's theoretical commitment to settling all citizens within unquestioned moral (b)orders make that response impossible. The American inequalities and cultural cleavages he will not render are precisely those that disrupt his account of cultural order and moral ties. The gaps that perplex the empirically oriented historical critic of *Democracy*'s cartography make sense when we understand the Tocquevillian imperative to contain the unruliness of democratic politics. While the previous chapter read "association" as a practice that democratizes struggle, we now see important limits to the work that association can do, the struggles that Tocqueville finds fit for democracy. The problem, in short, is that he leaves no room for democratic contestation over fundamental structures of society, culture, and identity.

Recognizing the problem is crucial to the reading of *Democracy*, but I believe it would be a mistake to use this recognition to resolve or even to stabilize the tensions that mark Tocqueville's enterprise. *Democracy* remains cleaved by ambivalence, pushed and pulled between contending intellectual forces. Though it seeks to provide democracy with unassailable foundations, the ground chosen turns out to be traversed by fault lines, composed of shifting plates. Tocqueville's way of securing democracy militates against the reading of him I have developed so far, but one can still forge a path across this fissured ground, pushing into territory the author did not imagine or tried to avoid. The route followed in this chapter begins by passing through several of the most important sites at which Tocqueville carries out his policy of containment, each site bringing us closer to the policy's sources. Once these have been identified and surveyed with some care, it becomes possible to take further liberties with the text and overcome some of its obstacles. But only some: this chapter ultimately confronts the limits beyond which even an ironic reading of Tocqueville cannot take us. The best place to begin an inquiry into these limits is a section of *Democracy* that has been much praised by latter-day commentators but which—through a regrettable complicity with Tocqueville's rhetorical maneuverings—is rarely linked to the text's deep theoretical structure. I will suggest that the praise should be qualified considerably, and that the best means of doing this is to connect the section's imperfections with the commitments and strategies shaping the book as a whole. The section is *Democracy*'s chapter on "The Three Races that Inhabit the United States." The fundamental problem is Tocqueville's effacement of the constitutive relations between American democracy and American racial formations, an effacement that undercuts the political critique he elaborates there.

"Being American But Not Democratic": Textual Segregation

A reader more sympathetic to Tocqueville's mapping of Jacksonian America might resist this characterization, suggesting that the most important "gaps" are of my own making.[4] After all, "The Three Races" is *Democracy*'s longest chapter, and its account of the enslavement of the black population and the steady dispossession and devastation of the

"Indians" lays bare the most appalling conditions of American inequality. The chapter's portrait of life in America is at once severely critical and despairing. Tocqueville bluntly predicts that the white settlers will destroy the indigenous population, noting with caustic irony that, because the work of destruction has been carried out "legally," it has not led to America's condemnation in the court of world opinion.[5] He argues that the American version of slavery is far worse than those forms found in the ancient world: the American masters employ a "spiritualized despotism and violence" that aims to crush the slaves' inner lives and prevent even the desire to be free; they keep slaves "as close to the beasts as possible." For these and other reasons, the legal code on slavery in the southern states is an "unprecedented atrocity," an expression of a system that "violate[s] every right of humanity."[6] These are strong words, and they demonstrate Tocqueville's critical stance toward the most profound oppressions in American life. But even here there are occlusions, and, even here, there are substantial limits to Tocqueville's democratic enterprise. These are found throughout the chapter, but a brief look at his handling of slavery reveals the major problems.

Tocqueville does not treat race as a minor or superficial part of American life. He presents slavery as not only a legal system but a culture, and he argues that the culture corrupts whites even as it oppresses slaves. The problems are worse in the south, but the culture of slavery has harmed the nation as a whole, and the damage comes both from the way slavery divides whites and the ways it unites them. On the one hand, the cultural differences between slave and free states are so severe as to threaten the existence of the Union.[7] On the other hand, the long history of black slavery on the American continent has shaped mores nationally: "race prejudice" is deeply embedded everywhere. This prejudice is "much more intangible and tenacious" than slavery itself, and it will not disappear even if slavery is abolished.[8] In fact, "Race prejudice seems stronger in those states that have abolished slavery . . . and nowhere is it more intolerant than in those states where slavery was never known."[9]

Such observations lead Tocqueville to a despairing analysis of American political prospects. He concludes "there are only two possibilities for the future: the Negroes and the whites must either mingle completely or they must part."[10] Yet he sees little chance that either choice can be realized. He fears that, even after the emancipation that he assumes will eventually happen, the integration of the races as equals will not be possible: the prejudices run too deep. Barriers of caste are always difficult to dismantle, and this is still more true when these barriers are based on the "visible and indelible signs" of race.[11] And the prospects for a complete separation of the races are far smaller: the races cannot live in isolation within the same territory, and the idea of a black return to Africa is a mere fantasy.[12] From Tocqueville's vantage point, it is no wonder that the danger of a racial conflagration "is a nightmare constantly haunting the American imagination": his survey suggests no likely way for the nation to awaken and resolve the problems of racial subordination.[13]

There is much that is astute and unflinching in this account: as Andrew Hacker reminded readers in his recent best-seller on contemporary racial politics, Tocqueville saw and said much that other commentators would not—and still do not—acknowledge.[14] The chapter places race relations and prejudices at the center of the American experience, thereby showing how troubled and troubling that experience is. Yet the chapter is marked by a peculiar dissonance, a tension between the moral import of Tocqueville's explicit judgment that the atrocities of slavery "violate every right of humanity," and the political effects of his way of talking about these degradations and the avenues for redressing them. If racism and slavery are unjust, Democracy never gives one the sense that they are injustices that should be resisted. They are problems that provoke sadness and resignation more than anger and action: the discussions of race are governed by the disabling logic of fatality. Though Tocqueville writes, "God protect me from trying, as certain American writers do try, to justify the principle of slavery," he immediately adds that "those who formerly accepted this terrible principle are not now equally free to get rid of it" and he soon goes on to ask, "if, to save their own race, [whites] are bound to keep the other race in chains, should one not pardon them for using the most effective means to that end?"[15] The question is essentially rhetorical, the pardon granted. Tocqueville does not cease to call slavery outrageous, but his account removes slavery from the reach of practical confrontation in the present—which is to say that it does not in fact work to outrage its readers.[16] Democracy presents slavery as on the retreat, mentions, in passing, states that seem to be on the brink of abolition, and speculates on what will follow slavery's eventual end; but the discussion of these matters is oddly free of agents or struggles, as if there were no politics involved.[17] It is not surprising, then, that at least one leading black abolitionist, James McCune Smith, accused Tocqueville's writing of aiding "the perpetuation of American slavery."[18]

Of course, Tocqueville can hardly be taken to task for offering no sanguine remedies for the problems of American racism. None were at hand, as contemporary readers—who have seen just how right he was in remarking that racism would persist long past abolition — can well appreciate. But his evasion of the politics of actively confronting slavery is more than a refusal to invent easy and fanciful solutions to complex and stubborn problems; it amounts, despite his moral distress and the acuity of his analyses, to the subversion of his condemnations, to a backhanded legitimation of this condition. In seeking to understand that legitimating resignation, it might be a mistake to dismiss the power of the conventional racial condescension that Tocqueville displays throughout the chapter. If, in Tocqueville's characterization, the whites' treatment of slaves is inhumane, there also seems to be something almost subhuman about American blacks themselves. They are presented as brutish, servile, incapable of hearing the voice of reason, libidinous and licentious, and — hence — unable to use freedom wisely.[19] Such characterizations work to distance the problem of American racism, removing the reader from critical engagement by sustaining the sense of fatality and futility, of the incorrigibility of race.

Whether these characterizations are rooted in personal prejudices, however, is not the crucial point for understanding their role in *Democracy*. What matters are the theoretical imperatives they express and the tactical purposes they serve. As Stephen Schneck argues, America's racial politics present Tocqueville with a difficult rhetorical dilemma: how can the desired image of a homogeneous and equal America be preserved? Unlike many of the other differences obliterated by *Democracy*, race relations were too significant and too undeniable to be hidden altogether.[20] Schneck reads Tocqueville as solving this problem by placing blacks in a subordinate category of being, by treating them as creatures "to be explained by a science of nature rather than a science of democracy."[21] That *Democracy* turns to a science of nature is arguable,[22] but Schneck is entirely correct in suggesting that Tocqueville must do something to prevent race from disturbing his other analyses — and, as we have already seen, the rhetoric of degradation and inevitability is one powerful tactic.

Tocqueville also responds to his rhetorical dilemma through the way he places his observations on race in the larger structure of *Democracy*. "The Three Races" comes at the end of Volume One. Little is said about the problems of racism before that chapter, and the reader who continues on through Volume Two will have few occasions to be reminded of these problems and will certainly not learn how they affect other dimensions of American life. In Tocqueville's framework, racial subordination is analytically and politically segregated from democratic politics. As he puts it in introducing "The Three Races," race relations "are like tangents to my subject, being American but not democratic, and my main business has been to describe democracy."[23] This act of textual segregation is what enables Tocqueville's evasion of constitutive tensions in American political life. The evasion is costly. It keeps us from seeing, in Sean Wilentz's words, "how slavery could have underwritten the expansion of democracy for southern whites in the 1820s and 1830s," how the egalitarian and participatory features Tocqueville chronicles were made possible by, rested economically on, subordination.[24] We will also miss the ways racism shaped the specific problems of democracy in the free states. Though Tocqueville notes the pervasiveness of northern racism, he does not grasp its full political and cultural significance *for whites:* he does not show how whites, north as well as south, constructed the cultural meaning of American identity and the political meaning of citizenship out of their fearful and at times violent encounters with racialized others.[25] The fear and violence are discussed in "The Three Races" chapter, but their formative role in the shaping of American democracy is not explored with any rigor in *Democracy.* Through this masking of democracy's underside, the text works to obscure the political costs of Tocqueville's policy of containment.

That policy, I have been suggesting, expresses the fundamental structure of his thinking about politics: Tocqueville's analyses of the cultural preconditions of democracy *require* him to contain the issue of race. He cannot conceive of means of redressing the injuries of racism that are consistent with the principles of democratic order. If he makes blackness — that "indelible sign" — signify the very disorder that confounds those principles, the deeper theoretical problem is with his conception of order itself. His democracy must have a solid undisturbed cultural bedrock. We know that American democracy in his day was in fact imbricated in a host of contests, struggles, acts of violence, that the cultural foundations were always fractured. Yet the fault lines cannot be shown on Tocqueville's map. It is not simply that he is unwilling to show them, but that his approach precludes the survival of a political democracy in which there are sharp struggles over substantial inequalities and cultural differences (and perhaps even a polity that agreed to extend democratic rights to all, across racial lines and cultural divides, would strain the limits of his theoretical imagination).[26] Why? So far, this chapter has not offered much of an answer. I have insisted that a fractured culture and the overt contestation of social subordination are incompatible with Tocqueville's conception of a democracy's needs, but I have not shown why he construes those needs in this way. The beginnings of a more satisfactory explanation can be gleaned by turning from a case of the tacit and essentially rhetorical acceptance of subjugation to one in which subordination is explicitly justified—the case of gender and the family. There, we see how the containing of democracy proceeds from one generation to the next.

Wives and Citizens: The Gendered Reproduction of Political Virtue

Like the circumstances of blacks, the condition of women is not often explicitly at the center of *Democracy*'s analysis. Discussion of that condition is again largely confined to one specific point in the text (here, a few brief chapters on family life). This time, however, Tocqueville makes it clear that he is exploring a topic that is inextricably bound up with—indeed constitutive of—the character of democracy itself.[27] While the particular American problems of race are treated as highly local, American gender relations are presented as relevant for Tocqueville's French readers as well. Throughout Europe, the broad historical movement toward equality has narrowed the difference of status between men and women, a narrowing that will continue. As the nation that has most fully transformed the family in and for the democratic condition, America may, once again, teach something about the future of other nations. The future that Tocqueville's America recommends to his contemporaries is one marked by a distinctive form of separate and only selectively equal treatment.

In *Democracy*'s account, the key to understanding this new form is the disjuncture between the lives of American girls and those of American women: first there is unmatched openness, then extreme constraint. Nowhere are young daughters less inhibited than they are in America, where they are raised to think, speak, and act freely.[28] While this education for independence—a calculated response to the requirements of life in a democratic age of freedom and equality—equips women to navigate the dangers of the new social terrain, it is also in tension with the character of married life: "In America a woman loses her independence forever in the bonds of matrimony. While there is less constraint on girls there than anywhere else, a wife submits to stricter obligations." Raised in and for freedom, the American girl grows up to live a—freely chosen—adult existence in a home that is "almost a cloister," in which she is kept "within the little sphere of domestic interests and duties."[29]

Tocqueville considers American gender arrangements exemplary precisely because of this dissonance between the stages of women's lives. He endorses the way each stage is structured. The early education is fitting, but so too is the American decision to keep women out of commerce, political life, worldly affairs. This is an arrangement that does not "degrade" either men or women.[30] By offering girls an emancipating education yet assigning them to their subordinate place within the patriarchal family upon adulthood, Americans allow "the social inferiority of woman to continue . . . [while doing] everything to raise her morally and intellectually to the level of man." By organizing social relations in this way, Tocqueville famously concludes, Americans "have wonderfully understood the true conception of democratic progress."[31] While slavery and racism must, at all costs, be fundamentally distinguished from the problem of democracy—while they must not be allowed to disturb the image of a democratic order that is at once equal and harmonious—a certain kind of gendered subjection seems to advance the democratic cause.

Given who he was and when he wrote, that Tocqueville's enthusiasm for democracy does not extend to the thorough democratization of family life and gender relations is, like his racial condescension, hardly surprising. Nor should it be surprising, by this point, that his map of those relations in America again obscures important political activity and conflict, neglecting both the organized associational life of women and the resistance some offered to the ideal of marital subordination.[32] Yet his discussion of family life remains illuminating—not for his particular conclusions but for the reasons behind them and the way these reveal the pressures of containment, the requirements of his (con)founding of democracy. Most immediately noteworthy is the reasoning *not* offered. Though Tocqueville defends America's gendered hierarchy, he makes little use of the most obvious defense: as Delba Winthrop points out, his argument does not turn on "natural" differences between men and women. Winthrop concludes that "He thereby suggests that woman's designated place in the home is a matter of convention."[33] Yet *Democracy* does not defend this convention with the authority of tradition, either, for the American approach is not at all traditional. Neither the order of the universe nor the weight of history are enough to account for Tocqueville's American family; in his account, the gendering of the body politic results from a modern political choice justified by its continuing political consequences. Tocqueville contends that the separation of "the functions" of men and women is best understood as an efficient application of the division of labor, that "great principle of political economy."[34]

What efficiencies are created by this division of labor? And what goods are thereby produced? Tocqueville's concern is less with economic matters than with the political effects of the domestic work performed by women in their capacity as moral educators. As nurturers and child-rearers, women become expert in the reproduction of virtue, in the preservation of mores.[35] The combination of broad, egalitarian initial education and eventual domestic specialization suits women to the vital work of shaping the responsible, stable, coherent selves that democracy requires.[36] The goods produced are civic virtue and moral consistency: without women's playing this role in family life, there would not be the right kind of citizens in the polity. Tocqueville thus defends the American family as a social form necessary to the founding and replication of democratic order. The clearest expression of this argument comes earlier, in Volume One, when he contrasts the effects of European and American families on stability. In Europe, with its far less chaste and orderly family lives, individuals become restless, unstable, destructive; thus, "the disorders of society are born around the domestic hearth." In America, families promote a tranquil and self-limiting politics:

> When the American returns from the turmoil of politics to the bosom of the family, he immediately finds a perfect picture of order and peace. There all his pleasures are simple and natural and his joys innocent and quiet, and as the regularity of life brings him happiness, he easily forms the habit of regulating his opinions as well as his tastes. . . . The American derives from his home that love of order which he carries over into affairs of state.[37]

It is women's assigned role in the shaping of mores that enables this love of order to flourish, that prevents the formation of destructive selves and the concomitant unleashing of too much political turbulence, and it is this containment that sustains democracy; mores are the key to democracy's success or failure.[38] When Tocqueville closes his discussion by remarking, "I think the chief cause of the extraordinary prosperity and growing power of this nation is . . . the superiority of their women," he is serious: acceptance of the nineteenth-century American cult of domesticity is required by his commitment to a homogeneous and stable cultural foundation.[39] The ways Tocqueville's gender politics respond to the pressures of containment thus not only parallel but also help to explain his evasions on the politics of race, for the question of gender takes us deeper into the sources of his theorization of order: overt racial conflict would threaten those very foundations of democratic order that Tocqueville expects the family to maintain. Given the need for specialists in the reproduction of virtue, democratic struggles over the shape and structure of family life would challenge his core understandings of politics more fundamentally than would active struggle against the evils of slavery and racism: loose women are even more destructive than insurgent slaves and their abolitionist allies.

These arguments about family life are drawn from a familiar political repertoire, a standing army of republican tropes. Many a republican defender of civic virtue has supported a similar gendering of familial authority and public and private functions on the basis of its usefulness in the production of citizens capable of self-government, and the maintenance of ordered liberty. Many defending the freedom of republics, European and American, ancient and modern, have figured uncontrolled femininity as a fatal source of political disorder or corruption.[40] But if the arguments seem utterly familiar (with the important exception of Tocqueville's refusal to play the trump card of natural male supremacy), their place within *Democracy* is more complex, ambiguous, and provocative than a routine invocation of traditional republicanism suggests—precisely because Tocqueville is not a traditional republican. His project is not to produce a sovereign center of individual and collective *will*, and his conception of civic action requires a restless unsettling of political order. Yet here the thinker who—however ambivalently—valorizes the unruliness and multiplicity of democratic political life seems to be concerned only with stability, safety, docility. The thinker who worries, repeatedly, about the tyranny of public opinion, its pressures to conformity, the ways it reaches into the recesses of the self, is now intent on ensuring that citizens limit their own opinions, that their imaginations are fundamentally constrained. There is much about the construction of commonality in this discussion, and little about resistance to the commons. In such passages, politics itself appears to be the greatest threat, for Tocqueville's worries about disturbance are worries about the intrusion of politics into places— parts of culture and parts of the self—it does not belong. While Tocqueville's gendering of the American polity follows a familiar script (albeit with the odd plot twist here and there), it forces us to sharpen a question more peculiar to his enterprise: how is the specifically Tocquevillian politics of democratic association served by these depoliticizing limits on the arts of combination and contestation? How is this docile culture of citizenship to be distinguished from the conformity he fears and loathes? Having examined the most significant sites and effects of his policy of containment, we see that Tocqueville feels a need to dampen conflict not only between social groups but within the civic self, that he considers the larger structures of order he wishes to preserve to be essential to the fashioning of effective democratic agents and the preservation of genuine freedom. But we have not determined whether there is something fundamentally contradictory about these various needs and wishes. We still have not resolved the question of why he forges the links between order and disorder in the particular ways he does, where he is trying to go when fleeing the dangerous ground of politics, or how that flight affects the opportunities to employ his work today. It is time, then, to look more closely at the form of authority that Tocqueville found(ed) outside political contestation.

The Puritan Foundations of Democratic Politics

In Chapter 2, we saw that Tocqueville finds local freedom thriving in the townships of New England, and that this achievement seems to be paradoxical. The paradox is that such freedom requires particular mores that could only have flourished under the protection of the right laws, and yet the necessary laws could not have been enacted without the influence of those very mores. The cultural authority *Democracy* invokes seems to be an impossible artifact, the theoretical equivalent of an M. C. Escher image in which a pair of hands draws itself or water runs at once uphill and down. In my earlier discussion of this point, I noted briefly that the text thus seems ready to founder on what Connolly has presented as a more general "paradox of political founding," a paradox that tends to give rise to violence as the theorist seeks to make an apparently impossible authority possible by refashioning people and populations. I also noted that Tocqueville appears to evade the paradox and avoid violence by treating the freedom of the American locality as a form that arose "of its own accord . . . almost in secret," without a singular founding moment.[41] But the appearance is deceptive, my prior reading overly generous. Tocqueville's refusal to provide a discrete founding for freedom does not soften his insistence that there must be foundations; and as our examination of slavery and gender relations indicated, violence and subordination remain in his America. He tries to mask or legitimate these features of the nation's life by treating his foundations as if they simply arose gradually, imperceptibly and almost naturally, but he cannot in the end remove the constitutive exclusions and subjugation on which American order rests. If race and gender are the occasions for some of Tocqueville's most consequential attempts to conceal the costs of democracy's foundations, religion provides the most important materials out of which the foundations are constructed. It is in discussing religion that Tocqueville most actively insists upon the necessity

of a certain kind of homogeneity and placidity: this discussion is the theoretically decisive moment in his (con)founding of American democracy.

Democracy's commentary on local freedom and life in the townships
proceeds through a chain of synecdoches: the nation is revealed in New
England, and New England, in turn, embodies Puritanism. This move
is justified with the claim that America's origins were Puritan, and that
origins invariably reveal the main characteristics of a mature society.[42]
Tocqueville thus effectively makes the Puritans America's founders.[43] But
the purpose of his synecdochical substitutions is less to make a historiographical point than to enable him simultaneously to construct a culturally
coherent America and to forge a strong link between the "spirit of religion" and the "spirit of freedom." Though many thinkers would oppose
these spirits to each other, and though, as he acknowledges, these spirits
are in fact in opposition in many places, Tocqueville argues that they
are happily combined in the essentially Puritan "Anglo-American civilization."[44] Because Anglo-American civilization always already had the appropriate mixture of laws and mores, it provides freedom with the foundation it needs in order to flourish in a democracy. Religion ensures that
political invention will be accompanied by moral restraint. (Women are
effective in and necessary to the reproduction of virtue precisely because
religion "reigns supreme in [their] souls.")[45] The Puritans who shaped the
political life of New England brought this combination of restraint and
invention with them: they were at once "held within the narrowest bounds
by fixed religious beliefs" and "free from all political prejudices."[46] The
result was a political order that was bold, democratic, republican. The
early settlers bequeathed a spirit of innovation and action to their descen-
dants, but that spirit must not extend beyond the boundaries of politics.
Religious consensus does the most important work of containment.

Faithful to its Puritan origins, the homogeneous America mapped by
Democracy retains that relationship between political openness and moral
fixity: "Thus, in the moral world everything is classified, coordinated,
foreseen, and decided in advance. In the world of politics everything is in
turmoil, contested, and uncertain. In the one case obedience is passive,
though voluntary; in the other there is independence, contempt of experience, and jealousy of all authority. Far from harming each other, these two
apparently opposed tendencies work in harmony and seem to lend mutual
support."[47] The result, as Tocqueville adds later in Volume One, is that
"the human spirit never sees an unlimited field before itself; however bold
it is, from time to time it feels it must halt before insurmountable barriers. . . . The imagination of the Americans, therefore, even in its greatest

aberrations, is circumspect and hesitant."[48] The point is not that organized religion seeks influence within institutions of governance: American religious authorities understand that they would diminish themselves were they to bid for direct political power. Nor do sectarian passions intrude into political life in Tocqueville's America, for all Christian religions teach the same practical moral doctrine and duties.[49] Christian consensus does its work below the level of political life, and therein lies its importance: fixing the limits of the moral imagination, it shapes the ideas and passions, the expectations and characters, the forms of discourse, that are capable of entering the political arena. By refusing to interfere in political struggles, while setting the terms within which struggles can take place, religion establishes itself as "the first of [American] political institutions."[50] It is precisely when religion is not directly involved political life that it "teaches Americans the art of being free."[51] Religion's role in America is a fortuitous historical outcome, but it demonstrates a general truth: in democratic societies, freedom cannot do without faith.

Tocqueville invokes this uniform faith that admits of no fissures, that provides foundations without cracks, out of a commitment to freedom. How is freedom served by the imposition of these cultural constraints? Here, too, we encounter ambivalence. The guiding thread through *Democracy*'s various arguments is that faith provides defenses against tyranny, but the defenses sought and dangers feared shift over the course of the book. In Volume One, the primary fear again seems to be of wild politics, too much popular empowerment, self-destructive excess. The danger is that, without the moral restraint imposed by religion, people will accept the idea that "everything is permitted in the interests of society," a doctrine that can only lead to the political overrunning of individual rights and liberties.[52] Thus, religious constraints on action not only serve the cause of justice but also work, over the long run, to preserve freedom and the greatest practicable scope for independent action. But, particularly in Volume Two, the case for the necessity of religion also plays an important role in those moments when depoliticization is presented as the most formidable danger. Once again, the sources of Tocqueville's fear of the erosion of politics are the corrosive individualism and materialism born of equality. Individualism, as we saw, increases the possibilities of both the tyranny of public opinion and of the new despotism. The isolation and everyday, unselfconscious Cartesianism fostered by individualism give rise to skepticism of any individual's claim to truth, but also force people to place excessive trust in the opinions of the majority as a whole.[53] The withering of civic ties in the single-minded quest for material advantage leaves the field open for expansion by the tutelary state. Religion helps to guard against each of these dangers.

Tocqueville's explanation of the protective role of faith amounts to a critique of the rationalistic presumptions of Enlightenment. To those who draw absolute distinctions between liberating reason and enslaving faith, he replies: "somewhere and somehow authority is always bound to play a part in intellectual and moral life." [54] Authority is what gives meaning to human communities and activities. Very few individuals are able to probe the deepest foundations of belief, for most people lack both the time and the capacity to do so. To go about the daily business of living, we must have the firm ground of certainty under our feet. The only question, then, is what ground we will stand on. *Democracy* proposes that religious belief can be the soundest foundation, particularly for democratic societies. Though he acknowledges that religious authorities have sometimes stifled political liberty, Tocqueville insists that the absence of faith is still more likely to do so. With the rise of religious skepticism, "doubt invades the highest faculties of the mind and half paralyzes all the rest." [55] When the loss of certainty over spiritual foundations permeates a culture, there is a frightening and desperate moral turbulence and open-endedness. In such a situation, human will is weakened and the loss of freedom follows swiftly: when people find "everything on the move in the realm of the mind, they want the material order at least to be firm and stable, and as they cannot accept their ancient beliefs again, they hand themselves over to a master." [56]

The ultimate aim of Tocqueville's case for religion, then, is to show that, of their own workings, democratic and egalitarian societies can produce too much—indeed unprecedented—constraint. The political freedoms and even the intellectual horizons of individuals will be destroyed by an excessive and self-undermining openness, by the very form of life that at first looks like an emancipation. Compared to that ultimate narrowing, to the constricting powers of the tutelary state or an omnipotent majority opinion, the constraints of faith are a force for breadth and freedom. Against the major threats of tyranny, religion provides a counter-force, a reserve of strength, a standard of critical judgment. It locates a source of authority outside the transitory positions and possibly excessive powers of mass sentiment; it restrains the materialism and guards against the instabilities that fuel the search for despotic authority. It thus blocks potential dangers to civic life while also leaving that life alone. For this reason, the authority of religion is a "salutary bondage," one that makes the citizen able to "make good use of his freedom." The depoliticization of foundations, the removal of moral authority from contestation through the uniform rule of

Christian faith, is what keeps active democratic politics alive. Those who would rock these foundations must, whatever their intentions, confound freedom and democracy in a way that exceeds the constraints under challenge. Even when Tocqueville wishes to escape the dangerous terrain of politics, it is in the name of protecting that ground, making sure it is not ultimately overgrown with tyrannies or despotisms of one sort or another.

Limiting Democracy or the Limits of (Tocquevillian) Democracy?

Depoliticization preserves politics. Constraint promotes freedom. What should we make of these propositions that are so important to the inner workings of *Democracy?* Even approached from outside the circle of Tocquevillian faith, there is something bracing about this analysis. Tocqueville does not run from the problem of authority, does not wish it away in the name of democracy as a certain progressivist secularism might be inclined to do. Arguing that the issue is not whether but how democracy will be confounded, he forces some compelling questions upon the reader. Does any political system or culture do without articles of faith? (Surely not.) How many individuals can, in fact, provide their own foundations for belief, their own answers to the deepest questions of life? (Nietzsche, that most astute and severe critic of foundations, thought that only a rare few had the requisite strength.) *Democracy*'s responses cannot be dismissed out of hand, especially as they reveal the essential religiosity that lingers on in many ostensibly secular arguments for the necessary cultural coherence of democratic America (for the form of Tocqueville's argument can be filled by content quite different from his version of the Puritan legacy).[57] Nor are there easy ways of rebutting the claim that political contests need limits. Push disagreement deep enough and you get overt violence, push violence far enough and you get war, let warfare run its course unchecked and the polity may be destroyed—as almost happened when slavery did meet with the all-out politicization that Tocqueville himself evaded. There must be some cultural accord, some framework of agreement within which discourse and discord take place. How could that claim be rejected, and how could accepting it not require setting limits on the differences a democratic polity can embrace?

I take that Tocquevillian question seriously. This chapter is, in large part, a response to it. But acknowledging the difficulties the question forces upon us is not the same as turning a blind eye to the inadequacies of Tocqueville's answer. The problems become evident as soon as we examine the answer in light of the gaps between his America and ours, for these gaps belie Tocqueville's claim that his constraints are less severe than the alternatives. Even amidst the raced, sexed, and gendered hierarchies of these times, it is hard to see how the cultural prerequisites he required of authority could be reestablished. If *Democracy* has seduced readers into accepting the accuracy of its cartography, if some can persuade themselves that there once was an America as free of fractures as Tocqueville would have us believe, the cleavages running through contemporary culture are too pronounced to be so easily denied or erased, though they can—and do—provoke a backward-looking resentment against the present (it is here that we can trace the Tocquevillian ancestry of the disciplinary projects of contemporary communitarianism).

Yet accepting, unmodified, Tocqueville's argument for an untroubled foundation would demand this violent erasure of histories, identities, and interests. His account of democracy's conditions necessarily excludes many from the democratic arena. The necessity to exclude and subordinate inheres in, though it is never explicitly acknowledged by, his account of Christian consensus. It is therefore not plausible to dismiss his homogenization of America as an easily correctable blind spot, an effect of his prejudices or context: if the particular figures employed and conclusions offered in his accounts of race and gender are historically specific (and even these, arguably, have lingered on into the present), the imperative to subjugate and the injunction against political struggles over fundamental inequalities are tied to the very structure of his thinking about democratic order. Embracing Tocqueville's approach to foundation entails accepting this imperative. Though offered as a bulwark against tyranny, his version of coherent authority and cultural concord requires intolerable oppression. To imagine the contemporary instantiation of that authority is thus to confront the profound political limitations of his argument. There is no way around it: the price he requires (some of) us to pay for democracy is too high.

To criticize Tocqueville's view of authority for its unpalatable political consequences is not to fault his idea that faith is a potential source of resistance to tyranny (for faith has sometimes been such a source, and if *Democracy*'s enforced homogeneity of religious belief is unacceptable, there is no reason to see faith, as such, as peculiarly oppressive). Nor is it to reject his concern with the moral ties of citizens (for any democratic polity will and should have such ties). Rather, it is to resist the particular role he assigns to faith and morality, the ways he seeks to escape the danger he fears by fixing them once and for all. We can take Tocqueville's question seriously while resisting his conclusion by saying that he slides too swiftly from the claim that there will always be authority to the insistence that whatever holds the authoritative place in a social or cultural system cannot be subject to change or negotiation. His argument misses a crucial step: though he rightly seeks an authority fit for democracy, he does not—at least when he turns from such matters as association to the problem of foundation—adequately confront the question of what it would mean to have a democratic authority. To locate the key problem here is to say, with Claude Lefort, that while Tocqueville understood many things about the distinctive problems of selfhood under the conditions of democracy and modernity, he did not fully recognize that, "modern society and the modern individual are constituted by the experience of the dissolution of the ultimate markers of certainty; that their dissolution inaugurates an adventure . . . in which the foundations of power, the foundations of right and the foundations of knowledge are all called into question—a truly historical adventure in the sense that it can never end, in that the boundaries of the possible and the thinkable constantly recede."[58]

Lefort believes that there is much in Tocqueville's work that helps us to understand that new adventure, but that Tocqueville himself "for some reason holds back from the idea" of the democratic contestability of modern foundations. But we have seen that Tocqueville thought he knew well enough the reason for resisting that idea: to subject those foundations to challenge was to pave the way for the merciless expansion of tutelary power. What I would characterize as the opportunity to democratize authority is presented by Tocqueville as destroying democracy's necessary ground. His reasoning should be borne in mind, for it is not yet clear whether my critique of the gratuitous severity of his way of confounding democracy in any way rebuts his worries about the reasons for the advance of despotism. That his fear of that advance was merited was my position in Chapter 2, where I used his arguments to illuminate contemporary forms of power. Taking Tocqueville seriously thus entails asking how that earlier use of his thinking can be reconciled with this chapter's critique of it. What commitments does one necessarily make when saying that the price for Tocqueville's democracy is too high? Must we face either the domination he wished us to avoid or the domination he wished us to accept—is the contemporary lesson of *Democracy* that we can we do no more than choose between the oppressions of enforced cultural consensus and those of the tutelary state? Is it possible successfully to resist the terms of that choice? Can taking liberties with Tocqueville aid the work of resistance? In short, (how) can Tocqueville's thought best be employed amidst late-modern dissolution, and where is the border beyond which one cannot push without leaving him behind for good? I will suggest that it is possible to move beyond the terms with which he would confine us. Democracy's strategies can be confounded. But the best means of doing this is to work more carefully through the bases of Tocqueville's fear of contested authority. This approach enables a both a deeper understanding of the problem and a sharper sense of the opportunities for striking off on a different course.

A helpful point of entry is provided by Connolly's argument that there are intrinsic and irredeemable limits to Tocqueville's conceptualization of politics. Although he takes Tocqueville to be a principled democrat and pluralist, Connolly construes Tocquevillian principles as incapable of fostering a plurality adequate to contemporary America. In his critical account, the core project of Democracy is the (largely successful) attempt to "code the mores through which a people is produced onto the space of a common territory" and to align the boundaries of that territory and its people precisely with those of the sovereign state.[59] Through this rhetorical and philosophical labor of alignment, Democracy records and participates in the construction of what Connolly calls the "civi-territorial complex."[60] As the boundaries of territorially rooted civilization are established, a common identity must be "burned into" all citizens. The pressures most responsible for this imposition of commonality are those inhering in the logic of democratic sovereignty: within the terms of the civi-territorial complex, democracy is reduced to the problem of popular rule, and this reduction is the key move setting limits to Tocquevillian politics, past and present. To equate democracy with popular sovereignty requires the containment of movement, disruption, difference, "impel[ling] you to ask first, How can a people become unified enough to rule?, and last, How can rule foster the unity of the people?"[61] The result is violence exercised on, and often constitutive of, "the internal other (those inhabiting the territory who do not belong), the interior other (the other within the self which resists such strong identification with the collectivity) and the external other (those who are foreign)."[62]

Unlike other critics of comparable sympathies, Connolly does see traces of the more unruly Tocquevillian theory of democracy that I described in Chapter 2.[63] But he also notes, correctly, that the turbulence Democracy celebrates is confined to surfaces, and he argues that this leaves the underlying civi-territorial complex and the identity it requires undisturbed. For Connolly, this is a fatal move because Tocqueville's territorialism thus produces problems that cannot be challenged from within its own terms. Refusing the homogenization and subjugation demanded by Tocqueville's America requires a reconceptualization of democracy as more than popular sovereignty, as an ethos and form of life in which "those affected have a hand or voice in modeling the cultures that affect them." On this revised account, democracy necessarily remains a matter of rule and borders, but it is also about the resistance to and transgressions of them. This nomadic, rootless, "rhizomatic," form of politics "applies new pressures to existing constellations of identity\difference by shaking the ground in which they are rooted; it challenges them to modify themselves to enable new possibilities of cultural co-existence and political negotiation." [64] The moment of disruption and redefinition is crucial to the coming into being of democracy. Facilitating this coming into being requires the elaboration of a pluralism that lies altogether outside the bounds of the Tocquevillian frame: a more democratic theory of democracy requires a turn to other thinkers.[65]

This account of the pressures exerted by territorialism and sovereignty extends our understanding of Tocqueville's confounding of democracy. In considering the possibilities for a contemporary reappropriation of *Democracy*, it is crucial to recognize that Tocqueville ties democracy too tightly to the imperatives of territory and overly restrains specific popular forces in the name of popular sovereignty: these are powerful obstacles to the democratizing impulse. To be of use for my political purposes, then, *Democracy* thus would have to be read against its sovereign territorialism. Connolly's analysis suggests that these confounding imperatives successfully govern *Democracy*, but I believe that a resistant reading is both possible and valuable—for the sovereignty problematic neither wholly encircles Tocqueville's text nor accounts for the deepest sources of his confounding of democracy. Given the range of his concerns, and the phenomena he analyzes, Tocqueville is, of necessity, attentive to questions of rule and institutional architecture (what comprehensive democratic analysis could afford to elide these matters?).[66] Yet if his attention to these matters at times underwrites his policy of containment, his conception of democracy is by no means exhausted by them. In approaching democracy, he is ultimately less concerned with the channels through which popular will is declared and obedience compelled than with the practices through which selves and relations are constructed and contested.[67] In cultivating politicization (too selectively) he is not so much observing the requirements of sovereignty as seeking to preserve specific modes of power and action: "Democracy does not provide a people with the most skillful of governments but it does that which the most skillful of governments often cannot do: it spreads throughout the body social a restless activity, super-abundant force, and energy never found elsewhere, which, however little favored by circumstance can do wonders. Those are its true advantages."[68] The concern with the unfettering of the modern subject, with the art of freedom and its broad dissemination, with associations and their role in democratizing struggle and constructing a solidarity that does not bind *too* tightly—these substantial elements of *Democracy* do not superimpose politics on the outlines of the state, and they are about more than the preservation of popular rule.

Recognizing this allows us to refine our account of the sources of Tocqueville's politics of containment. To say that Tocqueville purchases a certain kind of freedom and democracy at the cost of homogeneity is both true and insufficient. It is insufficient because, for all of his homogenizing moves, Tocqueville is deeply committed to the preservation of difference. Indeed, along with the freedom with which he sees it as essentially connected, human diversity is Tocqueville's highest value, one that he suggests is of divine provenance.[69] As we have seen, his greatest fear of modern order is that social relations will become too undifferentiated and that the forms of independent selfhood will become too weak to resist the pressures of conformity. His concerns about democracy grow out of that fear, but his enthusiasm does too, for he sees in the (limited) disturbances of democracy a promising response. As his comments on democratic association reveal with particular clarity, he wishes to secure the greatest openness to difference possible under the conditions of modernity, and he turns to (some forms of) democracy as the appropriate—if dangerous—means of doing so.[70] Rather than simply imposing conformity in the name of sovereign freedom, then, Tocqueville paradoxically imposes conformity in the name of difference, using freedom and democracy as the middle terms in this transaction. He argues, in other words, that cultural coherence of a certain degree and kind is necessary to free politics, and that, under modern conditions, the eclipse of free politics will lead to a conformity of self and society far more pervasive and invasive than anything produced by his cultural consensus. This is why both the forces pushing *for* conformity and those pushing *against* it course so powerfully through his text. Tocqueville does not valorize consensus, as such, does not make it the purpose and destiny of collective life; he seeks to establish a consensus that will allow dissension to flourish and endure. Though he does not leave room for nearly enough dissonance, though his understanding of the degree of democratic difference possible under the conditions

of modernity is not ambitious enough for our own diasporic and globalizing late-modern condition, his motivation is less a longing for union than
a fear of too much of the wrong kind of unity.

Understanding that Tocqueville's ultimate concern is with the problem of difference and that his ultimate fear is of excessive unity enables
us to identify the most significant source of the homogenizing imperative
in his thought. This source is not his concern with sovereignty but his
analysis of the problem of *struggle:* Tocqueville's worry is less that contestable foundations will make popular rule impossible than that they will
invite struggles of a kind that will make rule too despotic. Tocqueville
does not believe that the democratic powers and practices conducive to
the preservation of difference and the formation of resilient selves—those
powers and practices best sustained by the arts of associating—can survive struggles over the most fundamental social and cultural structures.
The fears born of this analysis of struggle are the deepest source of his
most noticeable cartographic gaps and unsatisfying political conclusions,
his erasure of American inequality and his containment of certain American differences. The problem of struggle profoundly affects the question
of (in)equality because, for Tocqueville, the attempt to conquer social
hierarchies through political means leads to still more pernicious forms
of subjugation: organized struggle against entrenched social power must
fuel the growth of tutelary institutions and practices, resulting in the bureaucratic colonization of much of the social world and, consequently, in
both the obliteration of difference and the erosion of freedom.[71]

Democracy thus cannot portray the full range of American social and
economic inequalities because they place Tocqueville in a theoretical
double bind: on the one hand, the structural differences in power cannot be challenged through political means without threatening to destroy
some of the best hopes for modern political life; on the other hand, *Democracy*'s account of those hopes, of civic activity and the shared exercise of
political power in America, becomes implausible if inequalities are too
great. While equality looms large as a threat to difference in his writing,
this threat can at least be managed by providing a wide array of political
spaces and by nourishing the art of being free. These are the very remedies threatened by attacks on structures of social inequality: while the art
of association democratizes struggle, the practice of that art is incompatible with cleavages that are too sharp, for those cleavages ensure that
political spaces will be squeezed shut by the pressures of the tutelary state.
Tocqueville's stories of the unstoppable historical drift toward equality,
though the source of some of his very real and powerful anxieties about

homogenization, are also convenient devices for fending off a problem that cannot find a democratic solution within the terms of his theorizing.

The same limits to the practice of democratic struggle shape Tocqueville's account of the cultural differences that must not be allowed to threaten the cultural foundations of authority (and indeed, many of the differences he views as most threatening are those, such as "racial" differences, that are produced or intensified by structures of extreme inequality). Bound together by the shared culture of Christianity, restrained from certain unwise actions or judgments by that culture's practical morality, America's citizens are capable of struggling actively, democratically, over all of the divisions that remain, resisting the tyrannies of the mass while participating in a common world. Here their political arts come into play, providing means of at once containing and fostering agitation. All this is possible once there are foundations without cracks. Allow the cracks and, as cultural formations shift and drift apart, differences will exceed the capacities of democratic practices and institutions, requiring more severe forms of authority to hold the social order together. The extreme uncertainty and turbulence introduced by radical moral pluralism will ultimately produce a longing for some more secure form of order, for an end to those struggles in which the stakes are the deepest foundations of belief and the basic contours of social life. The result, once again, will be still more troubling forms of enforced conformity, and, in the end, the confounding of democracy itself. With this last reconstruction of *Democracy*'s argument, we have reached the point at which we must at once borrow from Tocqueville and leave him behind for good.

Adventures with Authority: Returning to Dangerous Ground

We have seen that he demands at once too much and too little of democracy: too much because his conception of the democratic citizen asks the self to pay too high a price, to blend too smoothly into the prevailing cultural formation, to achieve too much coherent virtue; too little because democratic struggle is confined to too narrow a range of actors, topics, institutions, and forms of life. The two problems are mutually constitutive: selves are homogenized in order to minimize social disturbance, and social struggle is contained in order to shore up the integrity of the self. To secure foundations beneath the ground of politics and thereby evade the dangers he fears the most, Tocqueville must overlook other dangers, accepting the modes of subjection and violence his foundations entail: though he prided himself on being the most clear-eyed and unflinching of observers, the unfolding of his arguments leads him to turn away from certain consequences of his own thinking. To examine what he evaded is to be pushed into the adventure of uncertainty from which he pulled back. We must expand the terrain of democratic struggle, thereby taking politics over the barriers with which he would contain it.

There are elements in Tocqueville's text that, when turned against his more constraining conclusions, facilitate this effort. Despite the severe limits of Tocqueville's thinking about cultural consensus, I find something instructive in *Democracy*'s ways of revealing to the attentive reader the oppressions its foundations require. The instruction is greatest if we read the text's most severe homogenizing moves with the aid of the Tocqueville I took the liberty of constructing in Chapter 2, the thinker who would resist as well as create a commons, who refuses to purge dissonance because he knows that any settled order does violence to the world and the self, and—thus—that all foundations are cracked. (Why not allow him into the conversation? After all, he bears at least a passing resemblance to the advocate of compulsory consensus we have been discussing here.) That more unsettling Tocqueville enables us to conclude that *Democracy*'s homogenizations teach something not only about the politics of his book but about democracy itself. The lesson is harsh but simple: because democracy is inevitably (con)founded, subjugation is never wholly avoidable. All communities do indeed exclude, just as all are necessarily bound together (though not seamlessly, not without cost) by practices of authority. To refuse these propositions is not to pave the way for emancipation and a more generous way of living but to disable political analysis and struggle by masking some of the most important dynamics of human interaction. A more democratic understanding of limitation and constraint can only be reached by working through and responding differently to these dynamics, not by denying them. Agreeing with Tocqueville—both Tocquevilles, as it were—that there is no escape from these problems, that they are constitutive of politics, need not entail removing any particular exclusion or form of authority from the reach of political inquiry, challenge, and invention. If there will always be foundations that will necessarily foreclose as well as open possibilities, subordinating some (parts) of us even as they authorize and empower others, they need not remain uncontested or unchanging. Tocqueville's emphasis on disturbance can thus be read against his particular foreclosures, helping us think about how to use the inevitable fissures to struggle against the political evasions that necessarily mark such founding moments. We can recognize that whatever a given constellation of authority forecloses upon is sometimes that which is most in need of being drawn into the field of political inquiry and challenge; and that this act of challenge can be the most important move in the repertoire of democracy.[72]

This conclusion resists some of Tocqueville's most consequential rhetorical moves and refuses some of his most deeply held convictions, but it is still reached with his aid. To insist, against his quest for certainty, that democracy must extend all the way down to foundations, that no authority is permanently or on principle beyond contestation, is not to insist that democracy transcends the question of authority or that the problem of subjection is resolvable through the perfection of democracy. All elements of Tocqueville's thought show us that such resolution is unattainable, not only because perfection can never be reached but because even perfect democracy (whatever that may mean) would not do away with the dissonance that inevitably resides within selves and haunts their relations to social order. Ambivalent and conflictual creatures that we are, no social identity can be assumed without residue or resistance. Read freely, Tocqueville can teach us about the democratic politics that flow from a recognition of this inescapable dissonance.

Public and private freedom, solidarity and resistance, commonality and distinction—Tocqueville's democracy relies on all of these goods, valuing them both for the ways they complement each other and for the tensions between them. Both the tension and the complementarity are valued because both are necessary to the formation of democratic individuals who are capable of acting artfully under the conditions of modernity. At least before he reaches his too-solid foundations—foundations we need not accept on his terms—Tocqueville thus shows us a political world from which dissonance can never entirely vanish: the tensions meet with no theoretical resolution, and such practical resolutions as can be achieved will not be permanent. They will always be contingent settlements—accords, colonies, ways of stopping motion—and there will invariably be moments when the task of politics is to disrupt such modes of order. Thus, while public and private freedom are both important and at times mutually reinforcing, Tocqueville will neither deny their potential conflicts nor simply subordinate one to the other. And thus, while he insists on the necessity of lateral bonds that can take the place of the fixed hierarchies of old, he will not treat democratic practices as free from danger: both in its most robust forms and in its attenuation, democracy is a threat to certain individuals and certain aspects of individuality.

The artful democratic citizen, the one who has learned well how to exercise freedom, is best prepared to negotiate the dangers peculiar to modernity; but skill in the art of being free does not make the dangers go away. Civic identity, for Tocqueville, does not attune us perfectly with our fellow citizens, our natural destiny, or God's design. Even to learn the skills and become inculcated into the culture that allow artfulness to flourish requires a demanding apprenticeship, a working on the self that is not without its subjugations and costs. In my appropriation of Tocqueville's thought, even the practices and institutions that teach those skills may, themselves, have to be resisted. Like other identities, the identity of the citizen will, at times, weigh too heavily, constrict too much. (My) *Democracy* is to be read not in denial of that, but for the argument that, still, a world in which the skills and powers and places of the citizen are pluralized much more radically is one in which even these problems can be best addressed. The dissemination of political skill and the provision of political spaces, the openness to challenges to democracy's foundations despite the recognition that our beliefs are always, somehow, grounded — these are imperfect remedies for late-modern political ills, but that does not mean they are ineffective or that more perfect ones are available.

What does this recognition, this alternative approach to the (con)-founding of democracy, entail? If the task is to uncouple *Democracy*'s account of the practices and processes of democratic politicization from the specific conditions of Tocqueville's America, to appropriate his insights without also perpetuating his exclusions and constructing a nostalgic narrative of loss, then we must both extend and transform his hope by transposing the book's most enthusiastic accounts of the unruliness of democracy from the register of "politics" into that of "culture." We must multiply the sites in which democracy's disturbing shaping of selves and relations takes place, refusing to accept Tocqueville's cultural settlements and the specific forms of violence they engender.[73] His thought can be of use only if it does not prevent us from fostering struggles in the blank spots and forbidden zones of *Democracy*'s map. But focusing on these sites is not the same as returning to the Tocquevillian locality. The fundamental structures of culture, difference, and identity that he removed from politics touch us intimately, often bodily, but are not necessarily organized municipally or even territorially; though contesting the regimes of race, gender, and sexuality requires common action, those with and against whom we act need not be our neighbors. Once we are resolved to bring democratic struggle to structures of this kind, and to recognize the ways they exceed *Democracy*'s politics of location, then we can borrow from the text's rich understanding of the art of being free, of the use of association to promote both concord and discord, and of the workings of tutelary power. If we break with Tocqueville's form of foundationalism, and take a less constricted approach to the problem of structure and struggle, then Tocqueville's wary ambivalence and his unusually complex understanding of the political relationship between democratic individuality and democratic collectivity become rich resources for political theorizing that stays on dangerous ground.

But two important caveats are in order. First, this discussion would be incomplete if I did not acknowledge Tocqueville's cautionary tale, one that those of us who would pursue a more disturbing politics ignore at our peril. As we look back on a century in which statist assaults on difference have been more ferocious than he could ever have imagined, we cannot simply dismiss his critique of the social logic of despotism. Nor, in an age when polities in many parts of the world are being torn apart by their internal divisions, should we be too quick to dispense with his worries about the cleavages that a democracy can survive. Of course, from the perspective elaborated in this book, it would be a mistake to rest with Tocqueville's conclusions: after all, the relations that he would remove from political criticism are, as Chapter 2 argued, themselves riddled with tutelary powers and other despotisms; and today's destructive struggles over difference are often the legacy of yesterday's political investments in policies of containment, of attempts to anchor differences in monolithic foundations (attempts that were themselves marked by violence and subjugation).[74] Still, *Democracy* helps us see dangers that must be kept in mind, for the struggle to democratize difference and confront late-modern hierarchies has barely begun and has no certain methods or unproblematic precedents. If there is clearly more room for maneuver and less scope for unproblematic, foundational stability than Tocqueville indicated, he still offers a sobering account of the obstacles facing political thought and practice, reminding us that we must make our way cautiously. But make our way we must, nonetheless—and it is here that we reach the limits of being free with Tocqueville.

These limits prompt my second caveat: to think through this problem of struggle requires more assistance than Tocqueville can provide. If *Democracy* offers a rich panoply of concepts and analyses that can be employed once we transpose his approach to democracy to social and cultural registers, that transposition can do only so much work. Read resistantly,

Tocqueville helps sharpen our understanding of what democracy can look like on these other terrains, but there are crucial lacuna when we look to his work for ways of thinking about *democratization*. To seek democracy in American social and cultural life is to confront manifold and powerful undemocratic habits, structures, sensibilities. In his reflections on the art of association, Tocqueville gives us a brilliant (if, as we now see, too limited) account of the democratization of struggle; but what is most needed when theorizing a post-localist and ironically Tocquevillian radical politics is an analysis of the struggle to democratize. That analysis is what is most lacking in Tocqueville's thought, even though his work is a response to (what he understands to be) the grand historical democratizing currents of modern life. Though he plumbs, with unmatched depth, the dangers that attend political challenges to social hierarchies, one unfortunate result of his acute sensitivity to these dangers was his elision of the struggles out of which democratic conditions—including those he admires—arise. Democratic association is a practice that grew in response to hostile forces and that continues to do its most important work in struggling against them. Without a better understanding of such self-consciously political struggles to democratize, we will remain caught in some of the impasses that mark *Democracy:* if the goal is to accept the inescapability of dissonance within polities and selves, to elaborate a democracy with more room for the play of differences, and yet to think about the politicization of structures of social and cultural subordination, then one needs resources that cannot be found in this text.

My wager has been that pushing the limits of Tocqueville's analysis can illuminate not only the character of Tocqueville's remarkable book but also some of the deep and relevant dilemmas of democratic thinking. I have tried to suggest that the book is useful not only despite but *because* of the difficult, resistant work that a radical reading requires. That work throws our problems into sharp relief while also forcing us to confront some of the dangers and self-deceptions that have all too often marked more conventional political radicalisms. Still, it is time to admit that this project can be taken only so far with Tocqueville, and to see how other thinkers move the work along. Arendt will ultimately provide us with an example of political thinking that is less fearful about the contestability of foundations, and that abets a more vigorous exploration of the democratization of authority. I first turn, however, to Marx, who was centrally preoccupied with theorizing and fostering struggles against hierarchy. We thus move from the deepest of democratic, counterrevolutionary thinkers to revolution's most ambitious affirmative theorist. While Marx is arguably democracy's most astringent radical critic, he is a crucial interlocutor for any effort to think through the tasks of democratization. If it will prove necessary to resist both his theorization of revolution and his aspiration to take radical politics beyond democracy, his writings about political struggle are ideal sources for sharpening our sense of the transpositions for which I have called but which, working only with Tocqueville's texts, I have invoked in rather abstract ways.

CHAPTER FOUR

Reading Freedom, Writing Marx: From the Politics of Production to the Production of Politics

Rational logic may not find it easy to explain how . . . two apparently contradictory discourses can coexist within the same position. Ideology, however, works according to "logics" of its own—ones which are capable of sustaining apparently mutually exclusive propositions, in a discursive structure closer to the dream-work than to analytic rationalism.

—Stuart Hall

The language of critique is effective not because it keeps forever separate the terms of the master and the slave, the mercantilist and the Marxist, but to the extent to which it overcomes the given grounds of opposition and opens a space of translation: a place of hybridity, figuratively speaking, where the construction of a political object that is new, *neither the one nor the other*, properly alienates our political expectations, and changes, as it must, the very forms of our recognition of the moment of politics.

—Homi K. Bhabha

All I know is that I am not a Marxist.

—Karl Marx

Talking with the Dead

That these are not auspicious times for Marxist theory is a conclusion well on its way to becoming a cliché. Innumerable critics, and not just America's End of History triumphalists, declare that Marx's social thought is every bit as dead as the "actually existing socialism" so recently swept away by the people of the former Soviet bloc. Even if the obituaries are once again premature, the critics would appear to have a point: the signs that Marxist theory has fallen upon hard times are visible just about everywhere. Reportedly, interest in Marx has disappeared among Eastern and Central European intellectuals since 1989, and has undergone a precipitous decline among Latin American militants as well.[1] Nor is the Old Mole faring much better with Western academics. Even on the left, the abolition of markets, long considered to be the essential core of the Marxist vision of a post-capitalist world, is an idea with virtually no serious adherents today. Outside the domain of economy, many radical theorists concerned with the workings of power in institutions and culture some time ago forsook the Marxist problematic for insights drawn from Foucault, Lacan, the later Baudrillard, the vast range of non-Marxist feminist theories, and other sources. Among those theorists with lingering ties to the socialist tradition, "post-Marxism" has been the ascendant paradigm for over a decade—long enough, in a time when academic fashions change as swiftly as those for other consumer goods, to make one wonder whether post-post-Marxism can be far behind.[2] There *are* unreconstructed Marxists among the professoriat, to be sure, but their numbers dwindle and their isolation grows.

At this historical juncture, it may seem perverse to return to Marx's corpus, at least if the reason for the return is to seek counsel rather than to perform an autopsy. Nevertheless, such a return is the purpose of this chapter: it is my contention that, even as the late-modern condition erodes familiar certainties and obscures many traditional intellectual signposts, Marx's writings offer contemporary readers valuable political guidance. I take Marx to be an important teacher on the subject that was of the greatest concern to him throughout his life, human freedom: his works still help us to think about where and how to be free.[3] Furthermore, despite the ambivalence and even confusion that mark his thinking on this topic, Marx's works also remain an essential intellectual resource for those confronting the problems of democracy and democratization. Of course, these works are fundamentally problematic; and among the most important of their limitations (and thus among the sources of the contemporary flight from Marxism) is a pattern of political evasion and homogenization that mirrors the strategies we have already seen in the writing of Tocqueville and his communitarian acolytes. Though one task of this chapter is to explore Marx's variations on those strategies, to trace their origins and assess their consequences, an awareness of the politically tragic shortcomings of his theories should not blind us to the lessons that still can be found in his writing. These lessons illuminate crucial problems in contemporary theory in a way that enables us to extend the inquiries and arguments of the previous chapters, refining our understanding of the ways political agency and subjectivity are created in and through struggle, and thereby sharpening our picture of the politics of democratic dissonance. Perhaps the most relevant place to begin an exploration of Marx's enduring political pedagogy, then, is by noting some of his departures from the assumptions and commitments of theorists such as Tocqueville.

While lifting Tocquevillian themes out of the context of the early American locality requires difficult—and, to some ways of thinking, dubious and disreputable—hermeneutic labors, no such effort is required to place Marx's work on a larger political stage. Not long after *Democracy in America* hailed the New England township as an exemplary modern instance of the practice of democracy, Marx suggested that such places and practices were already anachronistic: they were inadequate to the work of freedom because they were incapable of negotiating the primary conflicts and harnessing the fundamental social forces of the new era. While Marx's formative early encounters with republican notions of citizenship left a lifelong stamp on his work, from his earliest significant writings onward he sought to criticize and move beyond these notions—indeed, beyond *all* inherited conceptions of civic freedom.[4] Though the motivations for and expressions of this critical effort were multiple and complex, two arguments are particularly important for my purposes: republican politics necessarily preserves structures of social subordination, and the republican polity cannot be the sovereign center of political life in a world in which power relations are increasingly transnational. As Marx's thought developed, both insights were articulated together in a project that asserted the primacy of class. It is here that his project poses the most fundamental challenge to Tocqueville's *Democracy*, to my critical appropriation of that text, and even to democracy as such.

By the early 1840s, and before class emerged as a central and sophisticated category of his analyses, Marx was already developing his argument that radicals had to transcend republican (and liberal) ideas of citizenship.[5] Although the central objects of Marx's criticism were left-Hegelian philosophy and the Jacobin political imagination as it had descended from Rousseau and the French Revolution, the critique applies as well to the kind of argument Tocqueville pursued in *Democracy*. The inability to confront certain antagonistic differences, the masking or legitimating of the most fundamental inequalities, the insistence on the need for foundations beneath and beyond criticism—these are, on Marx's account, built into the very structure of existing democratic states. These states construct politics and democracy in such a way as to exclude "social" structures and problems, thus making freedom available only to certain people, in certain places and certain narrow forms. To make the fullest possible freedom available to all people, in all spheres of life, existing structures of thought and action must undergo a fundamental transformation: only by moving beyond this narrow preoccupation with and construction of the political can the task of liberation proceed.

As Marx's thought developed, this emancipating move soon came to be conceived as one not only within the social geography of the democratic state but across national frontiers as well. With Marx's conceptualization of the social totality as a mode of production, and with his identification of the capitalist mode of production as both the horizon of all previous modern political struggle and the object against which the war for liberation must now be fought, the lines of radical political alliance necessarily broadened outward.[6] When, to quote the famous and inflammatory rhetoric of *The Communist Manifesto*, the world has become one market and the global dynamics of capitalism bring "an uninterrupted disturbance of all social conditions," then "national one-sidedness and narrow-mindedness become more and more impossible": when the bourgeois enemy wields power on a global scale, and the interests of the exploited proletarians are similarly universal, it is time for "the union and agreement of the democratic parties of all countries," time for radicals to "everywhere support every revolutionary movement against the existing social and political order of things." It is only when radical class struggle traverses both of these boundaries—obliterating those distinguishing the institutions of "politics" from "society" and storming over those separating nation from nation—that it will become possible to win the revolution that shall, ultimately, make "the free development of each . . . the condition for the free development of all."[7]

The free development of each and all, then, is the goal: this slogan condenses Marx's vision of emancipation. But it is easier to recognize the central importance of this commitment than to unpack its meaning. What would the slogan's realization entail? How is the goal to be pursued? Immediately, we confront two problems. The first is that, though Marx's analysis of the global structures of capital and bourgeois power grew more and more comprehensive over the years, and though his own work as a political activist did indeed transgress national boundaries, he did not go very far in *theorizing* the structures and practices of transnational political action—staying, by and large, at the level of mere exhortation.[8] If the goal is to find direct practical recommendations for contemporary democratic actions that stray outside (while also working within) the confines of the sovereign, territorial state, then Marx has little to say to us that is of direct relevance. But even if we therefore put this problem of global scale aside and focus, as I shall for much of this chapter, on Marx's critique of conventional democracy's too narrow institutionalization of politics, and his corresponding illumination of the struggles and practices through which political identifications are constructed, a problem remains: Marx's accounts of the transcendence of older political structures and theories, and his conceptions of what the ensuing emancipation would look like, are often confusing and contradictory. To craft a concrete, unambiguous, and persuasive exposition of that famous call for free development is no easy task.

It is possible, of course, to speak coherently about Marx's emancipatory goals if one stays at a high level of generality. In all of its various moods and forms, his writing about freedom insists on the need to dismantle structures of heteronomy: human living together should be arranged so that activity can be self-generated and individuals become capable of developing their multiple talents and capacities with the minimum possible degree of imposition from external circumstances.[9] For Marx, this activity is always conceived of as taking place in a world rich with ties to other individuals since, as *The German Ideology* puts it, "Only in community [with others has each] individual the means of cultivating his gifts in all directions; only in the community, therefore, is personal freedom possible."[10] Given this emphasis on the cultivation of multi-faceted individuality, Marx is, at least in principle and on this high plane of abstraction, dedicated as well to the fostering of difference: he can be read as a committed pluralist, albeit one of an unusual kind.[11] But how persuasive or problematic is this reading? And, again, what does it *mean* to construct freedom in this way? Once we descend to the more concrete questions of reading and politics, to those that demand intellectual and practical struggle, we are required to face the conflicts and complexities confronting any thoughtful explorer of Marx's work. The Master's voice ranges across registers, inhabiting different personae and issuing contending edicts: we must come to terms with the ways in which Marx speaks against himself.

Contra Diction: Marx against Marxism

Karl Marx's writings span four decades. Currently, the English-language edition of Marx and Engels' collected works runs to forty-seven volumes.

This lifelong productivity confronts us with a familiar puzzle of interpretation. Many Marx scholars are convinced that the "early" and "later" or — depending on the critic's political and methodological point of view — "mature" Marx had substantially different things to say. Some even doubt that the two figures are on speaking terms with each other.[12] Other writers leave the impression that, though Marx's theoretical personality was indeed multiple, these two chronological selves are not the most relevant characters: for the young and the old Marx we may substitute, variously, the humanist Marx, the structuralist Marx, the rational choice Marx, the forces of production Marx, and so on.[13] For every period or genre of his work, there are hosts of warring critics, each offering a "definitive" account of this writing and its significance for our understanding of Marx's "true project."[14] Any attempt to solve a significant riddle in his thought thus immediately encounters the question, "Which Marx?"

There is something to say for all of these constructions of Marx's work, and a great deal to say for some of them, but my purposes are best served by writing about Marx *without* saying any of it, by taking the liberty of setting all of these characters and their champions aside. The argument pursued here does not *replace* the standard interpretations — does not offer yet another totalizing and authoritative rendering of Marx's *oeuvre*, or discredit those that already exist — but explores the possibilities that emerge when these figures are temporarily *displaced*. Reading with a certain freedom, I search for material that extends our exploration of a politics that stays on dangerous ground. Marx provides such material, but engaging it requires us to tell another story about him, one that locates and probes a rather different tension. This tension concerns the meaning of freedom and its relationship to democratic struggle.

If the goal is to foster individual development within an open community rich in self-sustaining relations — if, as with Tocqueville, the aim is to tie individuals to others without crushing individuality, to contest structures of subordination without shutting down space for the flourishing of difference — there remain different ways of pursuing and even conceiving of this end. In Marx's thought, as I read it, we can identify two contending approaches: the one more obviously at the center of his work can be called "freedom as transcendence"; call the other, less obvious, conception "freedom as a political practice." The accent in the latter formulation is on the "political," because these two conceptions of freedom differ most in their respective approaches to politics. Viewed from the perspective of the first conception of freedom, not only inherited understandings of politics but *the political as such* must be transcended. There are foundations beneath the political, and the tasks of emancipation require their reconstruction: politics can be transcended because the exploitation, subjugation, division, and conflict that make it necessary can, through the completion of the revolutionary project, be overcome for good. Transcendent emancipation can bring about complete *transparency:* when the structural bases of social contradiction and the power of person over person are dissolved, relations between and within selves will lose all opacity.[15] Because of the understanding that is made possible when individual life-projects and collective planning become fully transparent to participants and observers, it will be possible to create an enduring and fundamental harmony.[16] It is this conception of transparency-transcendence that underwrites the much noted, often criticized, and deeply problematic Marxist call for a world in which all problems become purely administrative.[17]

Yet though this call is, indeed, a significant and enduring part of both the Marxist inheritance and Marx's own work, it is important to listen for and to the other voices in his texts. The one calling for what I have termed freedom as a political practice does not lull us into imagining an end to or evasion of struggle. This alternative conception of freedom seeks to make good on the (hitherto) delusional promises of democratic citizenship by extending the democratic construction and exercise of power across the terrain of social life, turning every site into one where the struggle for emancipation can be waged. Here, the goal is not the transcendence but the radical transformation of politics, the renegotiation rather than the abolition of conflict, the proliferation of sites for the expression of democratic dissonance instead of a healing that makes democracy unnecessary by resolving discord once and for all: there is no secure foundation that can support a human world without power, and there is no reason to imagine that philosophy is something that can, seamlessly and with finality, be "realized." Marx's work calls for democratic struggles to reshape the structures and material practices of social life and for the radical—which is to say continuous and always contestable—democratization of the modern political imaginary; at its best, it shows how these two tasks are mutually constitutive.[18] Marx here makes democracy always at stake, always at risk, always underway, and, hence, always about democratization. In these moments, his writing offers us an understanding of freedom and politics that refines and extends the one that, reading against the grain and running up against certain ultimate limitations, I teased out of Tocqueville.

Does this comparison indicate that, unlike those Tocquevillian appropriations, the ideas to be explored in Marx's work are simply "there," manifest in "the texts themselves?" Not really. It is not as if Marx himself resorts to either of these names: "transcendence" and "practice" are terms of art I employ in order to think with some of the perplexities that mark his writing about freedom and politics. Perhaps these terms are best thought of as enabling fictions. Yet my claim is that they *are* enabling because they help us to identify and read a set of tensions, of ambiguities and ambivalences, in Marx's work. These tensions cut across the divisions so often (and perhaps with reason) used to classify that work: they run not only between Marx's texts but within them, marking writings both early and late, humanist and structuralist, philosophical and political, and so forth, sending the shock waves from the contention over freedom into such other crucial issues as the nature and explanatory status of class. As with the investigation of Tocqueville, it is in identifying the ambivalences, exploring the tensions, seeking to reveal and understand the pressures that drive Marx's cultivation and evasion of politics, that the most fruitful lessons can be learned.

This exploration at times requires (still more than with Tocqueville) careful attention to how the texts *work*. In the richest of Marx's political analyses, the most fruitful tensions are not so much between two contending theories or concepts as between explicit, propositional argument, on the one hand, and textual practice or rhetoric, on the other: we can learn much from the way Marx *writes* freedom and democracy, from the understanding of collective life that the writing *performs* in certain pivotal moments. It is in analyzing Marx's textual performances that my reading is most prone to disrupt the settled structure of received doctrines we now know as "Marxism." It is in these performances that—whatever its intended inflection and, indeed, whether it is apocryphal—Marx's disavowal of his Marxism speaks a truth more powerful than fact. And it is in such moments, which have received only scanty attention from political theorists, that Marx's texts become so valuable for thinking about the contradictions and possibilities of contemporary democracy and democratization.

Pursuing my argument for Marx's significance by exploring tensions between concept and contending concept, propositional theory and textual practice, I stage close encounters with three works. Concentrating largely on conceptual tensions with the first work, and adding an emphasis on the politics of rhetoric in the investigation of the latter two, I consider "On the Jewish Question," *The Communist Manifesto,* and *The Eighteenth Brumaire of Louis Bonaparte.* This is a small and unusual selection from such a formidably large and diverse canon of writings. If most of the arguments advanced in this chapter could be elaborated through examinations of other texts, it is also doubtless the case that one could arrive at a very different sense of the aims and character of Marx's work on the basis of different readings. Through the selection made here, Marx is primarily constructed as a theorist of political action—which turns out to mean a theorist of the actions through which the political is constructed, or, better still, a writer whose texts produce the political in a manner that enables readers to experience and investigate those processes of production.[19]

Though this Marx is not the most familiar one, he is well worth knowing. As the surprises and messy complexity of political struggle impinge upon his thought, the conflicts between rhetoric and theory intensify, his writing (of) freedom becomes exhilarating, and his (at times unwitting) illumination of the making and meaning of the democratic imaginary attains its greatest brilliance. Marx's writings on action sometimes contribute, as *Democracy* did, to our understanding of the specific state institutions in which freedom can be exercised, but that is not his most valuable contribution. Though texts such as *The Civil War in France* describe forms of governance that incorporate people and places missing from Tocqueville's democratic cartography, Marx teaches more—and more surprisingly—through his rhetorical demonstration of the political practices through which identities and hegemonies are constructed and contested, his illustration of the politics of textuality and the textualization of politics. This demonstration manages to subvert the familiar terms of Marxist theories of base and superstructure while, nonetheless, remaining rigorously attentive to the movement of material forces: Marx's writing enacts tensions—between invention and discovery, plasticity and obduracy, dissonance and consonance—intrinsic to politics itself, thereby offering unequaled accounts of the tangled intertwining of ideals, interests, and identities in collective struggle. Because they offer the most compelling performances, I devote the greatest attention to *The Manifesto* and *The Eighteenth Brumaire*.

But whatever the arguments for or against one or another approach to that still-mysterious political signifier, "Karl Marx," our method has surely been established by now: the task is to advance the work of freedom through the taking of certain liberties. Freedom? Liberties? What shall these terms finally mean? One of the most concise and powerful answers ever given in response to this question is elaborated by "On the Jewish Question." Though it lacks the rhetorical virtuosity through which the other two essays performatively produce the political, this more abstract and conventionally philosophical text is especially useful for revealing certain conceptual fault lines, for showing the tension between the two different ideas of freedom. It seems only fitting, then, to begin the inquiry there.

Emancipation and Subordination

"On the Jewish Question" is among the earliest of Marx's published writings. It is in this essay that his rejection of and attempt to move beyond the republican and liberal inheritance is given one of its first and most forceful articulations.[20] Marx here offers his sharpest early delineation of the limitations of established institutions and conceptions of the political, and begins to set forth an ambitious, though ambiguous and divided, alternative approach to freedom. Nominally a critique of the Left-Hegelian philosopher, Bruno Bauer, the essay uses Bauer's work as the point of departure for a critical interpretation of the structures of state, society, and subjectivity characteristic of modern, liberal, bourgeois orders. Marx proceeds by identifying and assessing the complex ensemble of changes — the reshaping of economy, power relations, and identity — that distinguish such orders from their feudal predecessors. On his interpretation, the most significant feature of the new dispensation is the separation between the state and an independent realm of civil society, the dissociation of political status from social condition. Naming this dissociation "political emancipation," Marx argues that it is a necessary but by no means sufficient step down the road to that full flowering of freedom that he calls "human emancipation."

For Marx, the modern separation of state from society *is* a significant emancipation because it turns the state into a sphere of "universality," a place where all are formally free and equal.[21] While the feudal world positioned each person in a hierarchy that was at once personal, social, and political, the liberal state gives all citizens, *qua* citizens, the same status, identity, rights, and responsibilities: substantive inequalities are confined to the ostensibly nonpolitical domain of civil society, and so, in politics — where we are no longer serfs or lords or burghers but simply citizens — we all stand, masterless, on the same footing. As citizens we therefore understand ourselves as "communal being[s]" bound by ties of solidarity. Modern citizenship would appear to be the realization of the noblest of human qualities and aspirations.[22]

Marx refuses to take this appearance at face value. He argues that the institutional separation of spheres constitutive of liberal modernity produces a profound dissonance between formal civic status and the substance of individual experience, giving each person a "double life." As a citizen one is merely "the imaginary member of a fictitious sovereignty": though citizenship promises a life of freedom in a community of equals, civil society in fact makes "the citizen . . . the servant of egoistic man" and treats the "*bourgeois* . . . as the *real* and *authentic* man."[23] The age-old problems of domination thus continue—or, more precisely, new and distinctively post-feudal forms of exploitation emerge. In civil society, where we work, "spend" our time, and carry out the daily "business" of living, money reigns supreme as lives are bought and sold. This primary sphere of life is experienced not as a locus of community but as a war of all against all, a struggle in which the individual "regards other men as means, debases himself to a means, and becomes the plaything of alien powers."[24] Under these institutional arrangements, liberty becomes merely the right of "man as an isolated monad" to move as he wishes, and therefore "leads each man to see in other men not the realization but the limitation of his own freedom." Equality is no more than "equal access to" that same egoistic and exploitative liberty.[25] Practically speaking, Marx argues, bourgeois rights ultimately amount to this: the preservation of *"private property."*[26] Held by some in great quantities and denied to the vast majority, private property becomes the crucial instrument and support of the power of human over human. The "rights of man" are thus revealed, in the end, as the state's codification and protection of the worst alienation and exploitation of bourgeois life.

In Marx's account, then, formal freedom and equality in the state are accompanied by material relations of inequality and power relations of command and rule in the rest of human life. The relationship between these two halves of the double life is not contingent but organic, essential: civil society becomes a realm of intense (but organized, disciplined) egoism at the very moment that a separate state is created; the state becomes a realm of universality precisely because it and its values leave the most important structures of civil society untouched. The double movement which places all citizens on a politically equal footing while making an inegalitarian civil society the primary locus of power is "not one step in the process of political emancipation but its completion."[27] Political emancipation unshackles civil society, releasing its imperatives. Politics is fashioned as a means for the preservation of the new social arrangements.

Marx's political summons follows directly from this diagnosis: it is time, he declares, to revolutionize *all* of the conditions which limit us while giving us the appearance of freedom. For humanity to be emancipated, liberty, equality, and fraternity in the state can no longer be accompanied by captivity, domination, and isolation in civil society. All of the noble ideals of community that remain empty fictions in liberal orders must be really, sensuously, embodied. The double life must be unified, and that cannot be done within the framework of bourgeois institutions: Marx's analysis of the relationship between the state and civil society indicates that the division between these two spheres, the defining characteristic of bourgeois orders, must itself be overcome. "On the Jewish Question" completes its argument with a call for that next step: "Only when real, individual man resumes the abstract citizen into himself and as an individual man has become a *species-being* in his empirical life, his individual work and his individual relationships, only when man has recognized and organized his *forces propres* as *social forces* so that social force is no longer separated from him in the form of *political* force, only then will human emancipation be completed."[28]

The Republic of Illusion: Two Escape Routes

What would it mean to pursue this fuller kind of emancipation? What would be the shape of an emancipated community, an emancipated and undivided individual life? We have not come to terms with "On the Jewish Question" until we have confronted these questions. Yet the pursuit necessitates an encounter with the essay's fundamental ambivalence, the clash between contending ideas of freedom and valuations of politics: it is possible to tell very different stories about what Marx's human emancipation entails. If we emphasize freedom as a political practice, then we will not take his relentless critique of political emancipation to be a critique of all possible forms of politics. Instead, we can read Marx's project as an attempt to show both why all of the conditions that constrain or deny democratic political community must be overcome and what must be changed for that to happen. This reading has one significant advantage: it is particularly able to account for Marx's evident conviction that the subordination of politics to civil society, citizen to bourgeois, is a grotesque inversion of priorities: politics has been "*reduced*" to a mere instrument for the pursuit of private advantage, and thus "the sphere in which man behaves as a communal being is *degraded* to a level below the sphere in which he behaves as a partial being."[29] Marx holds to a conception of emancipation which views others as necessary to the "*realization*" of our freedom rather than as competitors whose very existence is a "*limitation*" of it; and he seems to see politics as the practice through which we seek freedom with others. In these moments, we are reminded that the young Marx was a devoted student of classical political theory and the world of the polis.[30] How does this devotion shape his conception of freedom?

Early in the chapter I spoke of Marx's most relevant conceptual innovations as departures from his republican inheritance, yet I have so far characterized "On the Jewish Question" as a critique of *liberal* thought and practice. It may seem that, in elaborating that critique, Marx sounds classically republican themes. Politics is undervalued, egoism and private interest are out of control, and it is time to recreate community: is his refrain not the same as the one sung today by neo-republican critics of modern corruption? Is the conception of freedom as a political practice simply a republican moment in Marx's thinking? Though there are echoes of "On the Jewish Question" in those contemporary critiques, and though Marx borrows from the classical understanding of the centrality and dignity of political life, his argument is obviously more than an attempt to revive republican ideals. His critique of liberal ills establishes the inadequacy of republican remedies.

In all of the guises he assumes from "On the Jewish Question" onward, Marx argues that traditional laments over the betrayal of civic ideals fail to acknowledge that the political illusions of the liberal state are not primarily the products of bad analyses or faulty principles: these illusions are rooted in the actual conditions of modern life and they thus express a real truth, though in distorted fashion. If it is wrong to make citizenship a mere means, the wrong is deeply rooted in existing institutional structures and social forces: in the world produced by political emancipation citizenship is *necessarily* empty and degraded, and that degradation cannot be reversed through philosophical criticism or sheer acts of political will.[31] In thinking otherwise, moralizing republicans are themselves in the grip of a delusion produced by the modern separation between state and society. As a result, they can only be politically ineffectual: the quest to restore virtue and heroic citizenship, conceived of as such, is doomed. Political emancipation has brought about a world which renders old conceptions of public and private, *polis* and *oikos*, obsolete. There is more to human life than politics, and even politics itself cannot flourish without changes in the rest of human life. We need *human* emancipation because, in modern context, any pursuit of political freedom that stops short of social transformation is not only insufficient but destined for defeat:

> At those times when it is particularly self-confident, political life attempts to suppress its presupposition, civil society and its elements, and to constitute itself as the real, harmonious species-life of man. But it only manages to do this in violent contradiction to the conditions of its own existence, by declaring the revolution permanent, and for that reason the political drama necessarily ends up with the restoration of

religion, private property and all the elements of civil society, just as war ends with peace.[32]

The French revolution has already performed this drama, revealing, in its failure, the need to transform relationships and structures that lie well outside the bounds of the republican political imagination. A new radicalism is necessitated by a new world.

Yet Marx's (equivocal) embrace of what I am calling freedom as a practice suggests that this new radicalism is (sometimes), nevertheless, fundamentally political. He can be read as demanding an extension of the boundaries of politics, a politicization of the domains that liberals and republicans had classified as social or cultural.[33] He asks us how we can practice democratic politics when others govern us in so many aspects of our lives. How can civic freedom and the formal ties of equality be meaningful among those who also occupy differing positions in the chain of command? How can we be free when the contours of the human world are largely predetermined, removed from our influence, fortified against our power to act? In responding, Marx moves beyond the argument that democratic political community has certain social or cultural prerequisites, and so he breaks, for example, with the traditional republican call for constraining inequality through the promotion of Spartan simplicity, and with the kind of analyses represented by Tocqueville's account of the American family (Marx cites Tocqueville's work as compelling evidence for the ways in which the religious foundations of civil society are preserved after the constitution of a secular state).[34] Instead, Marx insists on a democratic revolution in social and cultural relations, a revolution that entails nothing less than a reconstruction of the relationship between state and society, a proliferation of political spaces in a redrawing of all previous cartographies. The human world is not to be divided into liberated zones and regions where questions of freedom and democracy are inappropriate: the struggle for democracy must be carried on everywhere. Only by making all significant social practices and institutions into concrete organs of democracy can there be human emancipation, for only under such conditions can humans realize their capacity to share in the power to constitute the world and direct their lives through conscious choice. The task of emancipation is to place that power in people's hands, and it is only through a process that resembles what we call "politics" that this can be done.[35]

In these moments, Marx thus offers a radical critique of Tocqueville's insistence on the need for non-democratic foundations beneath democratic politics. That insistence, portrayed by Marx as the constitutive move of conventional modern approaches to politics—liberal and republican alike—is here revealed as a bastion of servitude, a fundamental constraint on the practice of freedom. Resistance to that move requires us to accept this proposition: politics goes all the way down. A reading that emphasizes freedom as practice draws particularly strong links between the workings of power and imagination. For the imaginary identifications of citizenship to be more than mere diversion or delusion, they must be constructed through material structures that are themselves democratic; for the transformation of material relations to be genuinely emancipating, it must be linked to a radicalization of the political imaginary. Marx, then, appears to argue for the very transposition of democracy from "politics" to other registers that I called for in Chapter 3, and he seems to offer us a theoretical framework well suited to pursuing that task.

For all of the promise of this framework, however, there is a lack of concreteness, of specificity, to Marx's evocation of the political practices of freedom. The critical force of his rejection of liberal and republican foundations is greater than that of his alternative. There are limits, then, to even this most politicizing impulse in "On the Jewish Question" (which is one reason it is crucial to bring the essay's arguments into conversation with those of the two texts considered below). Perhaps those limits reflect the dilemma into which that impulse drives him. The emphasis on freedom as a political practice necessarily carries with it either a utopian aspiration to perfection (an unjustifiably high expectation of what the practice can achieve) or a resignation to the persistence of unfreedom. If heteronomy is unfreedom—as it always is in Marx's thought—then the attempt to democratize the field of power can never make us *completely* free. The shape of power can indeed be transformed through struggle, for the structures of human coercion can be challenged, the forces of normalization resisted, and individuals can thereby acquire a greater capacity to shape the conditions of their lives and selves. But can this project of democracy ever fully triumph? And, if so, can that triumph eradicate all obstacles to freedom? Unless we hold to the "Rousseauian" conception of democratic interaction, unless we imagine a democracy purged of all difference, dissonance, and conflict, and a form of selfhood beyond all opacity, ambivalence, and ambiguity, then (as we have already seen in considering Tocqueville) the answer must be, "No."[36] Marx, who is engaged in an effort to confront and overcome the Rousseauian legacy, sometimes knows that politics does not work this way. Freedom as a political practice thus names a project of struggle, an attempt to open space for freedom through perpetual and *necessarily* imperfect contestation. This freedom is inevitably attended by ambiguities and resistances. It is a freedom that is never guaranteed for good and is never available to all selves in exactly equal measure or with entirely commensurate (or even commensurable) satisfactions and successes.

The uncertainty of this project is evidently more than Marx can bear. Torn between a utopianism that cannot entirely persuade him and a resignation to imperfection that cannot altogether fulfill him, he is impelled toward other approaches, other solutions, utopias that can satisfy his longings while better assuaging his skepticism. There is a conceptual opening: what cannot be had through politics might be had by other means. The right reconstruction of the social world might remove all those obstacles, within the self and outside of it, to harmonious communion and unhampered growth. If Marx cannot conceive of a politics that will render even struggle unnecessary, then he will, at times, seek a struggle that shall take us beyond politics—and *therefore* beyond conflict, dissonance, and, in the end, beyond heteronomy. The yearning for this more ambitious and secure emancipation, this freedom as transcendence, finds powerful expression in "On the Jewish Question," becoming the essay's dominant aspiration.

Where does this yearning take us? What would it mean to move beyond politics altogether? In beginning to sketch an answer, it might be best to return, for a moment, to Marx's closing claim that we will be fully free only when "individual man has become a *species-being* in his empirical life, his individual work and his individual relationships." The language of this claim reminds us that the essay is not only an extension of Marx's prior efforts in his *Critique of Hegel's Philosophy of Right* but an anticipation of arguments that would soon take a more elaborate form in his *Economic and Philosophical Manuscripts*. The vision of emancipation that closes "On the Jewish Question" hints at and seems to presuppose that subsequent treatise's theory of alienation. The lure of transcendence and the appeal to transparency that shape this idea of emancipation are here bound up, in other words, with a philosophical anthropology that makes labor—broadly construed—the essential human activity, the form of conduct that reveals who we are as individuals and what we are as a species. Based on this anthropology, Marx argues, famously, that when we labor under conditions and for ends determined by others, we are estranged from the products of our labor and from ourselves, others, and the natural world.[37] Our most basic capacities confront us as alien powers, sources of servitude. Thus is our capacity for "species life"—for recognizing our uniquely human and shared capacities and making them the bases of our conscious reflections and deliberate choices—distorted and our freedom denied.[38] It is for this reason, of course, that Marx proposes overcoming the system of private property: his analysis suggests that only this overcoming can set us free.

This set of assumptions and arguments produces a much more radical decentering of the political than does the idea of freedom as a practice. While the latter requires an expansion and reconceptualization of "political" life by insisting that the qualities of a free political community be sought in all social institutions, including those of labor, the former suggests that political community is an insufficient model for thinking about emancipation because politics is not and, in the modern world, cannot be the primary locus of freedom. The capacity to be free is rooted in a deeper level, in productive activity as such. Full emancipation, here, is not merely a matter of struggling to transform specific relationships and institutions; to be completely free is to leave alienation behind, ending all forms of estrangement, returning to harmony with our selves and union with humankind. This entails not only going beneath politics to change things at the deeper level of production, but an emancipation from politics, a harmony that renders those relationships we call "political" unnecessary and even inconceivable.

Reading "On the Jewish Question" as a quest for this emancipation enables one to make sense of certain troubling features in Marx's critique of the "Rights of Man." That critique certainly retains some of its original force. If we are now familiar with the argument that formal freedoms are empty when combined with severe substantive inequalities, that rights to private property are often rights to control and constrain the lives of the propertyless, our familiarity is deeply indebted to Marxist arguments given early and powerful expression in this essay. But the essay's critique moves beyond these points, beyond challenges to domination and the bourgeois forms of the distinction between state and society. At certain moments, Marx makes the very existence of rights, of formal individual claims against the community, both a cause and a symptom of our lack of freedom. Such rights are expressions of our egoism, of our regrettable "separation" from others and from our "species life," a sign that our lives are not whole.[39] Ending that separation would eliminate the need for rights.[40] In this strand of his argument, Marx seems to suggest that difference *as such* is a symptom of alienation. Civil society, for example, is described as no longer being the locus of community *because* it has become "the essence of difference" and hence, we can only infer, the essence of unfreedom.[41]

Now only a tendentious reader would view Marx as launching a direct and deliberate attack on individuality and difference. In this essay, as elsewhere, Marx (like Tocqueville and, of course, Hegel) wishes to subvert the stark opposition between individual and community, to show that extreme hostility to community can hinder individuality and that certain forms of collective life can cultivate more robust and distinctive individual selves. He wishes to point out how individuality is stifled by existing conditions and how individual development could be unfettered by revolutionary social transformation. He clearly believes that, in an emancipated community, individuality would flourish in all of its most original forms as human beings developed in many different ways and bonded on the basis of, rather than in opposition to, their rich diversity. It is because of these aspirations and convictions that some readers have found in Marx a model of "political individuation" and a vision of radical cultural pluralism.[42]

Yet what shape do these aspirations take, what plausibility do the convictions carry, what blind spots mar this vision? Marx's genuine desire for the development of many different kinds of selfhood is severely undercut by his stipulations about the conditions of emancipatory development. A comparison with Tocqueville is instructive here. Where *Democracy* worries anxiously and endlessly about the relations between community and individuality, playing forms of freedom and claims of right or obligation against each other, seeking to leave room for artful subjects and find means of fostering resilient subjectivities, "On the Jewish Question" appears to suggest that such anxiety can be dissolved permanently because the problems that motivate it can be transcended. If Tocqueville's fears about the growth of despotism in the soil of cultural uncertainty lead him to undercut his commitment to difference by removing aspects of self and society from the reach of political challenge, Marx's search for a secure and complete freedom serves a homologous function in his thought, and does so more effectively—which is to say with still more unfortunate results. Marx seems to imagine that once the struggle for emancipation is won and relations have been so transformed that people have "become species beings in their empirical lives," then everyone will be in unalienated relationships to their human powers and to other human beings: self and society will be transparent. Political thought need not concern itself with the institutional preservation of liberties or sites of struggle and dissonance because no forces hostile to freedom will remain.[43] Nor, therefore, will politics remain—whether politics is understood as the public contestation and mediation of contending interests, the confrontation between principled versions of the good life, or the conflictual negotiation of identities and differences. Decisions, of course, will have to be made, but human emancipation is the transcendence of the social bases of conflicting interests and, as a result, conflicting principles and identities as well.[44]

It is hard to imagine the texture of such an unalienated and unconflicted life. In its most ambitious formulation, Marx's idea of emancipation strains against intelligibility (thereby making it difficult even for ordinarily lucid commentators to give a clear account of his argument).[45] This is not, of course, a novel claim: both critics of Marxism and anti-humanist Marxists have often argued that Marx becomes hopelessly entangled in metaphysics when he links emancipation to species being and the theory of alienation.[46] It is also a commonplace among liberal critics that he is dangerously utopian and coercive in his proposed obliteration of all boundaries between public and private, self and citizen, state and society. Marx, the argument goes, proceeded from his acute perception of the freedoms denied to most members of the bourgeois societies of his day to the disastrous conclusion that all of the rights and liberties that could be found in such societies were *themselves* "bourgeois"—and thus dispensable. There is something to this argument, but my point is different: though "On the Jewish Question" does indeed undervalue rights and private liberties, the central problem with the essay is *not* that it is "inimical . . . to liberal values" because it gives absolute priority to democratic politics.[47] The largest problems of individuality and difference in Marx's thought are rooted in his yearning not for the *triumph* but for the *transcendence* of politics. His ideal of a transparent community obliterates all notions of democratic contestation and governance at the very moment it dispenses with the problem of individual claims against community: these two moves are mutually reinforcing, indeed mutually constitutive. When he succumbs to the lure of his most illiberal visions of transcendence, he shares the anti-political attitude that is central to many of his liberal critics.[48] Marx's early essay does not give us a clear or substantive enough account of the material conditions of freedom's enactment.

The tendency to dispense with politics or to pay insufficient attention to the uncertain and imperfect practice of freedom is even immanent in the essay's sovereign category, "emancipation." While I have so far used emancipation interchangeably with "freedom," that approach is misleading. To ask how we might practice and preserve freedom is not the same as asking what would emancipate humanity. To be emancipated is to have been *set free*, released from a condition of servitude or slavery.[49] Often the release is won through one's own efforts, which is to say through struggle, and so there is a moment of activity or practice in this category, too. But once emancipation has been achieved, the struggle presumably ends: the concept leads us to focus our attention on the difference between life before and after, on freedom as a stable condition or achievement that follows the throwing off of oppression. The reading of freedom as something that calls on us to be artful and committed to political contestation must therefore fight against the very language Marx uses: to speak of emancipation is, almost inevitably, to hold out the hope of transcending the practice of freedom.

To carry out our project with the help of Marx is then, as with Tocqueville, to use tools in ways not envisioned by the manufacturer. Yet, once again, this labor of taking liberties has its pleasures and opportunities: if one must work against basic inclinations in Marx's work, there is still much to learn. Once the tensions in his thought are identified, Marx's writings about political action are the best places for probing the pressures that push him to embrace the quest for transcendence and for pursuing his conception of freedom as a practice. Though his search for secure foundations in many ways parallels that undertaken in *Democracy in America*, his commitments and motivations differ from Tocqueville's. Exploring Marx's turn to class analysis and the theorization of History adds to our understanding of how this search proceeds and how it can be resisted. *The Communist Manifesto* and *The Eighteenth Brumaire of Louis Bonaparte* are ideal sources of such instruction, for they open a privileged window onto the problem of writing. Taking up that ostensibly recondite literary problem turns out to be the best way to comprehend the means by which Marx both depoliticizes and politicizes: it shows us his most extreme acts of foreclosure and his richest insights into the multiple spaces and practices of struggle. Following the rhetorical operations of these texts ultimately allows us to find ways of thinking democratically with the constitutive tensions of political life. Marx's literary masterpieces thus enable us to move from reading him to writing him, from an attempt to understand what he is "trying to say" about freedom to a perception of the ways he can be used by those willing to take liberties with him.

Revolutionary Theory and the End(s) of History

The Communist Manifesto, Marx's[50] most famous theorization of history, is of course no academic treatise on historiography: it is a call to arms and a political program. But the program and the exhortation are grounded in an elaborate understanding of the nature and ultimate destination of historical development. Marx stakes his claim to historical knowledge at the very beginning of the text, and he repeatedly and explicitly uses this claim to establish political authority and discredit rival theoretical analyses. The famous opening passage informs us that communism, the "spectre haunting Europe," a challenge to the prevailing structures of political, social, and economic life, is the culmination of a process that has governed all of human civilization. Compressing an entire philosophy of history into an epigram, the *Manifesto* proclaims, "The history of all hitherto existing societies is the history of class struggles." [51] As Marx amplifies this assertion, we see that his understanding of history decisively shapes—or simply becomes—his conception of politics: "Freeman and slave, patrician and plebeian, lord and serf, guild-master and journeyman, in a word, oppressor and oppressed, stood in constant opposition to one another, carried on an uninterrupted, now hidden, now open fight, a fight that each time ended, either in a revolutionary re-constitution of society at large, or in the common ruin of the contending classes." [52]

The combatants change from period to period and locale to locale, but the structure of the encounter persists across time and space: politics is always and everywhere a kind of war, a ceaseless struggle between enemies who *must* be enemies. The stakes of the struggle could not be higher: the losers are destroyed, the victors shape the world to suit their own needs and purposes. The *Manifesto* trumpets Marx's claim that this war of classes has reached an unprecedented stage, its climactic moment. All of the old complexities and illusions have fallen away, and only the naked struggle of two adversaries now remains. Modern society is—transparently, undeniably—splitting into "two great hostile camps . . . Bourgeoisie and Proletariat." [53] The burden of Marx's historical argument is to show that these two camps are being drawn, irresistibly, into a final battle. The political question of the day, indeed, of the struggle for the future of humanity is: "Which side are you on?"

This question is not to be answered by mere subjective will, for the political identities at war are not primarily the products of conscious choice or allegiance. It is the logic of capital that has placed these two characters on history's final stage and determined which actors get to play what roles. The pursuit of profit has *required* incessant "revolutionizing the instruments of production, and thereby the relations of production, and with them the whole relations of society." [54] The Bourgeoisie has thus been *driven* to expand its empire around the world, destroying all parochial identities and local loyalties, and placing more and more of humanity in the camp opposing it. The social logic of capitalism has also ensured that this growing class of proletarians has begun to recognize its interests and its strength, as individual struggles have turned into class struggles and localized conflicts have been centralized through the creation of "an ever expanding union of workers." Soon the pressures of its social circumstances will lead that union to launch a frontal and final assault on the citadels of bourgeois power. Because proletarians are precisely those whose specific class-interests carry a universal significance, the assault will bring about the emancipation Marx seeks: the proletarians can only triumph by transcending themselves and the bases of exploitation, by "abolishing their own mode of appropriation, and thereby also every other previous mode of appropriation." [55] If History is the struggle of class against class, then this abolition, by eliminating classes themselves, shall bring History to the fulfillment of its purpose, to its terminal point—its End.

There is more, of course, but why tell this story yet again? The details are surely familiar enough: the *Manifesto* is the most famous document in all of Marxist literature, and even many people who have never read a word of Marx can produce a reasonable facsimile of its main points. Still, at a time when the confidence of the text's assertions provokes easy irony (which may—depending on the reader's allegiances—be tinged with sorrow, bitter humor, indignation, glee, or contempt), these points deserve a brief rehearsal, in order to remind us not of this or that detail but of the distinctive form of the argument. Though Marx is hardly the first pamphleteer seeking to inspire action through a historical appeal, his particular way of invoking history breaks with the generic conventions of previous political works. As even our brief summary makes clear, the *Manifesto* does not remind readers of the political maxims or commitments that have emerged out of a shared past. Nor does it produce a litany of rights and privileges that have been arbitrarily or unfairly abrogated. The text is neither a particularistic defense of a specific people nor a declaration of timeless, universal principles. Instead, it offers political argument in the form of universal History.[56] This form of argument, a pivotal development in Marx's critique of previous democratic thought, is crucial terrain for our exploration of the drive toward transcendence. Though the *Manifesto*'s particular version of the argument is not Marx's most refined theoretical product—this is a popular text, a simplification that lacks the complexity of his most philosophically or economically ambitious work—it is useful for that very simplicity: it lays bare its own theoretical architecture, enabling us to see, with particular clarity, the structures he creates in order to support certain political platforms.

Switching metaphors, we might also say that the *Manifesto* is an important extension of Marx's cartographic project. The vague characterization of alienation and domination in civil society offered by "On the Jewish Question" has given way to a precise survey of the forces and institutions that keep people in chains. By showing how economic relationships fundamentally shape the practices of state and by analyzing capitalist production as form of class rule, Marx maps "the economy" as an organized structure of political power. The newer terms employed by the *Manifesto*—forces and relations of production, means of production and exchange, class struggle, and so forth—are the instruments of his cartography.[57] Even as this mapping project sharpens Marx's earlier critique, it introduces the new one as well. His picture of domination and exploitation under capitalism is not simply a more precise rendering of the appalling social facts he had addressed in his critique of political emancipation; it also advances a methodological claim about how to understand the workings of social orders, the sources of social change, and the standpoint of revolutionary theory. The *Manifesto* is an account of how the diverse practices, institutions, beliefs, social relations, and technical instruments, though contradictory, form a totality, a whole. By naming the capitalist mode of production and situating it within a larger narrative of historical transformation, Marx argues that a social totality can only be understood in relationship to the one that preceded it and the one struggling to be born from within it. In tracing the contradictions between forces and relations of production, and between class and class, he provides an explanation of how that process of transformation works.[58]

The central ambition of the *Manifesto* is to persuade its readers that political struggle cannot be successful unless it is guided by this explanation. Radical political criticism is at best irrelevant and at worst harmful if it cannot identify the conditions and actors who are demonstrably capable of realizing its emancipatory vision—and only the theory of history present in the *Manifesto* can identify those conditions and actors. No struggle is liberating if it does not advance historical movement toward its ultimate destination. No change, no matter how painful or destructive, should be resisted if it furthers that movement. This is not only strategic advice but a claim about the epistemological status of strategic advice and the political relationship between this advice and normative judgments. In this text political ethics essentially disappears into strategic analysis. Marx's narrative is both shield and sword, protecting its possessors from the assault of nostalgic sentimentality and enabling them to pierce the veils of political illusion.

While other thinkers had offered similar services (think, for example, of Machiavelli's advertisements for himself), the *Manifesto*'s claims are particularly ambitious: when it rends the reigning political perceptions, the intent is not simply to debunk this or that proposition but to dispense with deceptive appearances once and for all. Illusion, Marx insists, need not accompany political struggle: comprehending universal history enables political actors to invest their hopes in and attune their struggles to the real moving forces of human life. Marx's analysis of the emergence and looming dissolution of capitalism supplants or refashions all of the local-ized popular stories of struggle and sacrifice, heroism and betrayal, right and obligation. National identity, ethnicity, and religiosity, sources of the deepest feelings of collective belonging, are laid bare as deceptions which must be abandoned; the conflict between bourgeoisie and proletariat is revealed as the actual battle of the current age; the international working class is recognized as the authentic source of collective interest, the effec-tive agent of change, and the appropriate object of commitment and iden-tification. To accept these changes of perspective and allegiance, the text suggests, is to trade mysticism and mistaken interest for undistorted com-prehension. In the very process of unveiling a "scientific" terminology which can analyze the observable processes of social life, the *Manifesto* en-dows the whole of the human past with a plot, a destination, and a moral.

In a sense, the text is even *about* this transformative interpretive act: the subject of the *Manifesto* is not only the epic drama of class struggle, but also the unique theoretical and political vocation of the "Communist." In-deed, the latter is essential to the former, for the proletariat's success in the drama's final scene comes under the direction of the communists. The communists are, precisely, those who understand the arguments outlined in the *Manifesto*, those who have "raised themselves to the level of com-prehending theoretically the historical movement as a whole" and who put this understanding at the service of the international proletariat.[59] Com-munists differ from other proletarians not by having distinctive interests but in their superior perception of the common interest of the working class as a whole. Because the working class gains its interests from its place in the structure of capitalist production, it is possible to specify, objec-tively, what those interests are. Communists ensure that the proletarian class struggle pursues these objective interests and does not fight against the tides of history. Knowledge enables them to move beyond the poli-tics of moralism and subjectivism, to reach conclusions based not on "in-vented" theoretical "principles" but on "actual relations springing from an existing class struggle."[60]

The *Manifesto* thus tries to efface its author's (prodigious) creativity even as it casts him in a heroic role: if the text is "about" his hermeneutic reconstruction of the whole of human history, it can be so only deviously, through a medium (as the younger Marx might have put it). The text's claim to authority dictates that communist innovation in the pursuit of freedom must be portrayed as a submission to historical necessity, for it is obedience to History's forces that distinguishes communist politics from all previous socialist thought and practice (the communist's most original claim is, thus, to have invented nothing). While socialists of various stripes have long dreamed of a world beyond bourgeois property, they have hitherto lacked any idea of how to bring that world into existence. Even the best of them, writing before the struggle between bourgeoisie and proletariat emerged in all its starkness, necessarily lacked a conception of the historically-produced revolutionary subject. They thus remained trapped in a delusional voluntarism in which, "future history" is imagined as no more than "the propaganda and the practical carrying out of their plans" and strategy is reduced to the issuing of moral appeals addressed to the whole of existing society.[61] Communists provide not superior appeals but an authoritative replacement for the moralist method. If the utopian socialists had not existed, Marx would have had to invent them: they stand for every radical and democratic political illusion from which the text attempts to free us.

Anchoring Identity

There is much to be learned from this form of political criticism, even today. The *Manifesto* forces us to focus on the links between social structures and political forms, conceptual ideals and their historical conditions of possibility. It fixes our attention on the question of which particular historical agents in what precise social locations will be encompassed or ignored, fortified or repressed, by radical argument and practice. It reveals a past and present political life criss-crossed by struggles and structured by violence, thereby making it difficult for us to tolerate the particular kinds of subordination sanctioned or accommodated by *Democracy in America*, while also, like Tocqueville's text, leading us to place the fundamental forces of modernity at the center of political inquiry and evaluation. Marx's analysis of these forces has the added advantage of showing how globalization undermines the state's claim to be the inevitable and controlling center of political life and political loyalty. Far more than "On the Jewish Question," this text pushes us to engage the perplexing issues of loyalty and belonging in our own, late-modern and diasporic global condition. And yet, of course, the *Manifesto* does not stop there. The argument goes beyond these worldly cautions and insights, propelling an otherworldly metaphysics of historical motion: Marx seeks in History a guarantee of his greatest hopes, a balm to his most profound anxieties, a means of removing the most vexing political and theoretical tasks from view. He offers us the faith that History will ultimately resolve our dissonances and contradictions, conclude the quest for freedom, and spare us the work of inventing new forms of power and struggle. Though he differs from today's American triumphalists in the depth and breadth of his learning, in the originality, scope, and power of his vision, and in the radicalism of his confrontational stance toward prevailing privilege, Marx shares their use — or, rather, they offer degraded and unintentionally parodic imitations of his use — of History to contain politics and close off the open horizon of the future.

If the ideal of transcendence resolves the uncertainty and cures the imperfections that must necessarily accompany the dissonant practice of freedom, if the embrace of struggle now must be linked to the project of overcoming struggle itself, History becomes the vehicle of this resolution. History is what makes the vision of complete transcendence a more plausible utopianism than the radicalization of democracy. History does this not only by providing a direction and a reassurance of ultimate victory, but by anchoring the identity necessary to transcendence. Marx's story about the historical move from battle to battle, character to character, epoch to epoch — culminating, as it does, with the emergence and anticipated triumph of the objectively revolutionary subject — provides the ideal of complete emancipation with the necessary conceptual fortifications. If victory will require a struggle, and if the struggle demands Marx's strident call to arms, the parties pursuing the struggle are already and *necessarily* there, provided by the structure of production and the historical logic of its development. The proletariat is not fundamentally a political production; class is the solid ground on which politics (temporarily) takes place.

History thus does the work, here, that Tocqueville's cultural foundationalism did in *Democracy*, grounding the possibility of a present identity and future society beyond the need for democracy and struggle, just as Tocqueville's exclusions and evasions of struggle worked to make political democracy possible. As Tocqueville's democratic self was protected from threatening others and vertiginous moral uncertainties, the *Manifesto*'s revolutionary identity is protected against contingency, rendered capable of overcoming all opacity while shedding every inconsistency. The philosophical longing for communion that runs through "On the Jewish

Question" here receives, in the analysis of the politics and historical development of production, a "materialist" veneer. The narrative structure
that impels us toward a time beyond scarcity, exploitation, and necessity,
thereby points us to a world beyond politics. Marx's teleology brings to
the surface what Tocqueville artfully concealed. The explicit teleology,
with its soothing resolution of Marx's political anxieties, must be resisted;
it demands a reading that, as with our approach to Tocqueville, brushes
against the grain. We must see how Marx's writing dislodges the anchors
placed by his teleological theory. But such resistant rereading requires us
first to trace the consequences Marx's flight from contingency has for his
thinking about political practices and institutions.

The consequences are visible on the surface, too: Marx's evasion of
politics can be seen not only in the way that proletarian identity is shielded
from unauthorized reconfigurations in the present but in the institutional
program and pronouncements directed toward the future. True to its
understanding of the communist vocation, the *Manifesto* does not shirk
the task of directing the proletarian struggle: it lists ten concrete steps to
be taken at the moment of revolutionary victory. If we read off the text's
approach to emancipation from this bill of particulars — the now-familiar
litany of state policies such as a progressive income tax, universal free
education, centralization of factories and institutions of credit, and the
like[62] — we would conclude that, though concerned with destroying the
bases of servitude, Marx is not primarily preoccupied with the political
practices of freedom or the spaces in which these practices can flourish.
Of course, these programmatic steps are presented as responses to very
specific historical circumstances, and Marx himself insists that "no special stress should be laid on them."[63] They are not the ultimate content
of emancipation, but simply transitional measures. But ask the question,
"Transitional to what?" and the answer is difficult to give with any clarity:
one cannot say what spaces and practices of freedom will accompany a
fuller emancipation. Marx's reticence about the shape of an emancipated
society is, of course, well known; that it is linked to his invocation of
History is also obvious. It is crucial, however, to situate Marx's reticence
in the context of his commitment to the certainty and closure of revolutionary identity and the corresponding ease with which he imagines the
dispensability of politics in a fully free order.

The following words provide the step by which the *Manifesto* moves
from its immediate and concrete revolutionary proposals to its more ambitious but vague vision of a society marked by the free development of

each and all: "When, in the course of development, class distinctions have disappeared and all production has been concentrated in the hands of a vast association of the whole nation, the public power will lose its political character. Political power properly so called, is merely the organized power of one class for oppressing another."[64] Politics, as a sign of our corruption, shall fall away when our corruption is cured: in passages such as this, the faith in History and the faith in transcendence and transparency are one. The forms and practices of freedom among the members of that "vast association," the means and manner of negotiating conflict and struggles within it, are placed beyond the scope of inquiry because history will overcome the circumstances that make them relevant. The coming end of politics means the present end of certain types of political reflection—and both ends are anchored in Marx's conceptualization of a self-certain revolutionary agency/identity impervious to schism and beyond any need of contested renegotiation.

One might explain such evasions as the results of Marx's commitment to a dubious "sociological hypothesis." That hypothesis—that class is the sole structural basis of the dominance of some over others—seems to be the basis of the knowledge claims advanced on behalf of the communist theorist (communist theory provides the understanding that can only come from a complete cognition of the structured bases of power). This thesis has been so roundly and effectively criticized from so many quarters that there is no need to add to the quarrel now. But it is important to note that Marx's difficulties go beneath the merely empirical: if he is offering us a sociological claim, it is one with deep metaphysical roots, one that reflects commitments important to him before his work took this analytical turn.[65] Behind the easy notion of specifiable objective and unitary interests is the dream of transparency and the longing for a transcendence that will enable the dream to be realized. Perhaps, however, the etiology of this problem is less important than the role of evasion in shaping the *Manifesto*'s strategic commitments and tactical narrative choices. If the text develops a cartography of more scope and detail than "On the Jewish Question," if it offers reminders to attend to questions of political agency and location, and an acknowledgment of a global predicament that seems more relevant now than when the text was written, the *Manifesto* nonetheless seems to say little about the practice of freedom or the cultivation of politics. Its use would appear to be primarily diagnostic: the pamphlet tells us more about the pressures that prompt Marx's foundationalist moves than about the opportunities for appropriating his thought. Or so it would appear.

Revolutionary Rhetoric: Inventing Identity,
Constructing Class

Is that appearance accurate? Is there no more to say on the *Manifesto*'s
behalf? Is the text so fissureless, so successful in establishing the incontestable foundations it seeks, that it offers no openings for rereading, rethinking, reusing? Must we look elsewhere for an approach to freedom
richer and more useful than the freedoms of transcendence? Some have
suggested as much. Even Claude Lefort, an interpreter sensitive to the
ways in which "Marx's work does not coincide with itself," is convinced
that the *Manifesto* is an unfortunate exception, a self-consistent and "self-
contained" work that "leaves the reader outside." Marx's passionate summons toward an emancipatory future in which human life would be transformed now reads as a repository of dogmatic Marx*ism*, as "the mauso-
leum he built with his pen."[66] And so it must read if we treat this pamphlet as a sequence of propositional arguments, a collection of various,
now-improbable or oppressive theses on the relationships among history,
knowledge, identity, and action. At this discursive level—as an essentially
"social scientific" explanation of class, politics, and change—the *Manifesto*
is as crude, mechanical, and one-dimensional as my account has so far
rendered it. But the *Manifesto* appears inert only if we concentrate exclusively on what it "says," paying no attention to what the text "does:" the
text is dead, closed to us, only if we ignore its rhetorical dimension and
fail to examine how the writing works. This oversight, common enough
in recent responses to Marx, blocks access to a fertile field in which we
could cultivate the art of being free.[67]

   While it is a mistake to overlook the rhetorical dimension of any political document, the mistake is particularly impoverishing in this instance.
The very title clues us into what we are in danger of missing: Marx's pamphlet is, after all, a "manifesto"—which is to say that it is at once a public
proclamation, a denunciation of existing evils, a declaration of intent, a
summons to action, a piece of evidence, a kind of proof. In the service of
authorizing action in the present and future, it aims, through its own activity, to "manifest" the fundamental facts of our political condition, to
demonstrate what is, in Marx's words, already "going on before our own
eyes."[68] That is the rhetorical task the genre in question gives the author;
and yet not all eyes are accustomed to seeing what Marx would have us
see. He must refer to what is "obvious" while writing against prevailing
perceptions of reality. A text that works in such a situation must be fundamentally *performative:* it must work to constitute the world it purports

to describe. Marx's remarkable act of constitution can teach us something about the practice of both textual and political freedom; the relentless and ferocious performance given by the *Manifesto* offers instruction about the reasons and opportunities for resistance to the productivism of Marx's own doctrinal account of the communist transcendence of politics.

In a brilliant assessment of the performance, Marshall Berman suggests that, if we yield to the claims of Marx's narrative, we will find ourselves "hurtled along with a reckless momentum, a breathless intensity. Marx is not only describing but evoking and *enacting* the desperate pace and frantic rhythm that capitalism imparts to every facet of modern life. He makes us feel that we are part of the action, drawn into the stream, hurtled along out of control, at once dazzled and menaced by the onward rush."[69] By emphasizing its performative dimension, Berman is able to read the *Manifesto* as at once a classic of literary modernism and a significant contribution to the making and meaning of modernity. No mere stylistic appreciation, this reading opens fundamental theoretical questions: Berman suggests that the essay's modernist writing of modernity subverts some of Marx's most familiar conclusions about the course of modernization. Once we pay attention to the ways the text rhetorically positions us in the swift, even violent, flow of its prose and imagery, "we are exhilarated but perplexed; we find that the solid formations around us have melted away."[70] The experience of reading the *Manifesto* works against (some of) Marx's own explicit intentions and pronouncements by showing us the power of modernity's corrosive or "melting" forces. If we reflect on what that experience suggests about these forces, if we pay attention to what happens to us when we are subjected to the rhythms of the text, we come to suspect that these can never be contained or come to an end: terribly fast, they are corrosive, powerful, unstoppable, driven by pressures that have no opportunity to dissipate or find some total culmination. We thereby end up doubting that we can reach the solid, post-historical ground Marx envisions.[71]

Let us take up this suggestive insight into the importance and self-subverting character of the *Manifesto*'s writing, turning, however, to political and theoretical problems tangential to Berman's focus on modernization. What does the *Manifesto*'s rhetorical performance tell us about Marx's account of political identity and struggle? What politics inheres in the way Marx's writing works (on) his readers? Start with this: that work is both wide-ranging and powerful, extensive and intensive. The language reorients us in the human world, changing the fundamental contours of that world even as it does so: our sense of who we are, where we come from, and where we are going are all subjected to Marx's efforts at re-description. The very name given to the (revolutionary and grammatical) subject of the *Manifesto*'s narrative of emancipation was, as Peter Stally-brass demonstrates, the product of an "extraordinary rhetorical . . . labor" of transvaluation: Marx's writing in the 1840s fundamentally changed the connotations of "proletarian" and "proletariat," moving them from "vile" to "virtuous," "poor" to "working class," passive to active, "parasite upon the social body [to] the body upon which the rest of society was a para-site."[72] We might take this change as a clue to both the nature of Marx's larger project in this pamphlet and the character of the world in which that project was able to meet with a certain degree of success. In its transvalua-tion of "proletariat," as throughout the text, the *Manifesto* is engaged in the discursive construction of identity—a construction that would appear to be one of the decisive moments of politics, for, as identity is renegoti-ated here, its political valences and opportunities, the interests that can be attributed to it, change as well. The point is not simply that Marx is con-tinuing the connotative shift charted by Stallybrass but that he is trying to draw a potential category of persons into being. It is not wholly clear that Marx is even addressing an existing community of people: he speaks to and for the "workers of the world" (when he is not speaking, more narrowly, for the Communist League), but it is unlikely that such a "community" could be aware of its own existence were it not for the theoretical frame-work and rhetorical positionalities that the *Manifesto* itself provides.[73] The text works to constitute the audience it addresses; the identity anchoring present struggle and future transcendence turns out to be itself a textual-ized political production.

The bourgeoisie and its "gigantic means of production and exchange" are figured as a highly potent force—here a "sorcerer" no longer able to control its products, there an "epidemic" sweeping through the popula-tion—that is necessarily obliterating the meaning of existing groups and identities. On every page, the text works to "hail" its readers as persons who, whether old or young, men or women, already organized or as yet still isolated, can only meaningfully identify themselves as proletarian. Listen again, then, to these famous words:

> The bourgeoisie, wherever it has gotten the upper hand, has put an end to all feudal, patriarchal, idyllic relations. It has pitilessly torn asunder the motley feudal ties that bound man to his "natural superiors," and has left remaining no other nexus between man and man than naked self-interest, than callous "cash payment.". . . All fixed, fast frozen re-lations, with their train of ancient and venerable prejudices are swept

away, all new-formed ones become antiquated before they can ossify. All that is solid melts into air, all that is holy is profaned, and man is at last compelled to face with sober senses, his real relations of life, and his real relations with his kind.[74]

In such passages the *Manifesto* does what it says capitalism does: it unmasks illusions and simplifies antagonisms. Marx's writing (if the text succeeds) "pitilessly tear[s] asunder" the ties that bind his readers to existing social relations. It is the *Manifesto* that constructs, rhetorically, a (model of the) political world in which all meaningful conflict is reducible to the naked conflict between two hostile camps. This piece of writing is thus not only a call to action; in its textual production of identity and difference it is itself a political action. We can therefore read even the famous totalizing proclamation quite differently: "The history of all hitherto existing society is the history of class struggle" functions less as an empirical proposition than as an axiom helpful to the pursuit of Marx's political project. The crucial project here is the fashioning of a proletarian movement, which requires not only the mobilization of readers around the appropriate political agenda but the provision of the appropriate political subjectivity.

That ideology is a powerful force in the politics Marx analyzes, and that mobilization is the task of the *Manifesto*, are obvious and well known. But attention to *how* the mobilization proceeds and *what work* "ideology" does (if ideology is an adequate term for the rhetorical/discursive positionings charted here) suggests conclusions less obvious and more disruptive of our familiar sense of Marxist doctrine. The model of political life implied by the workings of the text destabilizes the formal theoretical edifice found in the *Manifesto*. This implicit model suggests that there is no unassailable ground in which the anchors of identity can be permanently fixed: if the world is such that Marx's rhetoric can be effective, then the work done by the *Manifesto* will be joined and opposed not only by other such texts, but by an essentially "textual" process of construction that runs throughout social institutions, formations, and struggles of all kinds.

Subject not only to discursive mobilization but to discursive construction, a political production located at the intersection of a host of contending projects of recruitment and constitution, identity here is something always underway and in conflict, something that can never achieve the innocence, self-presence, or closure sought by the more mechanically economistic moments of Marx's grand theoretical narrative. This account challenges those convictions that enable Marx to dispense with thinking about spaces and practices of negotiation "after the revolution," and to pay insufficient attention to the spaces that can be most empowering in the present. If, as the rhetorical workings of the text suggest, we are transformed in and by struggles that cannot be sealed off from the discursive, if political identities are not only the bases but also the products of action and speech—if politics is not simply an effect of production but also necessarily a rhetorical production itself—then the pursuit of transparency and transcendence are subverted. The proletariat does not so much come to know what the Marxist theorist already knew, but creates relationships, institutions, values, and subjectivities, through struggle, that could not have been known or anticipated before. A more open-ended and contingent sense of liberation, a more integral and irreducible understanding of struggle, is elaborated here through Marx's unwitting rhetorical subversion of History's meaning and mission. My writing (of) Marx thus suggests that transparency is an inappropriate and even harmful ideal, transcendence an impossible dream, and freedom a practice that cannot but be imperfect, ambiguous, dissonant, and political.

Where can we go from this reading? What does an approach based on no more than "implicit" models and rhetorical practices suggest for our thinking about what can be done with Marx's thought? Does this stress on the irreducibility of politics and the inevitability of the discursive moment mean that the field of possibility is always infinitely open, that politics is no more than the play of desire and will upon selves and situations of infinite plasticity? Is this reading itself a kind of rhetorical conjurer's trick that, within the confines of these pages, renders invisible the elements of force and the weight of material institutions that are so central to Marx's powerful critique of utopianism and idealism? Perhaps the best way to begin a response is to look at Marx's own attempt to rethink his approach to politics, class, and democracy in the wake of the *Manifesto*'s failure to anchor revolutionary identity and predict the course of immediate struggle. That rethinking finds its most ambitious outlet in what is clearly Marx's greatest work of self-criticism—and, to my mind, his most powerful work of political analysis—*The Eighteenth Brumaire of Louis Bonaparte*.

Forging Politics

In their innovative and influential theorization of democracy and discourse, Ernesto Laclau and Chantal Mouffe present their post-Marxist intellectual project as prompted, in part, by a "radical mutation" in the forms and bases of political agency, a transformation they characterize as "the decline of a form of politics for which the division of the social into two antagonistic camps is *an original and immutable datum, prior to all hegemonic construction*, and the transition towards a new situation . . . in which the very identity of forces in struggle is submitted to constant shifts, and calls for an incessant process of redefinition."[75] To accept such a change of focus is, on the conventional understanding, to turn away from the core political and philosophical commitments of Marxism. But is this post-Marxist position a departure from Marx's own work? Not entirely—at least not as I will read it here. Already we have seen how the *Manifesto's* rhetoric challenges the idea that the bipolar war of identities is an "immutable datum"; the point that must be pursued now is that Marx himself went on to attempt an explicit theorization of the fragmentary and fluid field of struggle identified by Laclau and Mouffe. In *The Eighteenth Brumaire*, Marx is forced to confront such "shifts" and "redefinitions" as he comes to terms with the defeat of the revolution he had summoned so exuberantly in the *Manifesto*, just a few years before.

Within weeks of the *Manifesto's* publication, Europe was swept by the epochal rebellions and revolutions of 1848. For a brief moment, it may well have appeared as if Marx's prophecy of imminent victory would be fulfilled. Such hopes, as we know, were soon disappointed. When "the most colossal event in the history of European wars"[76] ended in the bloody suppression of workers everywhere, Marx began to reconsider the "spectre haunting Europe," using the politically crucial events in France as his test case. While the *Manifesto* made a kind of delirious poetry of History's irresistible forward movement, *The Eighteenth Brumaire* confronts a struggle in which each new stage brings a more reactionary party into power, forcing Marx to puzzle over interludes in which motion seems to stop in a time altogether outside of the historical. While the former text presented a world splitting more and more into "two great hostile camps," the latter investigates the staggering diversity and complexity of identities, sketching a political struggle in which classes and class-fragments assume now this and now that configuration as political actors pass through tangled networks of alliances and enmities.[77] The *Manifesto* saw majority rule as an unproblematic stepping stone on the path toward socialism: if the proletariat could "win the battle of democracy," then it would be able to "use its political supremacy to wrest, by degrees, all capital from the bourgeoisie."[78] *The Eighteenth Brumaire* subverts this easy affiliation of democracy with socialism, chronicling the repeated use of "democracy" *against* the socialist project and the working class. Even the triumph of Louis Bonaparte, chief figure of authoritarian reaction, abettor of economic exploitation, was carried out in the name of "the people" and, indeed, on the basis of broad popular support. That triumph, and the related early disappearance of the organized proletariat from the struggle—events inconceivable from the standpoint of the *Manifesto*—are *The Eighteenth Brumaire*'s motivating intellectual problems. Faced with disappointment over the imminence of the socialist future, Marx revisits the problem of political struggle in the present and the ways in which that problem is shaped by actors' attachment to the past.

Marx's Bonaparte forges politics: he is inauthentic, fraudulent, a *poseur*. A person of indeterminate class position, protector of the interests of classes he claims to oppose, and ostensible spokesman for classes he does not, in fact, represent, he uses his famous name and dubious genealogical claims in order to gain support for a career and a government that can only produce a grotesque comedy of pettiness, corruption, and betrayal. Neither the inevitable byproduct of uncontrollable forces, nor an all-powerful agent who made his fate through no more than the force of his will and ingenuity, he is, rather, a sign of his times—a misrecognized actor for a historical moment of misrecognition, a forger for an age of forgery, a manipulator of class identifications who profits from a particularly difficult and confusing period in the class struggle.[79] *The Eighteenth Brumaire* reviews a historical stage haunted by ghosts and illusions. Actors on this stage misunderstand themselves and the conditions that shape their lives: they stray from their original intentions, without knowing why; they fail in their projects, without grasping the causes of failure; they stumble through events as if in a dream. Marx makes the hallucinatory politics of self-deception his great theme, charting the forces that lead groups to work against their own interests or will their own political repression. At each stage of the struggle and at each twist and turn of his narrative, he seeks to distinguish "between the phrases and fantasies of the parties and their real organization and real interests, between their conception of themselves and what they really are."[80] If Bonapartism is a mask for class rule, Marx will remove it; if Louis Bonaparte is a fraud, his forgeries must be exposed to the light of critical scrutiny.

What lies behind the mask? What can such exposure mean? In *The Eighteenth Brumaire*, such questions yield complexities and paradoxes not present in Marx's earlier work, making the answers both more provocative and more perplexing. Marx's essay engages not only forging as fraudulent representation but forging as a method of construction. To forge is to melt and meld materials. Though not an easy process, it is one in which— if the fire is hot enough—even hard, dense metal becomes malleable. *The*

Eighteenth Brumaire takes up this form of forging as it investigates the means by which class identity and structure can be reconfigured through the heat of political encounter. When Marx traces the careers of a diverse company of political subjects—not merely the proletariat but also "the financial aristocracy, the industrial bourgeoisie, the middle class, the petty bourgeoisie, the army, the Mobile Guard (i.e., the organized lumpenproletariat), the intellectual celebrities, the priests, the rural population" and others—he not only dispenses with older, simpler maps of class formation, but reflects on the ways in which classes are themselves the complex and contingent artifacts of political institutions, processes, discourses.[81] The relationship between the two forms of forging—between shaping or constructing, on the one hand, and bogus representations or identity-claims, on the other—is the central issue the essay investigates: To what extent do Bonaparte's misrepresentations enable him to reconfigure the materials of identity and class? To what extent can the state produce or embody class realities at odds with its explicit claims to stand for (some other segment of) the People?

The questions are pursued with such a dizzying combination of direct reply and evasion, virtuosic illustration and rhetorical displacement, that, by the end, it is not altogether clear how the modes of forging can be disentangled. When things get hot, the distinction between manipulatively *falsifying* political reality and artfully *creating* it is shrouded in a smoky haze. Real interests, authentic identity, true representation, material foundations—all of these crucial categories for sorting out the fraudulent from the legitimate are blurred by the end of the text. Though Marx sorts with great determination and with all of his formidable analytical powers, he also gives us reason to question the ground on which that search is conducted. Once again, we find that this author pursues contending projects and speaks in different voices, providing us with a text marked by both conceptual and rhetorical conflict. Once again, our sense of the status of politics and the content of freedom depends on which voice we hear—or how we orchestrate the dissonant voices.

It is crucial, however, not to simplify or condescend to this most complex and compelling theoretical artifact. If there are tensions here, they are rather different than those I found in the *Manifesto*. To reiterate, Marx's own program in this essay is, precisely, to think the relationships between materiality and rhetoric, what is given and what is produced, class structure and class content. Even in probing the plasticity of identity and the work performed by representations, he maintains a concern for the limits imposed by specific historical situations and the balance of forces that mark them.[82] Even when seeking to anchor political events in underlying material realities of class, he often recognizes classes as themselves political productions. The tensions within Marx's work in this essay are responsive, then, to the paradoxes and perplexities that mark political action itself. Politics can not be treated adequately either as sheer performance, pure invention, or as the straightforward discovery of and submission to the necessity of circumstance. Any attempt to dispense with one of these dimensions of political life is bound to be self-deluding and to smuggle surplus violence into its engagements with the world. And the attempt to think both moments at once, in all their ambiguity and dissonance, is necessarily vulnerable to imprecision and confusion. *The Eighteenth Brumaire*'s stresses and strains thus demand a more nuanced treatment than those in the *Manifesto*. They require a greater resistance to simply choosing one or another of its moments, and an awareness of the difficulties that come with resisting that choice. But the promises and problems of the essay are still best approached by disentangling its various strands or impulses. Let us begin, therefore, with Marx's more determined efforts to locate the class anchors of political identity.

Constructing Classes

The Eighteenth Brumaire investigates events in which the progressive parties exit the stage in the early acts, and so Marx's primary focus is on the forces of reaction, on the victories of, first, the party of Order and then Louis Bonaparte himself. Marx traces the political processes through which the class character of the Right was constructed and reconstructed as state power and the struggle for it took on a series of contradictory forms. The showcase of his analytical method, and a crucial narrative for his project of material explanation, is his account of contradictory interests and fractions within the bourgeoisie, the ideological investments and impasses that flowed from these interests, and the manner in which such contradictions and blockages provided the opening for Bonaparte's ultimate coup. This account reveals the Right to be at once astute about the use of force to advance its perceived interests and haunted by phantasms in its acts of perception, efficacious in its maneuverings and deluded in its sense of who it was and where it needed to go. Thus the Right's debates over the form and character of French government were shaped by forces which the debaters themselves understood only dimly, and Marx positions himself as the critic who can explain the course of events by revealing what those forces were and how they really worked.

The party of Order is presented as a coalition uniting the large landowners, the "aristocracy of finance," and the industrialists. These "heterogeneous social substances" were fused together during their successful effort to repress the initial proletarian insurgency. But in the parliamentary struggles that followed, "the mixture decomposed into its original constituents."[83] The arguments between factions were couched in terms of loyalty to the two royal houses, Orleans and Bourbon, and these allegiances were indeed *experienced* by the participants as the primary sources of conflict, but Marx sees a more basic clash beneath the royal commitments and identifications: the conflict "had no other meaning than that each of the two great interests into which the bourgeoisie is divided —landed property and capital—was endeavoring to restore its own supremacy and the subordination of the other interest."[84] "Orleans" was just another name for domination by the financial and industrial elites; "Bourbon" meant a return to the ascendancy of the agricultural bourgeoisie. Neither party adequately comprehended the material bases of its actions.

From the beginning, then, the forces inside the party of Order were both deluded and centrifugal. Yet despite their mutual antagonism and their misrecognition of its sources, neither faction could afford an open war against the other: neither alone was strong enough to triumph, and the disintegration of their coalition would open the way to radical insurgency. Though organized around passionate monarchical commitments, the factions were actually dependent upon the preservation of the parliamentary republic that had been established in the events of 1848: the republic was the one form in which the contending elements of the bourgeoisie could rule jointly. Joint rule was experienced by each faction as an unhappy, but necessary, compromise. Marx argues, however, that this "compromise" served their purposes even as it frustrated their desires: it allowed them to achieve more together than either faction could have achieved through the victory it wanted, for joint, parliamentary rule required the pursuit of the *general* class interests of the bourgeoisie and made it possible to dominate "the other classes of society more harshly and with less restriction than they could under the Restoration or the July monarchy."[85] The party of Order was hostile to the very political form that brought it the greatest possible social dominance. Self-perception and self-interest thus appear to go their separate ways in this account of unwitting political success.

Marx does not stop there, however, but adds another twist to his analysis: the hostility turns out to have a rational core, to be more than the legacy of traditional loyalties. The forces of Order "instinctively" recognized that the republic also posed a threat to the "foundations" of their social power by making that power more visible to subordinate classes and, hence, more vulnerable to assault. The yearning for (one or another) monarchy expressed an understanding that "the Crown" could help conceal the facts of class rule.[86] In the republic, the rule of the bourgeoisie was naked, pure, "completely organized." The material interests of capital had become "most intimately imbricated" with the "state machine," and this enabled the antagonism of subordinate classes to emerge in its pure form as well, "transform[ing] every struggle against the state power into a struggle against capital."[87] The majoritarian parliamentary regime thus became a fundamental threat, a source of contestation and unrest, encouraging direct challenge to bourgeois ascendancy even as that ascendancy reached its apogee. The republic's potential to provoke insurgency encouraged the party of Order to abandon the republic, but the divisions within the party prevented a return to the monarchy. Caught in "inextricable contradictions," the bourgeois parliamentarians could "neither tolerate the Republic nor overthrow it."[88]

This structural contradiction produced fresh ideological divisions, the most consequential of which was a split between parliamentary representatives and their constituents outside of parliament. While bourgeois parliamentarians desperately maneuvered to thwart Bonaparte's dictatorial ambitions, the financial and industrial sectors of the bourgeois populace denounced these maneuvers as disruptive of order. The bulk of this class had come to the conclusion that "its political power must be broken in order to preserve its social power intact." Their representatives must be renounced, the republic had to go: a powerful class had concluded that the political effort to "maintain its public interests" now amounted to "a disturbance of private business."[89] Though bourgeois enthusiasm for a coup could be viewed as the expression of a servile disposition—and this is how the petty bourgeois left viewed it—Marx's analysis reveals it to be a calculated pursuit of primary commitments. Enter Bonaparte, smiling enigmatically.

Through this analysis, Marx aims to establish that Bonaparte was neither the all-controlling producer of the situation nor the necessary result of historical law. Marx's Bonaparte responded to deep dilemmas in the structures and practices of class, but he exploited the situation in a contingent and tactically shrewd way. Consummate forger, he could pass himself off as (another) Napoleon because he was able to construct a class

constituency powerful enough to wield the requisite amount of force (or
was it the other way around?).[90] Acting on interests the bourgeoisie did
not fully recognize, perceiving the opening provided by the bourgeois
paradox and the paralysis it induced, he pushed through this opening into
power, with crucial backing from a substantial army deployed throughout
the streets of Paris. Bonaparte's shock troops were drawn from what Marx
calls the lumpenproletariat, a "class" made up of "the scum, the leavings,
the refuse of all classes"—high and low—including, among its compo-
nents, Bonaparte himself and

> decayed roués of doubtful origin and uncertain means of subsistence . . .
> ruined and adventurous scions of the bourgeoisie . . . vagabonds, dis-
> charged soldiers, discharged criminals, escaped galley slaves, swindlers,
> confidence tricksters, *lazzaroni*, pickpockets, sleight-of-hand experts,
> gamblers, *maquereaux*, brothel keepers, porters, pen-pushers, organ-
> grinders, rag-and-bone merchants, knife-grinders, tinkers, and beg-
> gars: in short, the whole indeterminate fragmented mass the French
> call *la bohème*.[91]

As both the diversity of the inventory and the remarkable pungency of
the language indicate, this class, crucial to the seizure of power, a class for
which the elusive *poseur* Bonaparte himself serves as the ideal figure(head),
is a thoroughly political production, and Marx's discussion of it is, as
Stallybrass argues, an exemplary account of the way that classes are forged
out of heterogeneous elements through processes of political articulation.[92]

Marx's analysis of the rise of Bonapartism thus serves two fundamental purposes. First, it establishes the role of force, the power of structure,
the material bases of political rule: Bonaparte could not have ascended
without the violent deployment of the lumpenproletariat and could not
govern were it not for the conditions and interests of the bourgeoisie. Second, it shows how the class forces shaping politics are themselves political artifacts, thus demonstrating at the level of explicit argument a point
that could only be teased out of the *Manifesto*'s rhetoric. Even the bourgeois parties of order elaborate their interests through a complex political
process. Marx's intricate account of the relationship between the given
and the constructed, clear perception and misrecognition, enables him to
make interest and material force fundamental conditions of political life,
without reducing actions to intentions, actors to transparency, or politics to the effect of material processes that lie wholly outside of textuality.

These are struggles in which stories and images wield enormous power, but which are not, despite that, fields of infinite play. Neither the effect of automatic and inevitable processes nor an arena in which good intentions and strong will are enough to overcome an unfavorable balance of power, politics becomes a contingent and dangerous game in which strategic thinking must be joined to narrative skills, the mobilization of pre-established forces to the force of (rhetorical) mobilization.

This conclusion matters, for it is one that Marx believes has hitherto been lost on the most relevant readers: his analysis is not simply an exercise undertaken in order to pursue interesting conceptual puzzles (though it *is* in part, a meditation on some of his own previous theoretical oversights), for it is offered—once again in pamphlet form—as a model for future radical political thought and struggle. One conviction Marx does retain from the *Manifesto*, and, for that matter, from "On the Jewish Question," is his belief that radicals consistently fail to do the hard intellectual work needed for strategic understanding and political success. His critical dissection of the composition and actions of the party of Order and the lumpenproletariat is supposed to model that work, showing what must be taken up and analyzed in order to cut through the mists of fraud and self-deception. To drive the point home, Marx also tells a cautionary tale of what happens when such analytical work is not done.[93] The subject of this tale is the petty bourgeois democratic Left.

The various contending advocates of democracy are presented as both less successful and more deluded than the forces of reaction, and none is portrayed more unflatteringly than the Montagne, the party of the parliamentary Left. In Marx's account, the radical democrats of the Montagne were afflicted with singularly bad timing, with exceptionally weak understanding of strategy and tactics. They became militant when forces were overwhelmingly against them. They limited themselves to polite parliamentary maneuvers when there was an opportunity to seize control of the streets. Always outmaneuvered by their opponents, they found their fortunes growing ever more desperate as the events unfolded. Each defeat left them entirely without illumination: they "sum[med] up the whole course of development in one slogan: 'reaction'—a night in which all cats are grey and which allow[ed] them to reel off their useless platitudes."[94] This is the intellectual sin Marx wishes to diagnose and avoid in his essay. He presents the Montagne's analytic incompetence and political impotence not as the contingent qualities of this particular group of politicians but as clues to the essential nature of a party of radical democracy.

Such democrats inevitably miss the persistence of force in political life, and cannot acknowledge the coercion that would be required to realize their own ambitions. Their sense that, like "the walls of Jericho," the citadels of power will simply "collapse" before them is rooted in an intellectually lazy populism: a simple, moralistic notion of "the people" substitutes for an analysis of class structure and class interest. Democrats acknowledge the existence of a privileged class, but insist that this class cannot long resist the wishes of the people united. When confrontation looms, democrats therefore "do not need to weigh up the means at their disposal too critically. They have only to give the signal for the people, with all its inexhaustible resources, to fall upon the oppressors."[95] Lacking an understanding of the complex, structured divisions among "the people," the democrats naturally have no understanding of the ways these divisions can be exploited—often in the name of democracy—for purposes of political reaction.

Marx's political pedagogy here is complex. He wishes not simply to catalog ineffective commitments and counterproductive habits of mind but further to discredit them by tracing them back to their roots. He thus provides a class analysis of the democratic failure to engage in class analysis: the radical democratic idea grows out of the distinctive conditions of the petty bourgeoisie. Because "the democrat represents . . . a transitional class in which the interests of two classes meet and become blurred, he imagines that he is elevated above class antagonisms generally."[96] The petty bourgeois democrats therefore mistake conditions that benefit themselves alone for those that will bring universal liberation. Out of the class-based denial of the determining reality of class comes the hybrid politics of social democracy—the search for "democratic-republican" institutions which will soften class antagonisms while remaining within the fundamental structure of bourgeois society. This politics cannot liberate the proletariat.

But the critique of the class basis of social democracy marks another tension within Marx's text, for it employs an approach to class identity and construction, and thus an understanding of the game of politics, less nuanced and complex than the one in the discussion of Bonapartism and the party of order. In the discussion of social democracy, Marx thinks of struggle in terms of force and strategy, mobilization and rhetorical maneuvering, yet he also conceives of liberation as requiring the transcendence of antagonisms, and an escape from these problems of calculating conflict. Though all of *The Eighteenth Brumaire* transforms his cartography of class structure, and much of it makes class a more complex kind of political artifact, the essay here appears to embrace the *Manifesto*'s overt foundationalist and teleological view of the nature and consequences of revolution. Revolutionary triumph will come only when a larger, more mature proletariat, acting as an essentially coherent political subject, decisively smashes its enemies. That victory will presumably spare the emancipated actors from the practices and problems of politics, for, though the timetable and the terrain have changed, Marx retains his faith in the meaning and destination of "the historical process."[97] Reflecting on the French events, he concludes that, while the proletarian revolution follows a different and less direct course than that suggested by the bourgeois model, it will still prove victorious once conditions advance to the point at which "retreat is impossible."[98] In France, the revolution has not quite reached this point, but it is well on its way: it will soon launch a battle to destroy the Bonapartist state and, hence, capital. The working class will triumph, but only after it has come to a unity that exists prior to political articulation and thus purged itself of the naive equation of revolution with democracy. Not immediately, but soon, History will reach its End(s); it is a force too powerful and purposeful to be denied.[99] It is as if all of the complexities that Marx now sees when his historical glance looks backward dissolve when he turns toward the future.

Taken alone, such arguments make it appear that *The Eighteenth Brumaire* offers no more than did the explicit assertions of the *Manifesto:* once again we find an ultimate anchor for politics and an imagination of transcendence. Can such a conclusion really be compatible with everything we have seen in the text? Can such a sense of historical destiny coexist with the narrative of reaction Marx offers? Can this resurrected model of the essentially unitary proletariat allow for everything Marx says about that class's strange, heterogeneous negative image, the *lumpen*-proletariat? Can the Bonapartist project, for all of its reliance on the laborious political recruitment of individuals into classes, be understood through these arguments that appear to reinstate the pre-political solidity of class? If Bonaparte is merely a fraud, what explains his power? If he has really succeeded in forging a class coalition, melding it out of diverse elements, does this not suggest the need for a rethinking of the model of class as well as the map, the form of revolution as well as its timetable? To make sense of these questions we must turn away from the moments of Historical bravado and toward other strands in the text.

Rhetoric and Representation

An entry point is provided by Marx's account of the petty bourgeois bases of social democracy. There, he does not claim that all social democrats are literally from the ranks of the petty bourgeoisie. He is aware that the leaders and followers of the Montagne came from a wide variety of social locations. Rather than suggesting that they are all are "shopkeepers," he argues that, regardless of their own material circumstances, they all *represent* the petty bourgeoisie: "What makes them [representative] . . . is the fact that their minds are restricted by the same barriers which the petty bourgeoisie fails to overcome in real life, and that they are therefore driven in theory to the same problems and solutions to which the material interest and social situation drive the latter in practice. This is the general relationship between the political and literary representatives of a class and the class which they represent."[100] But what is the "general relationship" described here? How *is* it that some are intellectually constricted by boundaries that map, flawlessly, onto the material circumstances of others? What is the nature of these intellectual constraints? In earlier work, such as the *German Ideology*, Marx had offered a simple, mechanical, causal model for answering questions of this type. Does *The Eighteenth Brumaire* also rely on this model?

At times, such a model is explicitly defended: "A whole superstructure of different and specifically formed feelings, illusions, modes of thought and views of life arises on the basis of the different forms of property, of the social conditions of existence. The whole class creates and forms these out of its material foundations and the corresponding social relations."[101] Yet this model, though offering a general account, still does not explain how or why some particular individuals of differing material circumstances come to share the illusions of those of other, less exalted, circumstances. Nor, as Sandy Petrey argues in his elegant exploration of the materiality of representation, does it make much sense of the situation, diagnosed so brilliantly elsewhere in Marx's text, in which bourgeois parliamentary and literary representatives were fundamentally "estranged" from the class they represented, in which the limits of a class's material circumstances failed to constrain the thoughts and actions of its leaders.[102] In no case can Marx tell us how specific people come to inhabit or stray from the limits of thought proper to a specific class, and his general account of the "necessary class belongingness" of those intellectual limits is not adequate to the most sophisticated moments of his argument:[103] the base/superstructure model cannot capture the complexities of identity and class formation— the problems of forging—that are so important to *The Eighteenth Brumaire*'s story. In much of the text, the anchors of identity are placed on ground that is far less solid than this simpler form of materialism allows. Marx has a problem: he wishes at once to rethink his understanding of class and politics and to cling to certain reassuring convictions that this rethinking jeopardizes. It is worth tracing both his attempt to hang on, and the manner in which he departs on a very different course of inquiry.

Despite its brilliance, Marx's extended account of the schisms within the party of Order is not a sufficient explanation of Bonaparte's power, for that account concerns only the most powerful ruling elites, not the bulk of the population. Nor can Marx's remarks on the lumpenproletariat, an essentially urban phenomenon, make sense of the events taking place in most of the nation. At the essay's close, he therefore turns briefly to the task of providing a class analysis of Bonaparte's popularity among the "most numerous class of French society, *the small peasant proprietors.*" And it is this task that leads him into his greatest difficulties. Marx maintains that Bonaparte "represents" this class, and is able to do so because of the uniquely insubstantial or underdeveloped class-formation of the peasantry. The small peasants are a class only insofar as their economic conditions "separate their mode of life, their interests, and their cultural formation from those of other classes and bring them into conflict with those classes." But in an equally important sense, they are *not* a class: they live isolated lives, have no distinctive community or political organizations, "do not enter into manifold relations with each other." This class, which is made up of the majority of the population, "is formed by the simple addition of isomorphous magnitudes, much as potatoes in a sack form a lump of potatoes." Due to their isolation and underdevelopment, the peasants "cannot represent themselves." They need a powerful representative who appears as both master and benign protector; their "political influence . . . is therefore ultimately expressed in the executive subordinating society to itself." [104]

We have here a materialist explanation of sorts. Yet compared to the richly conceptualized and precisely detailed account of bourgeois class-fragments, this is a thin and elusive characterization. This lack of solidity is a symptom of the analytical trouble the explanation faces. Perhaps Marx's famous image of "potatoes in a sack" suggests itself to him because he needs some kind of conceptual container into which he can dump this unwieldy intellectual problem as quickly as possible. And he must dump it, because he also asks the material circumstances of the peasants to do some very different argumentative work in his explanation. After all, Marx also reads the executive's triumph as a prelude to successful revolution, and that reading seems unlikely if Bonaparte indeed represents the interests of the vast majority. Marx thus also insists that Bonaparte is *not* their true representative. Because agriculture has been wholly drawn under the reign of capital, and the peasant is exploited in the service of bourgeois profit, peasant interests are fundamentally at odds with those served by Bonapartism. Marx still insists that this (non)class cannot represent itself, but he now maintains that its "natural ally and leader [is] the urban proletariat, whose task is the overthrow of the bourgeois order." [105]

If it turns out that the destiny of the peasantry is socialist revolution, if the Bonapartist state just sustains their oppression, then Marx has not in fact explained their political convictions. What led them to endorse Bonaparte? In the end, Marx's answer is that, "*Historical tradition* produced the French peasant's belief that a miracle would occur, that a man called Napoleon would restore all of their glory." [106] This answer may very well be correct, but, as several recent readers have noted, it subverts Marx's own account of what his analysis demonstrates, making "tradition" and illusion the prevailing forces in the pivotal struggle for control of the state.[107] Marx criticizes the spurious nature of the tradition — "it represents the peasant's superstition, not his enlightenment; his prejudice, not his judgment; his past, not his future" — but he does not offer a compelling materialist explanation of this tradition's hold on the populace. Of course, from the beginning, *The Eighteenth Brumaire* presents us with a political world in which *everyone* is shrouded in the fog of ideology — the "*brume*" on which, in French, the essay's title puns — and no actions are wholly transparent to the actors who perform them. Throughout, Marx demonstrates an especially acute interest in the intertwining of illusion and historical memory, for he is analyzing a revolutionary period in which "The tradition of the dead generations weighs like a nightmare on the minds of the living" and those seeking to create a new world "timidly conjure up the spirits of the past to help them." [108] But, in the case of the peasants, the conjuring appears more powerful than Marx can easily allow. As Dominick LaCapra writes, "Marx provides no explanation of why certain groups ideologically disguise *real* interests while other groups are seemingly motivated in political action by *illusory* interests that correspond at best to past realities." [109] Marx's descriptions of deceptions and illusions shatter the framework in which they are set. The chain of signification fails to find its solid anchor in the unmediated reality of class structure.

Yet, as we already saw in examining the party of Order and the lumpenproletariat, Marx has made the status of "illusion" and the character of "interests" more contestable than they were in the explicit pronouncements of his earlier works. The problematic of forging and political articulation that marks *The Eighteenth Brumaire*'s richest analyses is less threatened by his concluding story about the decisive role of tradition in securing majority support for Bonapartism. That problematic essentially breaks with the older model of ideology that Marx worked out in *The German Ideology* and sometimes transfers to *The Eighteenth Brumaire.* Ultimately, the latter text strains against the philosophical paradigm of representation itself.[110] It would be a retreat from what is best in the text to use the case of Bonaparte's hallucinatory hold over the peasantry in order to argue for an idealist reversal of the cruder forms of Marx's materialism. The essay does not show us that "ideas" are "causally determining," that politics is merely a matter of vision and will. Marx's account of popular Bonapartism reveals—if not altogether self-consciously—the discursive constitution of real effects, the political production of the peasantry *as a class.* It is the performative work done by Bonaparte's acts of representation that make this "non class" into something "real." Bonapartism *"constitutes* the very interests it signifies": they were not simply there, prior to this constitution, nor are they merely in the heads of individual peasants.[111] *The Eighteenth Brumaire* presents politics as a production, revealing a world in which people's lives and selves are inextricably bound up with "textual" processes, in which stories, if repeated frequently enough in the right places, acquire material density and institutional shape, in which one can explain a seizure of state power by identifying the form of drama that was on the political stage: "At a time when the bourgeoisie itself was playing the most complete comedy, but in the most serious manner in the world, without infringing any of the pedantic requirements of French dramatic etiquette, and was itself half duped and half convinced of the serious character of its own state proceedings, the adventurer had to win simply because he played the comedy as comedy."[112]

These words put the problem of rhetoric to us in more than one way. The substantive claim they make is that rhetorical form and generic convention are crucial political matters. But what of the form of Marx's own writing? Are not his words themselves, as we say, stagy? Responsive to dramatic convention but fully aware of the stakes of the action, they, like Bonaparte, carry out their role perfectly. In their virtuosic combination of epigrammatic compression and ironic inversion, in their attempt to produce assent through the sheer power of performance, they are characteristic of many of this pamphlet's plays on words. Those plays, like the rhetoric of the *Manifesto,* teach us something significant about the political stage, about the acts through which political power is produced, transferred, challenged, and lost. The scandalous power of representations to materialize through performance—scandalous because this power sits uneasily with both conventional Marxist theories of the superstructure and the bourgeois realist epistemologies Marx opposed—is best demonstrated by Marx's mode of writing.[113] Perhaps because these demonstrations subvert the theoretical framework he (sometimes) wishes to retain, they make their author visibly uneasy.

Both kinds of illumination offered by Marx's textual practice—insight into the textualization of identity that marks the production of politics "in the world," and insight into the ways in which his anxieties find displaced expression in his rhetoric—can, at times, be found in the same piece of writing. Consider the following remarkable passage, in which Marx characterizes the dynamics of reaction:

> This, then, was the Constitution of 1848, overthrown on 2 December 1851 not by a head, but by coming into contact with a mere hat; this hat was of course of the three-cornered Napoleonic variety. . . . The republicans of 1848 . . . made an invention . . . the state of siege . . . which has found periodic application in every successive crisis in the course of the French revolution. The barracks and the bivouac were thus periodically deposited on the head of French society in order to compress its brain and keep it quiet; the sabre and the musket were periodically made to judge and administer, to guard and to censor, to play the part of the policeman and night watchman; the military moustache and the service uniform were periodically trumpeted forth as the highest wisdom and the spiritual guide of society. Was it not inevitable that barracks and bivouac, sabre and musket, moustache and uniform, would finally hit on the idea of saving society once and for all by proclaiming the supremacy of their own regime and thus entirely freeing civil society from the trouble of ruling itself?[114]

The use of metonymy is striking. Marx employs this trope to make his narrative vivid, to convey the dizzying whirl of events. But Marx's rhetoric is more than an attempt to make his prose lively: it is not merely decorative. His use of figure is integral to, and even constitutive of, his sustained theoretical engagement with problems of reification and fetishism. He is chronicling events in which things are not what they seem, and— with more power than could be provided by any more abstract discourse on inversion or mystification—the passage *shows* us the systematic distortions of this inverted world. When the sword, the hat, and the moustache get up and move about, Marx's prose mimics those distortions. His text recreates the political world he observes, teaching us, experientially, what it means to navigate through a field of misrecognition while counterrevolution is being forged.

But if the effort is simply to unmask illusion, to explore misrecognition from within the simple paradigm of base and superstructure, Marx succeeds too much, beyond his intentions, more than he knows. In recreating that world, he subverts his formal pronouncements about its nature. Once he sets his metonyms in motion, they keep on moving until they have marched out of their assigned places: Marx's figures enact, before our eyes, the difficulty of keeping ideologies tied to their ostensible moorings in class. The figurative language gets unruly at a pivotal moment in Marx's argument and narrative: he is edging up to an acknowledgment of the theoretical embarrassment that, in France, History refused to move as he had anticipated, producing a period of "crying contradictions," and "history without events."[115] The mystification mimed by his figures is crucial to his explanations of this turn toward reaction, with its curious lull in "normal" progress and its odd rhythms, its "constant repetition" in a strange time beyond purpose or direction. Marx does, of course, attempt to account for the sequence of events through the more "material" class analyses outlined above. Yet in those moments when he retains his commitment to an ontologically prior economic "base," to interests that have a necessary class belongingness, and to class identities formed outside the forge of politics, he has difficulty keeping the two levels or forms of his analysis—that of interests and that of phantasmagoric delusions—connected.

Marx provides a perfect figure for his own difficulty, for the excessive success of his other tropes and turns of phrase, when he describes the most striking of the "crying contradictions": "Men and history appear as Schlemihls in reverse, as *shadows which have been detached from their bodies.*" This remark takes some of its resonance from the ghost imagery that recurs throughout this phantom-filled text. Though that imagery is intended to trope the actors' unfortunate fixation upon the national past, it also works as the device through which Marx revisits and reworks his past models of history and politics. And it here becomes the image through which his writing—behind his own back—undoes those formulaic aspects of the reductionist model that (a part of him, at least) still wishes to retain. Of course, Marx only says that the shadows "appear" to be autonomous; but try as he might, he cannot bring them back to the bodies to which they belong. These shadows dance away, moving to rhythms and purposes of their own, neither the epiphenomena of pure matter nor mere spirits in a separate sphere of ethereal entities, but potent forces that make things happen.[116]

Thinking (in) the Shadows

How do our central themes appear from the vantage point that this long and leisurely tour has provided? Marx's writing (on) action both contextualizes and deepens the question of the contending approaches to freedom. We have seen that the yearning for transcendence, with its fictions of transparency and its confidence in the dispensability of politics, finds its full voice when Marx turns to theorize History and its end(s). This not only extends our catalog of political evasions but illuminates the means and methods, hopes and anxieties, by which evasions are accompanied. When Marx follows the lure of transcendence, the most tragic consequence is his failure to pay sustained attention to the spaces in which freedom can be practiced, the resistances that must, inevitably, remain, and the dissonance that marks all forms of collective life. Marx is able to pass, too often and too quickly, over multiple spaces and practices of politics because he (sometimes) refuses to think that politics goes all the way down. Or perhaps he too often seeks ultimate foundations because he too rarely attends adequately to the production of political spaces. Either way, this inattention to political space is connected to Marx's failure to bequeath to us usable thoughts for dealing with a problem he did identify astutely, the globalization of politics. If I have left that crucial issue behind here, it is because Marx's profound insights into the ways global conditions were eroding traditional notions of belonging and governance did not produce comparable insights into new modes of belonging and practices of governance that might be created as the old forms weakened.

As we have seen, however, these great historical pamphlets undercut the longing for transcendence, even while encoding it in a metanarrative of extraordinary sweep and ambition. Read freely, the *Manifesto* proves to be quite different from the catechism that was commissioned by the Communist League. If it contains propositions that can be recited dogmatically and by rote, and if these send us on a destructive quest to anchor revolutionary identity, the work done by the writing suggests a very different approach to politics. *The Eighteenth Brumaire* not only extends that rhetorical subversion but (sometimes) brings this sense of the irreducibility of politics and the complexities of identity performances into its explicit theoretical formulations. These rhetorics and arguments have important implications for the meaning of democracy and the ways we can be free, for they both carry out and refine the conception of freedom as a political practice. This conception (found in works as early as "On the Jewish

Question" and as late as *The Civil War in France*) calls on us to extend the practices of democratic struggle across the social and cultural terrain, and does so in a way that sharpens our understanding of what it would mean to transpose Tocqueville's sense of democratic dissonance and the art of being free out of the narrow register of what he called "politics." Many of Marx's texts, even those as institutionally specific as Marx's analyses of the Commune or as "policy oriented" as his *Critique of the Gotha Program*, evade the deepest and most interesting questions that must be asked about the sources and means of the project of radically extending the practice of democracy. But the *Manifesto* and *The Eighteenth Brumaire*, when brushed against the grain, provide incisive explorations of the struggles through which such transpositions proceed.

Read for their (submerged) alternative approaches to class, identity, history, and textuality, these works' manner of figuring the political offers a stronger argument for the perpetuation of democratic spaces than was ever offered by Marx's more explicit theoretical proclamations, while also providing his richest accounts of the relations, difficulties, and possibilities to which such spaces must respond. Marx's way of writing shows us how and why the democratic imaginary is among the prime materials of political contestation and how contestation over the imaginary proceeds—indeed his way of narrating class struggle reveals more about the democratic imaginary than about socialism itself. The *Manifesto* and *The Eighteenth Brumaire* remind us that politics is often a game of force, that even the most ingenious and inventive performances are constrained by or reenact the violence of their staging ground; the works thereby show us that the practice of radical politics cannot be disconnected from rigorous strategic analysis. Yet they also illuminate the ways in which practice, in a world of contingency, inevitably exceeds what strategy can envision, and they show us how even the most material of constraints are forged, made up, and thus—with luck—susceptible to rematerialization when the temperature is right. In their irresolution, the texts enact the conflicts constitutive of democracy and the practices of freedom. My goal in taking liberties with Marx has not been to cancel these conflicts in some magnificently dialectical *Aufhebung*, but to register them and keep them alive— for only by preserving such tensions can we resist the depoliticizing evasions that I have identified. Those seeking to expand the scope of freedom and democracy can afford neither to make politics simply a matter of the discovery of imperatives (laws of history, balances of force, objective interests) nor to treat it as pure invention, unconstrained spontaneity (as if anyone could successfully pursue any interest in any historical situation). The Marx I have written here, against many of his own impulses, teaches us how to think the political without either debilitating reduction.

Despite my sense of the need to live with these tensions, I sometimes find myself thinking it a shame that Marx's more familiar foundationalist project failed. The failure leaves us with nothing comparable in sweep and grandeur to his largest promises, his summons to form the great movement that would unite people across the boundaries of state, and destroy, once and for all, the forms of exploitation and the forces of heteronomy. Marx was able confidently to imagine a world in which all would be harmonious and whole. Who can honestly claim to find nothing tempting in that vision? The perspective I have constructed out of my encounters with Tocqueville and Marx offers no equivalent reassurances or hopes. It provides no analog to the Marxist identification of the linchpin of oppression, no parallel to the project of transcending all of the structured bases of fundamental conflict, no reason to believe our lives can be utterly unfettered and our selves completely—without resistance, without residue—free. With the abandonment of transparency as either a goal or a regulative ideal, the more partial and imperfect freedoms that remain for us are clouded in uncertainty and stained by contingency.

But here, too, Marx poses a useful challenge to us. If we cannot hitch a ride with History, we must nevertheless confront the peculiar circumstances that mark politics in our time. If we cannot get much political guidance from the slogan, "Workers of the World Unite!" we also cannot ignore the late-modern global dislocations that Marx observed so early, so presciently. If we cannot reattach the shadows to their bodies, thereby erasing all doubts about the distinctions between the real and the fake, cause and effect, representation and the represented, we can take up the still undertheorized task of thinking (in) the shadows Marx identified. Marx has refined our tools, sharpened our goals. Yet some of the most critical work laid out at the end of my discussion of Tocqueville still remains to be done. To do that work—to think further about the transposition of democratic practices into registers beyond those recorded by Tocqueville, as Marx's writing (of) freedom pushes us to do—I turn to the work of Hannah Arendt, for her thought offers unusually rich reflections upon the themes with which I have ended this encounter with Marx.

CHAPTER FIVE

Acting (Up) in Publics: Mobile Spaces, Plural Worlds

The *polis*, properly speaking, is not the city-state in its physical location; it is the organization of the people as it arises out of acting and speaking together, and its true space lies between people living together for this purpose, no matter where they happen to be . . . . [A]ction and speech create a space between the participants which can find its proper location almost any time and anywhere . . . . For power, like action, is boundless . . . . Its only limitation is the existence of other people . . . because human power corresponds to the condition of plurality.

—Hannah Arendt

But one cannot . . . plead *simply* for plurality, dispersion, or fractioning, for the mobility of screening spaces or the subjects who occupy them . . . . How then to open the avenue of great debates, accessible to the majority, while yet enriching the multiplicity and quality of public discourses, of agencies of evaluation, of "scenes" or places of visibility, etc.? A wager, an aporia?

—Jacques Derrida

You will find the distance that separates you from them, by joining them.

—Antonio Porchia

Pure Politics

Wide-ranging, complex, elusive, paradoxical, and—hence—subject to interpretations that are mutually contradictory and yet supported by plausible textual evidence, Hannah Arendt's work is not easily or fruitfully reduced to a single commitment, conviction, or project. Still, I suggest that the most consistent and important object of her diverse inquiries is to illuminate the sites and occasions that make politics possible and to reveal what takes place in them. Arendt is this century's great theorist of political spaces. She tells stories of their creation and their closing, analyzes their importance and the reasons for their failures, and develops a distinctive and at times stunningly poetic terminology for understanding them. In her telling, political spaces are mobile, theatrical, unpredictable, both the result of action and an impetus to it. Wildly transformative, they bring new selves and relations into being. Even as they constitute common ground, Arendtian spaces sustain difference-preserving forms of distance between people, at once joining and separating those gathered in them. The actions that create them and to which they give rise disrupt processes of normalization. For Arendt, these qualities make spaces for action matters of inestimable importance: without such spaces, we cannot be free. She links totalitarianism, the most oppressive form of twentieth-century political life, to their absence, and she focuses her most radical criticisms on the normalizing forces and structures that overrun them even in liberal-democratic orders.

I take Arendt, then, to be a crucial theorist for thinking about politicized challenges to "regimes of the normal."[1] Building on her understandings of action, the spaces of freedom, and what she called "the social," I use her work in order further to elaborate a democratic sensibility that refuses to evade politics. My slide from "freedom" to "democracy" here is calculated, but not necessarily Arendtian. Her theorization of freedom is highly ambivalent about democracy; arguably, she is not a democrat at all.[2] Either way, she is an unreliable guide to democratic politics. I will show, however, that Arendtian freedom can be exercised democratically, and that only by treating it as a democratic practice—which is to say only by being willing sometimes to rework her conclusions about the substance of politics and its relation to social life—can the fundamental shortcomings in her thinking be overcome. This approach also allows a reading of Arendt to draw on and extend the insights of Tocqueville and Marx while helping us to push beyond their most significant limitations. Although Arendt's political theory is informed by her reflections on the Athenian polis and is often mistaken for either a doomed attempt to resurrect that inaugural political forum or a quietist lament over its irrecoverable loss, I engage her writings to think about the kinds of democratic spaces that can and should be constituted after the eclipse of the Tocquevillian locality and the unraveling of Marxist teleology.[3]

Arendt's ability to help us transform the work of Marx and Tocqueville follows from her rejection of their foundational moves: from her perspective, both Marx's attempt to anchor revolutionary identity and

Tocqueville's cultural containment of democracy are instances of political theory's abiding fear of the unsettling unpredictability of politics.[4] In the case of Marx, Arendt's rejection is clear and explicit: some of her most important theorizing takes shape in opposition to Marxist doctrine. She saw his account of history, revolution, and the force of material interests in political life as a denial of the capacity of action to bring about the unexpected and the unprecedented, a subordination of the human potential for freedom to the tyrannical rule of necessity.[5] Refusing his anchors, Arendt undertakes a theorization of the political enactment of identity, treating action as a form of revelation or invention in which we show "who" (our unique personal identities) as opposed to "what" (our ascriptive characteristics, our social positions) we are.[6] Through this account of enactment, she articulates and develops perceptions that Marx largely leaves implicit in his textual practice: it takes no interpretive pyrotechnics to recognize *her* politics as a performative production.[7] For Arendt, wherever there are people acting in public there is politics; and since Arendtian publics can arise through action itself, the practice of politicization can, in principle, be pursued anywhere. Taking up her work thus enables a fuller appreciation of the opportunities to initiate democratic struggle than can be derived from Marx alone.

Arendt's critical rejection of Tocqueville's strategies of containment is less apparent but equally important. Most obvious—though rarely acknowledged in the critical literature—is his influence on central Arendtian categories.[8] Her understandings of mass society and totalitarianism bear the stamp of his reflections on individualism, conformity, and despotism even as they confront phenomena unknown to him. Her approach to action has clear affinities with *Democracy*'s reliance on the art of being free as the medium for countering both the centrifugal forces of atomization and the centripetal pressures of conformity. Recognizing these affinities clarifies the importance of the major differences. For Arendt's most significant departure is her refusal to provide political art with Tocquevillian guarantees. She does not rely on anything like Tocqueville's religious consensus as the basis for organizing political belonging or establishing the limits of action, and she does not construct the kind of constrained subject required by his norms of stable moral virtue. Indeed, her account of the "in between" spaces of the public world is elaborated as an alternative to all subject-centered approaches to political commonality.[9] For Arendt, the imposition of a shared identity is not only unnecessary to public spaces but inimical to them, for they at once depend upon and sustain "the simultaneous presence of innumerable perspectives and aspects in which the common world presents itself and for which no common measurement or denominator can ever be devised." [10] Privileging common spaces over the common quality of subjects, she argues that a free political life cannot be secured through the forms of homogenization that Tocqueville found necessary. Instead, she seeks a political foundation for politics.

So far, Arendt's approaches to space and action appear to offer a politics that is more radically pluralistic than Tocqueville's and Marx's, in the dual sense that its locations are more diverse and that it can accommodate greater differences among actors. Putting the point that way helps us to recognize the centrality of her concern for the preservation of human plurality, "the twofold character of equality and distinction" arising from "the fact that men, not Man, live on earth and inhabit the world," which she sees as the basic condition of political life.[11] As an account of the political import of her work as a whole, however, the comparative judgment just offered is problematical: while Arendt can help us to advance the arguments of the previous chapters, to treat her thinking as itself a satisfactory response to the problems I identified there is to ignore some of its most noteworthy features. The politics she theorizes is as narrow and limited as it is mobile and plural. Like Tocqueville and Marx, Arendt employs strategies of evasion. Like their strategies, hers are attempts to secure highly valued ends. Yet what Arendt values most highly, and more obviously and unambivalently than do the other theorists, is politics. The very commitment that leads her to reject the kinds of evasions that mark the writings of Tocqueville and Marx—the commitment to a politics of pure enactment, founded upon nothing but itself—thus becomes the ultimate source of her own evasions.[12] The alternative foundation she seeks proves to be as unsatisfactory as those it would replace: Arendt's quest for political purity leads her to depoliticize much that Tocqueville and Marx have already demonstrated to be the stuff of politics. Too often, Arendt recognizes neither the elements of force that mark even the most unpredictable and transformative of political performances nor the contestable signifying acts that forge even the most ironclad of social forces. In her thinking, as a result, the tension between discovery and invention is not so much sustained as it is made the basis of a negotiated settlement in which only the latter is allowed entry into the precincts of politics. Figuring the political as a realm free of the impurities of constraint, force, and fixity, Arendt's writing often empties the public spaces that it takes such care to construct. Her theorizing thus shows just how difficult it is to perform the complex adjustments required in order to work through the obstacles we found in their texts.

Take, for instance, the problem of human needs. In seeking to avoid the submission to necessity that she (correctly) saw in central strands of Marx's theorizing, Arendt banishes all claims and considerations of need from political discourse and action. That move does not keep the pressures of necessity from weighing as heavily in Arendt's world as in any other; they have simply, through her drawing of boundaries, been left unchallenged by any politicized response. Similarly, in seeking to avoid the political imposition of a common identity, Arendt ends up placing outside of the political sphere many of the power-charged processes and practices through which such commonalities are imposed; but of course they, too, persist uncontested after their removal. The consequences of this narrowing of the political are profound. Through her exclusions, Arendt seems to deny political status to (among other matters) economic interests and arrangements of corporate power, questions of health and welfare, gender codes and structures of sexual subordination, and racist cultural hierarchies and the social practices that sustain them. Arendt's boundaries are drawn so narrowly that, as frustrated readers have noted repeatedly, it is sometimes hard to determine what *isn't* left out, what should be taking place in the Arendtian public realm, or who can meet her standards for genuine political action.[13]

Nowhere is the paradox produced by this simultaneous exaltation and evacuation of the political more evident than in her approach to sovereignty.[14] On her account, resort to the idea of rule is the quintessential evasion in political thinking. She argues that violence is lodged in all forms of rule. This violence flows from the fundamental conflict between pursuit of the "uncompromising self-sufficiency and mastership" demanded by sovereignty—no matter how democratically construed—and the human condition of plurality. Both the plurality between us and that within us (each individual's diverse potentialities, faculties, aspirations) are suppressed when action becomes execution, the carrying out of a unitary, coherent will.[15] Identifying the violence inherent in this suppression gives us compelling reasons to resist the reduction of politics to sovereignty, illuminating the problems that arise when theorists conflate the terms (think of the connections between Marx's tendency to equate politics with class rule and his vision of freedom as transcendence).

But when Arendt's drive for purity leads from an awareness of the violence in rule to the conclusion that ruling is incompatible with genuinely political relationships—when, in other words, her demonstration that politics inevitably involves more than violence becomes a stipulation that the inevitable violence of collective life plays no part in politics—

she places herself in an impossible position. The problem arises not only from the general implausibility of a politics purged of all elements of sovereignty (as if politics had nothing to do with the making of binding decisions, and as if such decisions had nothing to do with ruling) but from the more specific conflict between her philosophical rejection of rule and her serious concern with political structures of governance. Her work, especially *On Revolution*, underscores the power of action to constitute organs of government, and suggests that this capacity gives reason for political hope. Indeed, she takes the creation of governing bodies to be the most worthy end of revolutionary struggle and argues that theorizing the forms of political governance created by revolutionary action is essential to understanding the possibilities for initiating spaces of freedom in this century. Yet Arendt's account of non-sovereign politics appears to deprive her governing institutions of the ability to . . . govern.[16]

What could occasion such a curious position? Why is it so important to keep politics pure? Arendt's answer, simply put, is "freedom." Freedom is "the *raison d'être* of politics," something only politics can provide. This is because, as she conceives of it, freedom is not a property of the will but, rather, exists wholly in its worldly exercise: "to *be* free and to act are the same."[17] Her argument for identifying freedom with action is based upon her understanding of action's role in expressing or inventing personhood. As Bonnie Honig has emphasized to great effect, Arendt's actor is an unpredictable, internally divided performer—a self never fully revealed outside the theater of politics, and sometimes more the creation of action than its cause.[18] Through action, "we insert ourselves into the human world," changing it as we appear in it and thereby initiating novelties that cannot be predicted from precedent. This is why action creates the very plurality upon which it depends: human differences emerge through our entry onto the public stage and are sustained by the spaces of appearance that action creates. Arendt identifies the capacity to bring newness and difference into the world, which she calls our "natality," as distinctively human, and argues that it cannot be explained by either the pressures of necessity or the calculations of utility.[19] Indeed, any attempt to subject action to instrumental imperatives or concerns can only destroy spontaneity and invention. Not just rule, but *all* forms of making or fabrication impinge violently upon the revelations and performances of self through which we experience freedom. It is, then, to safeguard the enactment of freedom that Arendt purifies politics of instrumentality and force.

There are, to be sure, important counter-tendencies in her thinking, elements and moments that suggest a less exclusionary account of what is proper to politics. For instance, worldliness is not only the setting for Arendtian action but part of its content: she repeatedly insisted that action is about the realities confronting actors, that it cannot be political if it does not focus on the worldly interests at stake.[20] Later, I shall consider the ways these elements complicate the picture offered so far. But I have begun by emphasizing the drive for purity because it shapes the most important categories of Arendt's thought (including worldliness): her distinctions between public and private, political and social, labor, work, and action are all crafted with the purpose of securing a medium for the pristine enactment of freedom. To protect that medium, she often renders these distinctions impermeable, treating theoretical or practical efforts that cut across them as transgressions of the basic ontological structures of human life. And as I have been suggesting, both the placing and the rigidity of these conceptual boundaries disable politics.

My reading will therefore confound Arendt's categorical distinctions by resisting her impulse to purify. I draw on Tocqueville and Marx for assistance even as I use her work to revise their arguments. Arendt's illumination of the problems with Tocquevillian efforts to secure difference through homogenization becomes more helpful if we do not dismiss his understanding that no politics proceeds without the imposition of commonality. Her insights into the power of performance are rendered more complex if we recognize, with Marx, the inexpungeable force of necessity and the persistence of instrumentality in all political action. Only by being made responsive to its inherent impurities can Arendtian freedom be saved from becoming either incoherent or irrelevant. Altering Arendt's understandings of freedom and politics through an acknowledgment of the impossibility of purity both requires and enables the democratization of her thinking. And appropriating her in this way can indeed deepen our understanding of the spaces and practices of contemporary politics: if her texts are not taken as blueprints that establish the boundaries of public life or successfully design institutions of governance, they can become lenses that alter our perceptions of the powers through which we create and recreate our worlds. These lenses clarify our vision of the prerequisites and promise of democratic struggle by uncovering the extraordinary possibilities that inhere in ordinary situations and relationships.

My pursuit of this vision proceeds through several distinct stages. First, I provide a fuller account of the obstacles that my appropriation of her must overcome, focusing on her use of the category of society. Arendt's presentation of "the social question" and "the rise of the social" underwrites her most problematic and limiting conclusions about the possibilities for political action. But I go on to argue that her complex and confusing approaches to the social also offer resistant readers the best means of both understanding and overcoming her impulse to purify, thereby making possible an ironically Arendtian political response to contemporary regimes of the normal. While there are other theorists (Foucault most obvious among them) who require no such laborious reconstruction in order to recognize the political importance of challenging social normalization, I suggest that, suitably amended, Arendt's conception of publics and spaces offers singular and valuable ways of understanding how the challenges proceed. When rendered not only less pure but also more mobile, plural, and transient than she imagined, these spaces and publics help to engender the democratizations I have been seeking.

It is to exemplify the last claim that I conclude the chapter with a brief commentary on the formation and early flourishing of ACT UP. An Arendtian approach helps me to offer a critical appreciation of ACT UP's understanding of power, its construction of dissonant forms of solidarity, its genius for the creation of multiple, fleeting publics, and its use of these publics for disruptions of hegemonic codes of identity and belonging, disruptions that, particularly in the broader culture of queer insurgency that emerged out of such movements, pose a politicized challenge to normalization as such. But if Arendt provides a useful way of talking about certain dimensions of AIDS activism, that activism obviously strains the limits of her thought, scrambling her categories and cartographies. ACT UP successfully politicized the very things she thought least capable of genuine politicization—love, sex, bodies, needs, the administration of health—and did so through media and techniques that she believed to be unsuited to public spaces and worldly action. My reading of her work leaves me unable to ignore the Arendtian resonances of that politicization and equally unable to see how they can be acknowledged while staying within her terms. ACT UP's practices certainly do not exhaust contemporary democratic possibilities or resolve all the questions with which I have wrestled in this book, but the group provides an instructive and urgent example of how and why Arendt's work must, like that of Tocqueville and Marx, be turned against itself. That turning is easier to accomplish, however, if it begins with a more careful look at assumptions and arguments that cry out for creative appropriation.

Need, Normalization, and the Social

"The social" is where most of the elements of human life that threaten the enactment of freedom end up when Arendt purges them from politics: her claim is not that these elements do not exist, but that they are incapable of successful politicization. I say "successful," because she knows full well that most of modern thought and much of modern practice treat these elements as the central concerns of politics. She thinks that such prevailing perceptions are wrong, and that they lead to the destruction of action and its spaces. The social receives its most ambitious constructions as a category when she attempts to show how this destruction is wrought. The most significant attempts come in *The Human Condition* and *On Revolution*. The latter offers a reading of revolutionary history that purports to prove that when "the gates of the political realm" are opened "to the poor," that realm is necessarily "overwhelmed by cares and worries that actually belonged in the sphere of the household."[21] The former offers a broader and more philosophical account of what politics looks like when it is given over to "collective housekeeping."[22] Arendt's purposes are best grasped—and contested—when these two arguments are read in conversation with each other, but I begin with the earlier work, which offers her most nuanced and theoretically fertile argument on these matters.

By "the social," Arendt means "that curious and somewhat hybrid realm which the modern age interjected between the older and more genuine realms of the public or political on one side and the private on the other."[23] She elaborates her account of "genuine" publicity and privacy through a reading of ancient Greek views, in which the conditions of activity in the two realms were radically different. The household was where families were driven together "by their wants and needs," so that "necessity ruled over all activities performed in it." Mastering necessity there was the condition of entry into the public realm, but needs had no place in public.[24] The end of the public realm was the exercise of freedom: by acting in public, "men could show who they really and inexchangeably were."[25] There was no intermediate space between these realms: "the word 'social' . . . has no equivalent in Greek language or thought," for "society" did not exist.[26] When citizens moved back and forth between the household, which hid life's necessities in darkness and privacy, and the glorious light of the public, where free men appeared to each other through word and deed, the concerns proper to the each realm did not move with them.

"The social," which arises with modernity and takes its "political form" in "the nation-state," is a "curious hybrid," precisely because it combines what the ancient realms kept distinct, casting the illumination of the public onto traditionally "private" concerns and activities.[27] Where once the household had been the exclusive site centered on the preservation of life, the social "is the form in which the fact of mutual dependence for the sake of life and nothing else assumes public significance."[28] Labor, "the activity which corresponds to biological process of the human body" and is thus predominant whenever the overriding concern is with life, has escaped its domestic confinement and displaced action as the fundamental mode of public conduct.[29] With the modern creation of "societies of laborers and jobholders," the status and character of politics have changed fundamentally. We have come to see politics as a means to the end of protecting society and, thereby, "have almost succeeded in leveling all human activities to the common denominator of securing the necessities of life and providing for their abundance."[30] This central preoccupation with social matters is fatal to politics, for while properly political relationships are those in which we can be equals without being the same, "the social" is a realm or way of relating in which plurality yields to sameness: "society always demands that its members act as though they were members of one enormous family which has only one opinion and only one interest."[31] This "anti-political" insistence on homogeneity reflects the form of togetherness proper to laboring bodies: "far from establishing a recognizable, identifiable reality for each member of the labor gang, [unity in common labor] requires on the contrary the actual loss of all awareness of individuality and identity; and it is for this reason that all those 'values' which derive from laboring, beyond its obvious function in the life process, are entirely 'social.'. . . The sociability arising from those activities that spring from human body's metabolism with nature rest not on equality but on sameness."[32]

Arendt's fundamental concern, then, is with the public preoccupation with matters that destroy or cannot account for difference. She argues that as social matters have entered public life, as governments have made the management of the life process and the division of labor more and more their central activity, the forces that "normalize" identity and conduct have grown ever more powerful. The project of managing the life process requires standardization and regularity—and thus we experience a kind of coerced conformity, "the impos[ition of] innumerable and various rules." Hence, "the most social form of government" is bureaucracy, a form that is intrinsically hostile to action: its normalizing processes seeks to substitute "behavior" for action whenever possible because, in its singularity and unpredictability, action disrupts the regularities that bureaucracies must both presume and produce.[33] Arendt's point is not only that bureaucratic structures contain no spaces for free action, but that bureaucracy is a form of government that, in a sense, aspires to eliminate human actors altogether: it is "a kind of no-man rule," in which no one seems to be in charge. And it is rule by nobody that makes bureaucracy such an insidiously "tyrannical" form of governance. The problem is both that there is no one who can be held responsible and that "this nobody" who rules is really "the assumed one interest of society as a whole."[34] Given over to organizations bent on eliminating action, our socialized public life holds "statistical uniformity" as its "no longer secret political ideal."[35] Though Arendt tends to understand action as a faculty, as something of which human beings have always been capable any time and anywhere, she also believes that this faculty may not continue to survive the assaults that are being made on it.

How are we to respond to this threat? Do Arendt's reflections inspire a radical challenge to contemporary structures of normalizing power? In some respects they must: her account of the social is an indictment of tyranny, faceless rule, the denigration of action, the disregard for plurality, and the normalizing construction of unitary collective interests, all of which, she suggests, are found woven into the very fabric of contemporary society. We might assume, therefore, that the political task for Arendtian politics to is to reweave that fabric, using the unsettling pluralities of action to confront tyranny, give rule a face, and contest the imposition of uniformity. That assumption is warranted insofar as Arendt is working to incite our anxiety about structures and processes that we might otherwise take for granted, to present plurality as the proper condition of politics, and to foster care for action and more genuinely public spaces. But how should Arendtian actors confront the normalizing regimes she describes? Although Arendt presents action as an alternative to the behavior produced by those regimes, it is not clear that she stages a confrontation with them. Note how she presents the ancient world that, in this discussion, provides her example of equality without uniformity. On her account, the wealthy male slaveholders of the Athenian public realm were able to avoid the modern denigration of action precisely because matters of housekeeping, and those people concerned with them, were kept back in the *oikos:* Arendt is quite straightforward about the constitutive exclusions and subordinations on which Athenian freedom rested; she links its purity to these exclusions. Her discussion suggests that public preoccupation with matters of life will destroy that purity and ensure the normalizing consequences she decries. And "life" seems to encompass most of our relations—how we (do or don't) work, love, reproduce—and many of the structures of power in which they are enmeshed. Arendt is not summoning us back to an Athenian future, but whatever contemporary possibilities she envisions for freedom and equality would require us to acknowledge that these matters are not fit for political discourse and struggle: we can pursue action as an alternative to normalization and bureaucracy only if we do not make social subordination the focus of politics.

What would accepting Arendt's claims entail? What light does this account of the social shed on her drive to purify? The political import of her argument emerges more clearly if we turn for a moment to *On Revolution*, where she offers a cautionary tale about the consequences of modern, radical struggles that take up inappropriate political objects. Arendt offers far more than caution, of course, for her central purpose is to celebrate "the revolutionary tradition." Her reconstruction of this tradition, which she identifies with both the American Revolution and with moments of European popular insurgency throughout the nineteenth and twentieth centuries, uncovers instance after instance in which political action led to the spontaneous formation of new organs of self-government in a remarkable proliferation of political spaces. The names of these spaces— *Räte, soviets*, councils, communes—change but, in each case, we find "the amazing formation of a new power structure which owed its existence to nothing but the organizational impulses of the people themselves."[36] These are spaces, within the modern landscape, in which freedom can be exercised. For Arendt, these spaces are thus the most glorious political inventions of the modern era, inventions that must be remembered and understood if we are to expand the scope of freedom today. They provide a counterpoint to the modern tyrannies of the social, exemplifying those relations of equality and plurality that remain possible for us. But they do this precisely by refusing admission to social matters. Indeed—and here is where the tale turns cautionary—Arendt presents a sustained account of how revolutions that try to politicize the social, that challenge "the order of society," prove fatal to freedom. Freedom can be established only when the exclusive focus of struggle is, as in the American founding, "the form of government."[37]

In this story, rebelling against the order of society was the original sin of the French Revolution. When the Revolution took on the basic structures of material inequality, the poor, who (like those in the Athenian household) had "previously been hidden in darkness and shame," surged into the light of the public stage.[38] The results were tragic. The problems of the poor were problems of basic need, and making these problems matters of political concern brought coercion into the one sphere in which the experience of freedom is possible. Driven by necessity, action was subordinated to the "urgency of the life process," the "irresistible," "raging force" of nature—which is to say that it was no longer action in any meaningful sense.[39] Needs cannot be made the subject of genuine political action because when we are compelled by necessity we act as one: "the cry for bread will always be uttered in one voice."[40] Transcending any particular cultural or historical condition, needs are what we all have in common prior to our differences, underneath our uniqueness as individual human beings. All of the violent excesses and disasters of the revolution were immanent in the attempt to make these immutable commonalities and imperatives the basis of struggle.

Much of this echoes what we already saw in *The Human Condition*'s discussion of labor and the rise of the social, but *On Revolution* makes more explicit the argument that the substance of the social resists all efforts at politicization. Such efforts, Arendt would have us conclude, only hasten the destruction of politics by extending the rule of nobody. Because it is given over to matters that transcend all differences and lie beyond all disputes of principle, the social is, inherently, the realm of technical management and expertise—fit for administration rather than action.[41] Indeed, one could summarize both books by saying that the rise of the social crowds politics out of the public realm precisely by filling that realm with administrative forms and routines. Seeking to reclaim space for action, Arendt elaborates a politics that leaves the problems of social life untouched. Not merely a problem of her retrospective glance, this exclusion of the social marked Arendt's contemporary interventions, leading her, for instance, to oppose the struggle to desegregate the Little Rock, Arkansas schools as an attempt to remedy wrongs that, regrettably, were not a part of politics and were thus unsuited to action.[42] By a route very different from Tocqueville's, she thus ends up with a comparable exclusion of fundamental inequalities from political concern; she thus arrives at a position for which, as we saw, "On the Jewish Question" provided an anticipatory critique. Is her staging of the problem of political freedom more compelling than that critique would suggest?

The Need to Politicize

Arendt's story of the betrayal of revolution's promise through the submission to necessity makes it easier to understand her more abstract attempts to purify action and politics. Like Tocqueville, she helps us to understand how the project of leftist revolution persistently became one of administratively reconstructing the whole field of human relationships, and why that project had such disastrous consequences. Like him, too, she helps us see the continuities between those attempted reconstructions and the subtler forms of administrative rule that mark capitalist welfare states. These are not trivial perceptions, and they should be borne in mind by any reading that would offer democratic resistance to her categories. But as with the case of Tocqueville, acknowledging the dangers to which the work alerts us by no means dispenses with the evident problems and perplexities in its account of what is and is not fit for politics. Even aside from the continuing puzzle of determining how *anything* can gain admission to Arendt's pristine spaces of freedom, her argument is unpersuasive both as inventory of matters that *cannot* be politicized and as explanation of why they defy politicization. Attending to these problems provides an opportunity to reconfigure and redeploy her argument and, thus, ultimately to elaborate a fuller account of emancipatory spaces than could be extracted from the work of Marx, the thinker who harbored no such anxieties about the social question.

Arendt's way of distinguishing action from administration offers a productive point of entry. In her discourse, each term contains what is constitutively excluded from the other: while the enactment of identities is free of all instrumental concerns and defies the vocabulary of means and ends, administration is pure instrumentality in which the only question is what means will most efficiently accomplish given and unproblematic ends.[43] With administrative problems there is, in principle, an ideal solution — one that, if found, is beyond argument — while action, which poses no problem that can be "solved," is always contestable. Labor, bodies, needs, life are all assigned to the "administration" half of the dichotomy because, for Arendt, they are ruled by the logic of instrumentality and thus must defy disputes of principle. They occasion technical problems but not the enactments and the contests that occur in the field of freedom.

It is here, I think, that Arendt runs into trouble. Consider again her account of what happened when needs entered the political stage in the course of revolution: they burst in violently, brooking no discussion, dictating human behavior, issuing imperious and irresistible commands.[44] In some respects, this account is unobjectionable, even tautological. The oldest meaning for "need" listed in the *Oxford English Dictionary* is "violence, force, constraint, or compulsion, exercised upon persons." When violent compulsion is exercised upon persons, how — Arendt would ask — could there be an opportunity for dispute? But if we counter Arendt's question with another question, asking how we *know* when need has entered politics, the line she would draw so sharply begins to blur. As Nancy Fraser points out, what confronts us in any political struggle about "social" matters is an articulated *claim* or set of claims about the specific needs of concrete human agents: much of contemporary political life is comprised of "discourses about needs." Such discourses are not the same as unmediated Necessity, and unlike the forces of nature they can be argued with. In political life, as Fraser writes, "needs are irreducibly interpretive . . . and in principle contestable."[45] Indeed, many of the most momentous encounters between political actors and principles involve conflicting attempts to establish the most persuasive interpretation of needs. Much the same can be said for the other terms that Arendt would consign to the automatism of the social. But if all this can be said so simply, can't one say it in an Arendtian way? Are her distinctions in fact this rigid and untenable? Does her thought allow *no* opportunity for a political engagement with the imperatives she calls social? And if it does allow for them to be engaged, what does that engagement look like?

Many readers are, appropriately, disinclined to follow Arendt down the path I have sketched in these last few paragraphs. Those who are unwilling to join in these sweeping depoliticizations but do draw sustenance from her thought have often sought to find in it openings for a more generous and fluid account of the social. Hanna Pitkin identifies a particularly important opening by noting that Arendt's distinctions are not always ontological and unbridgeable, and that they need not be appropriated as if they were: social and political (and public and private, labor, work and action) can also be taken as mentalities, rhetorics, or ways of relating, rather than as domains of being.[46] In this account, "the social" is not defined by the necessarily mute irresistibility of its objects (e.g., the laboring body) but by whether and how those objects are discussed. A discourse or relationship is social if it treats contingent results of human conduct as if they were necessary, or if it demands homogeneity where plurality is possible. Thus, Arendt would exclude from politics not needs but a political rhetoric of incontestability, not labor but the presumption of the common interest of an organic collectivity. A politicizing struggle would challenge these rhetorics and presumptions. Read in this way, the social is no longer incapable of politicization; rather, it cries out for it. The vast terrain that Arendt's more inflexible pronouncements remove from struggle appears now as a potential stage for action.

Though there are moments in Arendt's writings that might sanction such an approach, the promise of this way of thinking can be realized only by overriding some of her most fundamental commitments.[47] Or, better, this approach makes it possible to turn her insights against much of what she has to say about the history of radical social struggles and about the social itself. To shift the definition of the social from one centering on domains or objects to one concerned with discourses and sensibilities enables overtly politicizing responses to the kinds of economic relationships ruled off limits in her account of the revolutionary tradition and, indeed, to all of the many forms of subjugation which get (at most) only a passing glance in her work. Honig, who has pushed the expansion of the Arendtian political farther than anyone, proposes that Arendt's distinctions be radicalized by taking them as an invitation to resist all claims to irresistibility. Rather than "reproducing and re-presenting 'what' we are," an Arendtian politicization of social relations "agonistically generates 'who' we are by episodically generating new identities."[48] The political task is to "unmask the private realm's natural or constative identities of race, class, gender, and ethnicity . . . to deauthorize and redescribe them as performative productions by identifying spaces that escape or resist administration, regulation, and expression."[49] Arendt thus points us toward a politics of democratic resignification.

This reading locates vital resources for diversifying the substance and spaces of Arendtian politics. Only by stressing action's ability to unsettle fixed social positions and relations can Arendt's work inform not only alternatives to but struggles against normalization. But if the task is to overcome Arendt's evasions, the argument for turning her insights into performance against the "constative" elements of social life tells only half of the story. Equating the political with the performative challenge to constation, and identifying action as that which eludes administrative regulation, reinscribes some of Arendt's own purifications back into politics. Arendtian politics is now better able to *contest* the elements of violence, force, and rule, but these elements are not really figured as part of the political itself.[50] This approach obscures the ways in which, as we saw in *The Eighteenth Brumaire*, all performances inevitably reveal "what" as well as "who" we are, carrying within them their histories of violent imposition. Marx understood that those impositions are not simply what politics resists, but are, themselves, crucial political moments. He showed that what we are is not only a congealed performance that can be unsettled but also something palpable and fixed by its position in an unequal structure of power relations. The constative is not simply a misrecognition of the performative; it is the power-laden consolidation of a way of being. To push beyond Arendt's purifying evasions, we must engage not only the problem of bodies or identities that aspire to illegitimate or duplicitous constation but also the problem of how any social location, any identity shapes and is shaped by those around it.[51]

Radicalizing Arendt on the political and the social, I am suggesting, requires us to acknowledge the inevitable interconnections between who we are and what we are, in a way that complicates her distinctions between them. Recognizing both the contestability of need and the violence of performance makes it impossible to sustain Arendt's separation between making and doing, instrumentality and enactment. Instrumentality is not merely a logic that action can evade or oppose; it is insinuated into democratic political action and entwined in conditions from which it proceeds. It is not that these distinctions lose their intelligibility (as if making a table were simply the same as the revelations of identity Arendt finds in the sharing of public words) but that the elements she would separate inevitably contaminate each other. The quest for purity is doomed. If the quest is abandoned, the administrative apparatuses invoked in *The Human Condition*'s account of "the rise of the social" not only emerge as potential sites of performative political resistance (though such resistance is crucial to the democratic enterprise) but also can be understood to be among the primary instruments through which *politics* in our time is carried out. While Arendt is concerned with the political as space of appearances, with what we reveal and what we initiate when we "are together in the manner of speech and action," the "social" apparatuses she sketches set the conditions from which enactment proceeds, helping to determine what revelations and inventions are possible.[52] In our time, the practices, discourses, institutions, and problems that she dismisses as no more than collective housekeeping are, to borrow a remark that theorist Cindy Patton offers in a different context, media in which "what is at stake is not [only] the content of identities but the modes for staging politics through identity."[53] Although Arendt argues that the revolutionary spirit is lost when the attempt to found new "forms of government" is displaced by a preoccupation with "the order of society," my argument is that the order of society is crucial to the governance of contemporary relationships and identities. Taking liberties with her work enables us to see this and, thus, to expand both the sites and the means of political struggle. Only by doing so can the plurality Arendt admires be fostered and sustained.

Despite the persistence and the centrality of the distinction between forms of governance and social order in Arendt's thought about revolution and political action, there are also instances where she begins to intimate what such a politicized response to the social entails. The most widely remarked upon Arendtian figure of such a politics is what she calls the "conscious pariah," a figure she constructs in her early reflections on Zionism and Jewish politics. *Conscious* pariahs struggle for freedom on the basis of the stigmatized identity that makes them marginal: Jews who adopted the perspective of the conscious pariah undertook a collective politicization of their subordination, fighting for the "admission of Jews *as Jews* to the ranks of humanity."[54] The fight, as Arendt presents it, was waged against both the injustice of an imposed inequality and the normalizing pressures of cultural assimilation. In such remarks, Arendt acknowledges that what we are can form the basis of those political struggles through which we reveal who we are. She further maintains that if these struggles are pursued properly the results can be explosive: "As soon as the pariah enters the arena of politics and translates his status into political terms he becomes perforce a rebel."[55] But while her use of the term "translation" here seems to offer a key that opens the door with which her more abstract theorizing blocks traffic between her domains, and though a number of commentators have therefore made the self-conscious pariah crucial to the elaboration of a more radical Arendtian politics, my purposes are not served by lingering over this figure of rebellion.[56] As often as not, Arendt's treatment of the conscious pariah reinstates distinctions I wish to blur, calling for the struggle against legal oppression while dismissing 'merely' social forms, and understating the complexities and contingencies that mark the production of pariah identities.[57] Furthermore, Arendt's own remarks on the processes of translation into political terms are sporadic and underdeveloped.[58] Rather than seeking in her work a satisfactory model of these processes, or claiming her authorization for politicized struggle against regimes of the normal, I will explore, particularly by examining the case of ACT UP, how they take place. But this exploration is enabled by a critical appropriation not only of Arendt's remarks on the rise of the social but, still more, of her account of the mobile and plural spaces of action. Once we have confounded her distinction between social order and forms of government, the Arendtian conception of political space becomes crucial to the contemporary art of being free.

Democratizing Arendtian Spaces

To claim that politics are at work in Arendt's social and to find opportunities for the opening of Arendtian political spaces is not to conclude that adequate spaces are already there. Far from it. While her argument is in need of interrogation and revision, she is persuasive in asserting that the contemporary practice of politics is often severely constrained by the dearth of forums for the pursuit of freedom. Surveying the American scene at the beginning of the seventies, she wrote: "Representative government itself is in a crisis today, partly because it has lost, in the course of time, all institutions that permitted the citizens' actual participation, and partly because it is now gravely affected by the disease from which the party system suffers: bureaucratization and the two parties' tendency to represent nobody but the party machines."[59] This absence of spaces for participation is not, on her account, a peculiarly American ailment. *On Revolution* had already suggested that such problems inhere in the way that liberal-democratic states have come to institutionalize the political: "what we call democracy today is a form of government where the few rule, at least supposedly, in the interests of the many. This government is democratic in that popular welfare and private happiness are its chief goals; but it can be called oligarchic in the sense that public happiness and public freedom have again become the privilege of the few." The core of her indictment of contemporary polities is her claim that they do not provide enough people with enough spaces in which that freedom and happiness can be exercised—a problem, she adds, that liberal democrats essentially evade by denying that these particular public goods exist.[60]

For Arendt, sharing in the creation and recreation of our common world by wielding political power is an essential part of being free. For us to lay claim to that freedom, we need access to the political stage: "without a politically guaranteed public realm, freedom lacks the worldly space to make its appearance," to "become a visible, tangible reality."[61] In the spaces she celebrates, from the polis to the revolutionary council, it is possible to generate and preserve the power that "springs up between men the moment they act together," to unite knowing and doing, and thus, through the "miracle" of action, to do the unexpected and the unprecedented, to bring newness into the world.[62] In the theater of politics, in the "shining brightness" of its publicity—with its "inherent tendency to disclose the agent together with the act"—actors experience a kind of "second birth."[63]

On this account, it is in the spaces of politics that human plurality emerges in all of its plenitude. This is not only because of action's individuating qualities but because of the distinctive ways in which politics can be a medium of differentiating connection. Despite her attempts to purge instrumentality from political life, to reject the very vocabulary of ends and means, she insists that action concerns "worldly interests," which, as she puts it in *The Human Condition*, "constitute . . . something which *interest*, which lies between people and therefore can relate and bind them, together."[64] The "in-between" of the public realm enables discourse and exchange among people of divergent locations and perspectives; indeed it is the spaces of politics that preserve those divergences. The "being seen and being heard by others" that mark the space of appearances "derive their significance from the fact that everybody sees and hears from a different position."[65] Arendt's valorization of action oriented to the common world between us flows, in large measure, from the way that this mode of relating serves as an alternative to the construction of a singular "common good" or a unitary political identity. Political space enables—and genuinely political thinking requires—one to learn to view the world and one's location as they appear from other positions, to consider "a given issue from different viewpoints, by making present to [one's] mind the standpoints of those who are absent . . . [which] is a question neither of empathy, as though I tried to be or to feel like someone else, nor of counting noses and of joining a majority but of being and thinking in my own identity where actually I am not."[66] A polity with a robust public realm rich in political spaces would enable the cultivation of such "representative thinking" and, hence, a way of preserving the distances between us even in joining us together.

These, then, are the qualities and possibilities that are jeopardized by the absence or eclipse of political spaces and a public realm. How great is our jeopardy? There is sometimes a sad and backward-looking air to Arendt's discussion of these possibilities, an implication that she can do no more than tell a vivid story about a "lost treasure" that can never return in its original splendor. But her conception of action also militates against that nostalgic impulse, holding out the possibility that new kinds of spaces might emerge in new circumstances. Her thinking about power and the space of appearances elaborates a marvelously generative tautology: the public realm that enables action to occur arises from action itself. On the one hand, Arendt argues that a space of appearances is necessary for action to take place, and that certain institutionalized spaces best stabilize and protect our opportunities for the exercise of freedom. On the other hand, she theorizes action as (to return to this chapter's first epigraph) "creat[ing] a space between the participants which can find its proper location almost any time and anywhere." Action is "the one activity which *constitutes*" the public realm.[67] Or realms: for it is possible to speak of publics and spaces in the plural precisely because they can be performed into existence by those who know how to act. This insight is what, above all, I wish to use in exploring the democratic politicization of the Arendtian social. What kinds of spaces can she help us to see, envision, and enact?

A starting point is provided by those hopeful possibilities that Arendt herself celebrates most fervently. At times, her perception of our ability to constitute spaces of freedom through action leads her to an extraordinarily expansive sense of political opportunity. We can take the measure of her fondest hopes from her remark that, "buried in the disasters of twentieth century revolution" lies the struggle for a way of enabling "every member of the modern egalitarian society to become a 'participator' in public affairs." [68] In her telling of this history of revolutionary aspirations and disappointments, she shows how, repeatedly and without the benefit of much theoretical guidance or a clear memory of their forerunners, the citizens who took part in modern revolutions found ways to "turn a more or less accidental proximity into a political institution." By creating institutions—neighborhood councils, committees of correspondence, and the like—flowing from and responsive to the fundamental "conditions of action," revolutionary actors made small-scale "elementary republics" available to anyone who cared to enter them. [69] Though local organs often arose independently of the organizing efforts elsewhere, they soon federated with other councils, and formed ascending levels of governing bodies. Though each level of the system was considerably more exclusive than the one before, each was constituted through deliberation in public space: "From these 'elementary republics,' the councilmen then chose their deputies for the next higher council, and these deputies, again, were selected by their peers, they were not subject to any pressure either from above or below." [70] She glimpses in these revolutionary moments the beginnings of an alternative to the modern, party-dominated, nation-state: they present us with a "new type of republican government which would rest on 'elementary republics' in such a way that its own central power did not deprive constituent bodies of their original power to constitute." [71]

Is Arendt suggesting that we can replace the political architecture of the nation state with structures of a fundamentally different sort? At times, she seems to do so. But she also repeatedly acknowledges how swiftly the revolutionary organs she describes were destroyed by the states and parties they opposed, and she balances moments of hope with those of despair over the opportunities for *any*, let alone such a heroic, politics. Perhaps her most frequent position, in this work and elsewhere, is that even if there is little hope of simply replacing the sclerotic systems of representative government, and even when there are only dim prospects for constructing a political geography in which "elementary republics" are the fundamental units of official civic belonging, the story of revolution tells us something important about the creation of meaningful spaces for action and freedom. Certainly the revolutionary councils serve for her as an example that can be emulated, if partially and in chastened form. Arendt argues that the council models the kind of publics that can spring up on smaller scales, with less coordination, in ways that are still useful for "breaking the modern mass society."[72] She hailed the practice of civil disobedience as an important way of pursuing that possibility in contemporary America, and she drew out the potential affinities between the civil disobedient and the revolutionary.[73] This seems an eminently practical descent from her loftiest aspirations. But here we must return to a question that has been raised, in other forms, several times already: what is to comprise the substance of their actions?

At first glance, Arendt's grandest hopes for a system of councils and her more modest hopes for episodic spaces complementary to the institutions of representative democracy may appear to confront us with opposing problems: the former seems too ambitious, even utopian, in its claims, the latter not ambitious enough. But upon closer inspection, the problems are quite similar. Even her grand vision leaves us uncertain what objects and problems would be fit for admission to the spaces of politics. The difficulties with these two approaches stem from a common source, the Arendtian drive to purify. The key problem, here, is her way of conceiving of the practice of freedom as essentially unrelated to democracy. Although her discussion of the revolutionary tradition is full of the discourse of "participation," it would be problematic, I think, to read even Arendt's version of the council system as "democratic." Clearly, she saw this system as admirable for the way it enabled people to exercise power and experience freedom. But she maintained (plausibly enough) that while anyone *could* enter these spaces of politics, most would not. The ascending tiers of councils would be filled by people "from all walks of life," but only on the basis of interest and commitment, of having "a taste for public freedom." The public's business would be done by this self-selected political elite. This, she adds rather casually, "would spell the end of general suffrage as we understand it today."[74]

What underpins Arendt's surprising comfort in the face of such an end? Why does the end of a basic mechanism of representation sustain the cause of freedom? In her writing about revolution, "democracy" tends to be paired, as a term of contrast, with "republic." Democracy is aligned, variously, with sovereignty rather than the non-sovereign space of action, with the leveling conformism of mass sentiment against the republican elevation of individual opinions through their refinement by public deliberation, and, as we have just seen, with domination by economic and social elites rather than the self-selection of political elites.[75] The crucial pairing is that of democracy with rule, for it is this alignment that makes democracy inappropriate to Arendtian freedom. Arendt's description of republican council government is an attempt to account for hierarchy and the making of binding decisions while, at the same time, keeping all actors party to any decision innocent of relations of rule. It is for this reason that it is so hard to determine what even the federated councils may legitimately do, in her scheme. Arendt's thinking about politics, then, tends to be both too tightly tied to problems of governance and not serious enough about them. Here, she stands in need of correction by Tocqueville. Where Arendt's notion of freedom as wholly non-sovereign requires her to refuse any conceptual links between freedom and democracy, Tocqueville's more ambivalent sense of the terms leads him to refuse to collapse democracy into rule while acknowledging their desirable points of articulation. What would Arendtian spaces of politics look like if reread with such a correction in mind?

Wolin has argued, persuasively I think, that Arendt's wariness toward democracy arises, in part, from "a correct intuition that the impulse of democracy has been to override" her distinction between social and political.[76] Yet it is just such an act of overriding that enables us to remedy the problems I have been identifying. Arendtian spaces can neither supplant the institutions of representative democracy nor be disconnected from the problems of governance. But to connect them to the problems of governance means not only to have them engage critically the policies and programs of state, but to engage the "social" forces and institutions that shape the construction of bodies and subjectivities. One crucial element of what I am suggesting is that we take the mass-mediation of everyday life as an arena of Arendtian intervention. Arendt's own tendency was to base her politics on a renunciation or an escape from that arena, a rejection of everything that makes up "mass culture."[77] She figures that culture as intrinsically normalizing, worldless, corrupting of genuine appearances, incapable of allowing action's requisite spaces, and, hence, necessarily a domain of behavior. Rather than responding as she does, we need to find Arendtian sites within the terrain of celebrity and mass-mediation that is such a huge part of contemporary American (as other) public life. We need to think of Arendtian action, in other words, not simply as an alternative to the sedimented patterns of mass-mediated culture but as a form of engaging, disrupting, and transforming relations in and through it as well.

Saying this adequately requires modifying Arendt in two ways. First, we must recognize that the spaces of politics must be more plural and mobile than she suggested. Second, we must also understand that such spaces will be more fleeting. If *The Human Condition*'s abstract reflections on the space of appearances celebrate the ways in which these spaces spring up and dissolve with the gathering and dispersal of actors, Arendt is also centrally concerned with the durability of publics: "If the world is to contain a public space, it cannot be erected for one generation and planned for the living only; it must transcend the life-span of moral man."[78] The great narrative of *On Revolution* is of the political quest for durable foundations for freedom. The argument I have been making renounces that commitment, or at least softens and transforms it. Clearly the spaces I have been pointing toward are less durable than the model of heroic founding requires. And yet the intention of securing freedom is worthy. Perhaps what is best drawn from Arendt's work, now, is the sense that the spirit of action and commitment to the creation of spaces must be sustained, even if the location of those spaces moves, and sometimes moves rapidly. Not one, but many: the Arendtian language of "the world," too, must be pluralized. Arendt's spaces are particularly fruitful under late-modern conditions for they are not so firmly rooted as were Tocqueville's in the locality. They are not only multiple but mobile, as they can spring up wherever we are.

Such an approach to the spaces of politics straddles and scrambles the distinctions between self-government and self-fashioning, instrumental action and symbolic display, care for the common world and care for difference. Therein lies its great utility in a time when the foundations of those distinctions are crumbling under the force of global changes in the production and circulation of information and images—when, as Bruce Robbins notes, "participation in the making, exchanging, and mobilizing of political opinion . . . [now takes place] to an unprecedented extent in the domain of culture."[79] With her emphasis on appearances and her attention to the ways that politics is about the construction of agency, the transformation of identities, and the contestation of differences, Arendt ironically offers much that is of use in thinking about the political possibilities opened up by this now global condition of mass-mediation. But she can help us come to terms with such spaces and forms of action only if we view Arendtian publics as necessarily heterogeneous and multiple, worlds as plural and only partially overlapping, and action as never about the actor's telos, unity, or "authenticity." Such a view is made possible by a resistant reading that has her transgress and democratize the codes of citizenship and community that governed conventional republican politics and still shape neorepublican forms of communitarian nostalgia.

When Arendt is approached in this way, one of the aspects of her politi-

cal vision that has often disturbed even admiring critics, its intense the-
atricality, becomes a crucial resource. In his critique of Arendt's hostility
to democracy, Wolin summarizes her failings by noting that she offers an
"agonistic" politics pursued by "actors and not citizens."[80] As my discussion should have made clear by now, this characterization is not entirely
accurate. Arendt not only repeatedly valorizes the practice of citizenship,
but at times insists that taking up the citizen's distinctive vantage point is
the *sine qua non* of perceiving the world from a political point of view.[81]
But Wolin also captures an important current in her thought: Arendt's
praise of agonistic action—with its emphasis on spontaneity, display, performance—often does present the political in a way that exceeds the sober
strictures of republican citizenship. Her actor is not *always* a citizen, and
citizenship thus does not exhaust Arendtian political identity. Though she
presents action as always preoccupied with the worldly matters that lie
between us, the actor and citizen exist in a complex and at times uneasy
relationship in her thought. In contrast to Wolin, I want to claim this
uneasy complexity as one the chief virtues of her thinking for a confrontation with democratic politics: as much as anything, it is Arendt's way of
relating actor and citizen that enables us to pluralize her political spaces.

Arendt herself points toward such a pluralization in a remark, at the
end of *On Revolution*, on the many unforseeable dramas that can take place
within elementary republics. Rather than specifying all of their legitimate
uses in advance, she suggests that it is "wiser to say with Jefferson, 'Begin
with them only for a single purpose; they will soon show for what others
they are the best instruments.'"[82] While some might see this ambiguity
as evasive, I see in it an admirable theoretical restraint, born of respect
for the creativity of action and the responsibility of those who undertake political struggle. This theoretical reticence opens up more room for
inventiveness in the politics of enactment; its appreciation for the uncertainties and mobilities of politics undercuts the Arendtian drive to purify.
Let us keep this Arendtian appreciation for the spaces and modalities of
politics alive as we explore a form of political struggle that is Arendtian in
character but that also stretches Arendtian politics beyond itself.

Remaking Space: Acting Up, Acting Now

October 11, 1988. The headquarters of the Food and Drug Administration
(FDA) in Rockville, Maryland are under siege. AIDS activists plaster the
building's facade with visually arresting and politically pointed posters,
turning it into a loud indictment of the agency housed inside ("The Gov-

ernment Has Blood On Its Hands: One AIDS Death Every Half Hour"; "We Die—They Do Nothing"). All day long, members of ACT UP affinity groups from around the country surge toward the building's entrances. Each time, the would-be intruders are stopped by the police, who drag them back while generally refraining from making arrests. The demonstrators are trying to get arrested. The successful ones are herded into buses; when the buses begin to leave, other demonstrators block the road. Police drag away these human roadblocks, too. Throughout the skirmishes, TV crews crowd around, jostling each other as the cameras roll. The protesters, many of them wearing elaborate costumes, oblige by scripting impromptu street theater, staging actions that will look good on the evening news. That night, the demo gets network coverage, and the reporting is, for once, informed about the issues behind the action. The activists have seen to that: ACT UP's Treatment and Data Committee prepared a forty-page critical analysis of the FDA's policies concerning the approval of new drugs, and the Media Committee condensed it into a press kit that was disseminated widely before the action began. Throughout the day members made their (previously scheduled) appearances on talk shows everywhere, explaining how government inaction lets the death toll mount. The protest has been " 'sold' in advance almost like a Hollywood movie." [83]

At the time of the protest, the AIDS Coalition to Unleash Power was a year and a half old. Nationally, ACT UP had already accumulated the breadth and experience that enabled its members to contribute so heavily to the event's success. After its founding in Manhattan in March 1987 as "a diverse, nonpartisan group united in anger and committed to direct action to end the AIDS crisis," autonomous chapters had sprung up in Atlanta, Boston, Chicago, Denver, Houston, Kansas City, Los Angeles, Nashville, San Francisco, Seattle, and other cities. Memberships ranged from the low hundreds in the smaller chapters through the approximately 3,000 people belonging to ACT UP New York.[84] Each chapter had been practicing a politics of protest. ACT UP New York alone, for instance, disrupted the workings of the New York Stock Exchange to call attention to the Burroughs Wellcome corporation's pricing and distribution of AZT, confronted Ronald Reagan's Presidential Commission on the HIV Epidemic, staged same-sex "kiss-ins" on street corners, and performed sexually explicit demonstrations of AIDS prevention materials for teenagers throughout the city. These actions, too, were conducted with a flair for the theatrical, an emphasis on visual style, and persistent attention to making news.[85]

The geographic breadth and the range of concerns revealed in this inventory of locales and actions highlight the distinguishing characteristics of the AIDS politics that I will discuss. My discussion focuses largely on ACT UP's activism of the late 1980s (hence the use of the past tense for a group that, in greatly diminished numbers and influence, survives today), asking what the encounter can reveal about the possibilities for democratic struggle in our era.[86] Most of the features of ACT UP that concern me can be seen in microcosm in the symbolic takeover of the FDA. The participation of affinity groups from across the nation exemplifies a commitment to direct insurgency, an emphasis on constituting democratic spaces in which each member could act. It also previews the complicated relationship to localism and nationality that are, I will argue, inherent in AIDS activism. The posters covering the headquarters reflect the unusually central role that striking graphics and slogans played in ACT UP's public performances. That "performance" is, indeed, the appropriate term is obvious in the staging and restaging of scenes. The ultimate success of the scenes, the slickness of the packaging, and the care with which the event was "sold," were expressions of the group's unusual savvy about the workings of the mass media. Both the professionalism with which the media were approached and the forty-page policy analysis upon which the press kits were based were products of the intense cultivation of expertise that are as crucial to defining ACT UP as its insurgent democratic ethos. And in that combination of know-how and unruliness, as well as in the uncertainties of audience inherent in this kind of mass-mediated performance, there is at least a pointer toward one of the most important features of all: the intricate ways in which urgent instrumental concerns about medical treatment were entangled with a wildly theatrical but equally urgent struggle over the broadest contours of the politics of sexual identity and difference.

Can Arendt's theory of theatrical politics help us make sense of these complex connections? There are reasons for skepticism. Although the activists who came together at the beginning of New York ACT UP were directly influenced by poststructural theory, the evidence does not suggest that many of them drew upon, admired, or even knew her work.[87] Nor is this surprising, given the issues she excludes from political concern. Arendt characterized love as the most anti-political of sentiments and virtually did not mention sex or sexuality in her published writing. If we add to this her principled assertion that "politics is never for the sake of life," and her convictions about the hopeless conformism of "mass society," then it becomes difficult to imagine a struggle more contrary to Arendtian concerns than the activists' politicization of AIDS.[88] Of course, the revolutionary councils she praises violated her strictures more fundamentally than she admitted, but those violations scarcely compare to the manner in which her categories are unsettled by the case of ACT UP.[89] Still, although she would never have approved of taking up that case, I propose that the pluralization of her politics carried out in this chapter both illuminates and finds illumination in ACT UP's struggles. There is much—even with the freest of readings—that her work cannot say about the political construction of disease and sexuality, but the work still offers important and distinctive resources for thinking about AIDS activism and queer insurgency.[90] The conscious politicization of pariah status, the ways in which power springs up among those who gather together through word and deed, the unstable relationship between the roles of actor and citizen, the intertwining of action and administration, who we are and what we are in the politics of enactment, and the crucial importance of mobile publics and spaces to the pursuit of that politics—these provide the terms through which my reflection proceeds, serving as both means and objects of analysis.

In beginning this analysis, it is helpful to note how ACT UP took its politicizing ventures deep into territory that the official Arendt would have us view as necessarily ruled by incontestable administration: the group's most pressing instrumental objectives concerned matters that, on her account, can become public only as a form of collective housekeeping. Starting with ACT UP New York's inaugural demonstration protesting the price of the then experimental drug AZT, the chapter centered its earliest efforts on the questions of how drugs were tested, released, and sold. During the first two years of ACT UP's efforts nationally, the overriding strategic objective was to "get drugs into bodies."[91] This goal necessarily drew activists along the intricate pathways connecting regulatory agencies, medical institutions, and powerful corporations. Success on these paths required the acquisition of "sophisticated technical information," in one commentators words, "about the structure and functions of the FDA and the U.S. Department of Health and Human Services (HHS); about the process and economics of developing, evaluating, and releasing new drugs; about the conceptual and statistical grounds on which standards for clinical trials are based; about drugs themselves—where they come from and how they work; about viruses in general and HIV in particular; and about AIDS, HIV infection, and how drugs might act to bring about prevention, retardation, and cure."[92] As activists gained this knowledge, it shaped their goals, for political objectives were often defined in terms of "the working procedures and principles" of the organizations being pressured.[93] The direct action at the FDA, for instance, was launched in order to change such things as the structure of the agency's Institutional Review Boards overseeing clinical trials, to abolish double-blind placebo trials altogether, and to rewrite the regulations on insurance payments for experimental therapies.[94]

That such struggles concerned matters Arendt thought "social" is doubtless more evident than that they generated an even ironically Arendtian politics. In beginning to identify that politics, therefore, it is worth belaboring the obvious by emphasizing that these *were* struggles: what many bureaucrats and health professionals presented as the necessary procedures of disinterested science were redescribed by ACT UP as matters of political interpretation and dispute. Treating research and medical procedures as intrinsically political, the group persistently fought to be involved in their formulation. These redescriptions and revisions produced real gains. Many demands were not met, but some important ones were; concerted action succeeded, for example, in changing the protocols of clinical trials and broadening the forms of participation open to the subjects of research.[95] But if noting this emphasis on the contestability of ostensibly neutral claims provides a useful introduction to this politicization, it does no more than that, for ACT UP's political relationship to the administration of health was quite complex. Even while approaching science and medicine as inherently political, the group did not view claims to expertise in these domains as pure mystification and thus did not claim that effective AIDS treatment could be arrived at through no more than assertions of political will. Certainly the hopes that coursed most urgently through the earliest responses to the discovery of HIV—hopes for a drug that would eradicate the symptoms of AIDS, cure HIV itself, or provide a preventive vaccine—were dependent on medical success and, thus, the possibility of scientific knowledge of the world. ACT UP's activism was not a romantic dismissal of science but a political intervention into and appropriation of it. At their most ambitious and militant, these interventions and uses were, in Paula Treichler's words, attempts to create a "radically democratic technoculture."[96]

Technoculture? The term would never have come from Arendt's pen, for the idea behind it is thinkable only through a confounding of her distinctions, particularly those between making and acting, what we are and who we are. But thinking this idea in relation to AIDS activism opens a space to focus our attention on important connections among technicity, performativity, and publicity under regimes of late-modern power. The connections can be seen in the ways that AIDS treatment activists sought to acquire and revise technical knowledge not only for its uses as a lever for moving the machinery of state but also as an intrinsic part of their struggle to elaborate cultural practices of empowerment and create spaces for action. Such knowledge proved vital not only to individual survival but to the collective invention and dissemination of practices of safer sex, and for much broader projects of education, including ACT UP's mass-mediated subversions. Technical competence was an essential part of the political challenge to prevailing constructions of AIDS as an intrinsically "gay disease," and of gay, lesbian, and bisexual people as "AIDS carriers." The wider battle against stigmatization necessitated confronting not only the most obviously hostile and polemical remarks of politicians (say, the speeches of Senator Jesse Helms) but also the most specialized discourses of health and disease.[97] Combating an "epidemic of signification," in a time when "gay . . . bodies are written by science" and immunology has emerged as a central practice for determining the boundaries between self and other, ACT UP's political struggles over health required both making demands about access to drugs, treatment, services, and tax dollars, *and* contesting powerful medicalized inscriptions of the body politic.[98] Radical AIDS activists pursued a democratic technoculture, in other words, because elementary matters of survival were imbricated with the most fundamental questions of cultural politics.

The turn to the technical, to discourses of what Arendt would consider making, was, then, necessary to ACT UP's struggle to create a politics of plurality, for this turn was integral to the group's resistance to the processes of normalization. This resistance was not incidental to its activism, but as several participants and observers have argued, was from the beginning central to ACT UP's mission and self-understanding.[99] Even while it often refused to be identified as a "gay group" and directed some of its most memorable graphics and campaigns against popular ways of linking "gay" with "AIDS," its actions relentlessly interrogated contemporary presumptions about sexual identity, exposing the often masked ways in which sexualities are constructed in American public life. Even when pushing for narrowly instrumental or material changes in specific institutions (Burroughs Wellcome, the FDA, etc.), it articulated the role of these institutional encoders and enforcers of homophobia. These exposures served as acts through which pariah status could be self-consciously reclaimed and reworked, and—through this translation into political terms—set the basis for a politics of enactment. More than a way of naming injustice or merely *asserting* selfhood, ACT UP's disruptive style of protest also staged performances through which new collective and personal identities could be *enacted*. Through these performances, and through its role as inspiration and incubator for groups such as Queer Nation, ACT UP was an important force for the development of an avowedly queer sexual politics.[100] This politics has helped to bring about a significant change in political subjectivity and allegiances, for at its most radical "queer" is a militantly anti-essentialist and anti-assimilationist way of naming a polymorphous grouping of people "united only," as Lisa Duggan puts it, "by a shared dissent from the dominant organization of sex and gender."[101] In this mode of radical dissent, Michael Warner argues in an analysis that invokes Arendt's work, queer politics rebels against the very idea of sexual "normality" and poses a fundamental challenge to the interconnected regimes of behaviors, expectations, and discourses described in *The Human Condition*'s critique of the rise of the social.[102]

ACT UP's insurgencies thus exemplify Arendtian political possibilities even while revealing basic problems with central Arendtian assumptions. The full extent to which these possibilities are illuminated through her work emerges only when we note the enabling conditions of ACT UP's challenges to normalization. To frame these challenges in terms of "resistance" and "subversion" is both correct and inadequate, because the contestation of normalizing power developed through activists' creation of spaces in which their own forms of power could be constituted and exercised. That power can be generated through collective action—that it "springs up between men when they act together"—was one of ACT UP's animating ideas, an idea inherent in the group's self-identification as a "Coalition To Unleash Power."[103] Neither ACT UP's "open, leaderless, grass-roots, anarcho-democratic" structure nor its style of demonstrating are fully intelligible without such an understanding of power through coalescence.[104] The basic organizational unit of the ACT UP demonstration, the affinity group, served as a kind of "elementary republic," bound together, as it were, by no more than "the strength of mutual promises." Small, mobile, and usually fleeting—sometimes arising for and dissolving after participation in a single demonstration—affinity groups are political bodies constituted for the sole purpose of making action in concert possible and creating a space of appearances.[105] Action was an end of the protests and not only a means toward them: it takes nothing from the intensity of ACT UP's commitment to fighting for changes in policies that effect basic questions of life to observe that its demonstrations were also always clearly about themselves, about the power created through demonstrating. The demonstration created publics internal to the movement while also changing those found on the streets: it created spaces in which forms of queer assertion could be invented and displayed. This was a

movement that, as Gregg Bordowitz put is, "create[d] itself as it . . . represent[ed] itself." [106]

The space of the demonstration and the form of the affinity group are
not, of course, particular to ACT UP; they are common to many post-
New Left radical organizations. To focus exclusively on these common
features at the expense of the more singular elements of ACT UP's politics of performance would be to miss much of what is most instructive
about its creation of mobile and plural spaces and publics—for ACT UP
did not simply put "queer content" or demands particular to AIDS policy
into conventional political structures. As Crimp and Rolston report, ACT
UP's struggles, particularly those of ACT UP New York, were waged to
an unusual degree through the visual arts. The striking "Silence = Death"
logo (inverted pink triangle, black background, bold white lettering) early
on became widely identified as a symbol of ACT UP, giving it a distinctive
look and serving as an "aid to organizing." [107] Graphics quickly became a
central medium of confrontation, as groups of artist-members such as the
collective Gran Fury helped to plaster the city with slogans and images
taking up and taking on the politics of AIDS and homophobia. Intermin-
gling the codes of merchandising with those of more conventional political propaganda, confronting problems of social practice, cultural attitude,
economic power, and government policy, inflecting their messages with
both rage and outrageous wit, these graphics were emblazoned on subway advertisements, wheatpaste posters on telephone poles, and stickers
that could be found on virtually any public surface. "10,000 New York
City AIDS Deaths. How'm I DOIN'?" (over a photo of mayor Ed Koch),
"Read My Lips" (two men kissing), "Sexism Rears Its Unprotected Head.
Men: Use Condoms or Beat It. AIDS Kills Women" (a dramatically lit
photograph of an erect penis, *sans* condom), "Liberty And Justice For
All.* *Offer not available to anyone with AIDS")—across the city, ACT
UP's graphic disruptions confronted passers by at unexpected moments.[108]

How should we read these confrontations? Although they provide "information" their primary purpose is not, in any straightforward sense,
to inform. The texts and images are challenges which, largely through
irony or surprise, aimed to undercut common assumptions and expectations, indeed to contest the larger symbolic structures through which
indifferent, sexist, and homophobic constructions of AIDS have been
constructed.[109] I find it fruitful—reading Arendt loosely and metaphori-
cally—to think of even these graphic challenges to viewers as attempts
to open political spaces. Spaces of affirmation and spaces of challenge.
Spaces of self-recognition and imagined solidarity. Spaces of distance be-

tween people and who they took themselves to be. Spaces of encounter between strangers. Spaces that could open or close with a moment's remark in a subway car, a passing glance. Such spaces are, at best, extremely fragile, transient. They might—and no doubt most often did—fail to arise at all.[110] At their best, though, these spaces enabled the most diffuse forces of violence to be rendered visible, be given a name, located at work in particular policies, practices, places, prejudices. They were spaces in which both a political movement and its targets could appear. I think something similar can be said of the group's approach to the electronic media. Here the instrumental attempt to inform was extremely important (we saw, for instance, that a central aim of the FDA action was to communicate ACT UP's specific complaints about federal policy to as wide an audience as possible), but the aim was also to create, in and through the mass media, momentary spaces of appearance in which normalization could be contested—spaces all the more necessary since the media were already crucial to the construction of sexual subjectivity and cultural hierarchy.[111]

The spaces opened by ACT UP's graphics and other media interventions were by no means only—or even primarily—for the actors and audiences presumed to be indifferent or hostile. The graphics and media interventions were part of a political project, of which the demonstrations were another part, to *lay claim* to public space and public status. Although assertions of the right to privacy have been central to anti-discrimination legal strategies over the last twenty five years, the anti-assimilationist actions of ACT UP and the queer groups that emerged out of it emphasized a "freedom to be public."[112] From the beginning, AIDS activists had to engage the question of who was to *count* as public—to challenge heterosexually coded rhetorics of "the general public"—but ACT UP's graphics were also a contribution to the broader struggle to make spaces for queers and queerness to appear.[113] The ubiquitous "Silence = Death" became a way of naming that struggle. A summons to resist policies that it constructs as a kind of holocaust, it protests against a death that is, of course, quite literal. But it is also an indictment of the closet, an indictment that figures exile from public speech and space as itself a kind of politically imposed living death. There is a queerly Arendtian resonance in this latter signification. Of course, the politicized fight against the closet would be unthinkable if her way of demarcating the boundaries between public and private, political and social, held sway. Read against those boundaries, however, the queer struggle for the freedom to be public is illuminated by her remark, in *The Human Condition*, that to be excluded from the space where we "appear to others as others appear to us" is "to be deprived of reality, which

humanly and politically speaking, is the same as appearance."[114] Queerness is a political production made real by acts of making space: as Cindy
Patton writes, "AIDS activists know that silence equals death but we also
know that this cannot simply be said, it must be *performed* in an anarchis-
tic politics that sometimes . . . seems simply mad in the traditional public
realm."[115] For all of her invocations of and selective borrowings from the
Great Tradition, and for all of the ways that she herself set limits on what
could enter into her public realm, Arendt's work helps to theorize the
public in which those performances make urgent political sense.

This discussion of ACT UP began with an event aiming to change particular government regulations and has ended up with what might appear
to be spaces of pure display. What makes ACT UP so instructive for my
purposes, however, is its very impurity, the tangled ways in which its concerns were intertwined. The most provocative qualities of the group are
lost if its combination of political concerns and forms is reduced to constituent elements. Obviously, no account of ACT UP can succeed if it
fails to stress that the group's mission and political practice were defined
by the goal of improving AIDS policy; but I think that ACT UP's politics are also misconstrued if we fail to note how the struggle over policies
led to a democratic confrontation with the larger structures of cultural
power. Targeting federal regulatory agencies, ACT UP engaged the state
without becoming statist; indeed, its actions against and demands on the
state were pursued through the creation of unruly spaces of action. ACT
UP created a politics of display and performance without ignoring questions of rule; indeed, its most theatrical performances were disruptions of
the processes—medical policy-making, insurance regulation, education,
televised accounts of what counts politically—that now govern the production of identities and differences. Mobile and multiple, its spaces were
neither reducible to governance nor innocent of it. If they help us to see
the possibilities that can be uncovered through reading Arendt against her
limitations, her exaggerations and purifications help us to identify dimensions in those actions that might otherwise be occluded.

Like (my appropriated) Arendt, these spaces were responsive to late-
modern dilemmas of political location and identification.[116] AIDS both
cuts across and is mediated through the geography of sovereign power.
AIDS is a global problem: political borders do not operate as effective
prophylaxes against the spread of HIV. Many of the institutions that research, profit from, or work to coordinate AIDS treatment are international in scope. ACT UP's targets reflected this. They were often highly

local (a particular hospital, a municipal official) and often national, but at times they escaped the sovereign frame. When American members of ACT UP took part with AIDS activists from other countries in demonstrations at the Fifth International AIDS conference in Montreal, they took their democratic struggle outside the boundaries of the democratic state. When ACT UP chapters formed in Berlin, London, and Paris, and when, for instance, ACT UP San Francisco and ACT UP London coordinated a simultaneous protest at English and American stock markets, that further illustrated the disjuncture between democratic imperatives and those of the nation. But the moments of coordination across national boundaries were far less important than the differences from context to context. The ways in which AIDS is experienced and fought were — and remain — fundamentally conditioned by the lines of sovereignty.[117] The policies which American ACT UP members worked to reshape were primarily those of their city, state, and nation. Even the cultural struggles over sexual identity, representations, and practices were distinctively American. Again, though, the channels of formal electoral politics were not the crucial ones for the constitution of the elementary publics constituted in these American struggles.

ACT UP thus exemplifies the necessarily shifting and uncertain relationship between the actor and the citizen. The instabilities of this relationship, so productive (if underthematized) in Arendt's thought, respond to the problems of globalization but are not reducible to them: the local and national actions show, too, why our perception of political possibilities is constrained if we insist on a decisive choice between these roles. ACT UP often (if ironically, subversively) deployed patriotic rhetoric and national symbols, making claims on Americans *as* Americans who should, as such, recognize specific bonds of obligation. AIDS activism articulated claims about the public good. It also strained against those claims, however, whenever they were too constraining: ACT UP's most radical challenges to cultural power at times exceeded the symbolic resources offered by American traditions of civic speech, for the American political imaginary leaves little room for the queering of public space. To confront the fundaments of homophobia is not only to turn the more generous of American political commitments against local betrayals of them; it is to interrogate those commitments by unsettling the political-cultural foundations of the nation. In this combination, ACT UP is again exemplary. It exemplifies the daunting demands upon and hope-inducing potentialities of, the democratic enterprise today, and it exemplifies the contribution

that Arendtian thinking about the arts of freedom can make to our understanding of that enterprise.

My wish to idealize the struggles I have been describing has made it easier
to illuminate the way in which the Arendtian politics of enactment and
the depurification of the Arendtian political require each other. Still, it
would be a mistake to ignore the limits AIDS and queer activism have so
far revealed. The recent history of this activism offers a bitter reminder of
the extent to which the forces of necessity and the press of circumstances
set boundaries to what can be accomplished through even the most concerted of struggles, the most artful of performances. The democratization
of AIDS expertise achieved by activists has disseminated knowledge of
safer sexual practices, changed the priorities of research and bureaucratic
regulations, affected the price and availability of drugs, and helped cultivate new ways of living with HIV and AIDS. But so far these efforts have
not produced a vaccine, a cure, or even a decisive revolution in means
of treatment.[118] This reflects no failure of political imagination: though
much about government policy remains, after over a decade of activism,
grossly inadequate, I do not see how *any* change in activism's political
course could have produced the medical breakthrough that activists hoped
for in launching their efforts. Locating Arendtian politics in the social—
finding that there are crucial points for contestation not only in the way
bodies are mapped and sexualities are publicly inflected but in the most
technical complexities of health administration—should not blind us to
the ways that this terrain defies any attempt to reduce it to pure politics.

Furthermore, as Marx showed so well, the constraints imposed by circumstance include the deadening weight of historical tradition, the inherited context of discourse. ACT UP's wit, anger, organizing skills, and
media savvy helped to open spaces in which important new sexual identifications and emancipatory forms of cultural power could emerge, but
the struggle provoked formidable counterinsurgency as well. It is by no
means clear that homophobia is less virulent today than when ACT UP
was formed. This persistence should give rise to caution, and still more
is suggested by the evident political limitations of ACT UP's organizational forms and practices. Despite members' concern with internal diversity and their efforts to forge a multiracial, cross-class struggle, chapters remained predominantly white and middle class.[119] Treating ACT UP
largely as a unitary subject, and speaking most often of an undifferentiated "queer" actor, I have elided the tensions and struggles internal to

the movement's organizations and actions. These led, ultimately, to the dissolution of a number of ACT UP chapters. In the nineties, as ACT UP struggled with the problems I have been identifying, there was also a shift in the focus and style of its activism. The links between AIDS policy struggles and the broader campaign against homophobia began to attenuate, and ACT UP activists began to concentrate more exclusively on AIDS as the anti-normalizing insurgency was taken up by groups such as Queer Nation.[120] The ACT UP that I constructed in the account above should not be burdened with more weight than it can bear. Even amidst an argument that many of the most important of political spaces, now, will necessarily be mobile and fleeting, the swiftness with which the politics I have described shifted course (and the alacrity with which many chapters of Queer Nation later dissolved) should make us wary of taking ACT UP as an unproblematic model of democratic publicity.

My reflections have not been a search for unproblematic models, however, and it would be a mistake to turn queer activism's construction of insurgent publics into another false form of generality, a figure for all forms of contemporary democratization. No one case can play such a role. The forms are too diverse, varying from problem to problem and location to location. To stretch the categories with which we theorize a democratic politics responsive to the multiplicity of contemporary struggles against oppression is not to establish one model of how marginalization is produced, lived, resisted, or overcome, but I do not wish this reflection on ACT UP and its legacy to be read as lacking broader implications, either. Though the forms of unfreedom and the dilemmas of politicized identity are heterogeneous, an ironically Arendtian reading of ACT UP can, I suggest, show us something about the places in which publics are constituted, the ways in which such acts of constitution proceed, and the performances they can enable. Neither the group's legacy nor the reading offered here offers an escape from the contemporary dilemmas of freedom and democracy. But neither escape nor transcendence is the goal. ACT UP is one specific example that, in its very particularities, instructs us about the pains and pleasures, perils and promises, of making space for politics.

Notes

Preface: The Art of Being Free

1. Michel de Certeau, *The Practice of Everyday Life* (Berkeley: University of California Press, 1984), p. xxii.

2. In his essay "Traveling Theory," Edward Said writes, "Like peoples and schools of criticism, ideas and theories travel—from person to person, from situation to situation, from one period to another. Cultural and intellectual life are usually nourished and often sustained by this circulation of ideas, and whether it takes the form of unacknowledged or unconscious influence, creative borrowing, or wholesale appropriation, the movement of ideas and theories from one place to another is both a fact of life and a usefully enabling condition of intellectual activity." *The World, the Text, and the Critic* (Cambridge: Harvard University Press, 1983), p. 226.

3. Michel Foucault, *Power-Knowledge* (New York: Pantheon, 1980), pp. 53–54.

4. My relationship to the texts of Tocqueville, Marx, and Arendt is "tactical" in Certeau's sense of the word: "A tactic insinuates itself into the other's place, fragmentarily, without taking it over in its entirety, without being able to keep it at a distance." In his account, strategies concern systems of control, maintaining property and propriety, while tactics work improperly and at times imp(r)udently within these systems. *Practice*, p. xix; see also pp. 35–39.

5. Donna Haraway, "A Cyborg Manifesto: Science, Technology, and Socialist-Feminism in the Late Twentieth Century," in Haraway, *Simians, Cyborgs, and Women* (New York: Routledge, 1991), p. 149. My sense of the uses of irony for reading political theory is fundamentally indebted to that essay, and to years of conversations about "serious irony" with Paige Baty, who also uses the term in her work.

6. Antonio Porchia, *Voices* (Chicago: Big Table, 1969), p. 14. The art of being free with texts must be partial in a dual sense—not only incomplete but engaged.

7. For an elegantly understated account of political thinking as a form of bricolage, see Margaret Leslie, "The Uses of Anachronism," *Political Studies* 18, no. 4

(1970): 433–447. On the AIDS quilt and the political uses of the past, see Marita Sturken, "Conversations with the Dead: Bearing Witness in the AIDS Memorial Quilt," *Socialist Review* 22, no. 2 (1992): 65–96.

8. See, for example, Hannah Arendt, "Tradition and the Modern Age," in *Between Past and Future: Eight Exercises in Political Thought* (New York: Penguin, 1977), and "Walter Benjamin" in *Men in Dark Times* (New York: Harcourt Brace Jovanovich, 1968). The latter essay, which describes the act of appropriating glittering fragments for our contemporary illumination and adornment—of retrieving intellectual treasures that, like pearl and coral, have undergone a "sea change" beneath the weight of history—is one of the further inspirations for my approach to texts here (which is *not* to say that my way of reading is simply modeled on or even congruent with Arendt's). See *Dark Times*, pp. 202–206.

1. Introduction: Making Space for Politics

1. I use "late-modern" as a term to mark the recent intensification and mutation of distinctively modern forms of power, while keeping some distance from the recent debates over postmodernity. Though much of the recent social theorizing drawn on in this book is commonly classified as "postmodern," I find little use in the periodizing argument over whether or not ours is a moment that breaks radically from the modern. Even at its best, the debate has tended to make modern thought and experience more monolithic and self-certain than I believe they have been, thus cutting off political thinking from some still-relevant modern sources; and whether celebratory or hostile, claims about postmodernity's rupture with the past have tended to ignore or obscure the particular problems of democratic thought that will be at the center of my argument. In my usage, then, "late-modern" should be viewed less as a rejection of postmodern theoretical discourses than as a tactical refusal to enter too directly into an increasingly hegemonic polemic; my hope is that this refusal will help me unsettle certain categories and assumptions, opening conceptual spaces that are often closed these days, and finding new wrinkles in some older works. This use of "late-modern" to characterize the present condition leans indirectly on the following: Ernesto Laclau and Chantal Mouffe, *Hegemony and Socialist Strategy: Toward a Radical Democratic Politics* (London: Verso, 1985); Agnes Heller and Ferenc Feher, *The Postmodern Political Condition* (New York: Columbia University Press, 1988); Claude Lefort, *Democracy and Political Theory* (Minneapolis: University of Minnesota Press, 1988); William Connolly, *Identity\Difference: Democratic Negotiations of Political Paradox* (Ithaca: Cornell University Press, 1991); Sheldon Wolin, *The Presence of the Past: Essays on the State and the Constitution* (Baltimore: Johns Hopkins University Press, 1989).

2. The *locus classicus* of "realist" analysis of the impossibility of popular rule is the work of a moonlighting economist: the most significant debunking tradition was inaugurated by Joseph Schumpeter in his *Capitalism, Socialism, and Democracy* (New York: Harper, 1950).

3. The constraints that the international political economy and other globaliz-

ing forces exert on states' capacities for self-government is a theme of much recent scholarly writing. In my framing of the problem, I have drawn particular benefit from Arjun Appadurai's account of global cultural flows and William Connolly's arguments about the gap between the power of contemporary states and their efficacy, and his account of the disciplinary consequences of the drive to fix politics to territory. By Appadurai, see "Disjuncture and Difference in the Global Cultural Economy," in *The Phantom Public Sphere*, ed. Bruce Robbins (Minneapolis: University of Minnesota Press, 1993), pp. 269-295; and "Patriotism and Its Futures," *Public Culture* 5 (1993): 411-429. By Connolly, see *Identity\Difference;* "Democracy and Territoriality," *Millennium: Journal of International Studies* 20, no. 3 (1991): 463-484; and "Tocqueville, Territory, and Violence," *Theory, Culture & Society* 11, no. 1 (1994): 19-40. I have also drawn on David Harvey, *The Condition of Postmodernity* (Cambridge, Eng.: Basil Blackwell, 1989); Barry Hindness, "Imaginary presuppositions of democracy," *Economy and Society* 20, no. 2 (1991): 173-196; R. B. J. Walker, *Inside/Outside: International Relations as Political Theory* (New York: Cambridge University Press, 1993).

4. Wolin, *Presence of the Past*, p. 155. (Wolin's remarks are presented in the context of an emphasis on the power of the state, rather than a discussion of limitations and counter powers.)

5. Appadurai, "Patriotism and Its Futures," p. 423.

6. Wolin, *Presence of the Past*, p. 162. Wolin's argument is that the politically exploitative use of the marginal often unites those who ostensibly differ over state policy and who clearly have contrary electoral interests. The few years since his essay was published have only served to make its claims more compelling. Presently, both American political parties struggle primarily over how swiftly and punitively the virtueless citizen is to be reshaped. For some of the crucial intellectual underpinnings of the newer disciplinary policies and discourses, see, for example, Mickey Kaus, *The End of Equality* (New York: Basic Books, 1992), and Lawrence Mead, *The New Politics of Poverty: The Nonworking Poor in America* (New York: Basic Books, 1992). The former offers a reform agenda from an avowedly liberal position, while the latter is self-consciously conservative; it says something important about the politics of our day that even a dedicated reader is hard-pressed to tell the difference between the two substantive agendas, and that, rhetorically, the "liberal" text is more obviously an exercise in *ressentiment* and the demonization of vulnerable others.

7. I wrote these remarks before the official launching of the campaign for California's Proposition 187. I trust that it is no longer necessary to consider my scenario speculative, and I fear that we will see many more such struggles in the years ahead.

8. The words I quote come from columnist Charles Krauthammer, who wrote them shortly before the collapse of the governments of Eastern Europe. In remarks that would come to typify the most prominent American response to that collapse, he argued, "The perennial question that has preoccupied every political philosopher since Plato—what is the best form of governance?—has been answered. After a few millennia of trying every form of political system, we close this millennium with the sure knowledge that in liberal, pluralist, capitalist democracy we have found what we have been looking for. . . . The triumph of the Western political idea is complete. Its

rivals have been routed. . . . Political theory, at least the part concerned with defining the good polity, is finished. The Western idea of governance has prevailed. . . . Yes, some details remain to be worked out. . . . We will always need the Kennedy School. But the basic question is definitively answered." Krauthammer, "Democracy Has Won," *Washington Post*, March 24, 1989. That these sentiments were pervasive and not particular to Krauthammer is best seen in the broad and sympathetic response to Francis Fukuyama's very similar remarks. See Fukuyama, "The End of History?" *National Interest* 3, no. 4 (1989): 3–18.

9. Fredric Jameson puts the problem of identifying new (b)orders well when he writes of "the incapacity of our minds, at least at present, to map the great global multinational and decentered communicational network in which we find ourselves caught as individual subjects." *Postmodernism, or The Cultural Logic of Late Capitalism* (Durham: Duke University Press, 1991), p. 44. The democratic dimension of these cartographic problems is captured by this remark of Connolly's: "Central to the project of retheorizing democracy to fit the circumstances of late-modern life is the task of rethinking the contemporary relation between sovereignty and democracy." *Identity\Difference*, p. 215. See also Michel Foucault's comments on sovereignty in "Two Lectures," *Power-Knowledge* (New York: Pantheon, 1980), pp. 94–108.

10. In other words, I argue for the importance of these three thinkers without denying the contingency and contestability of my selection. Probably the most obvious of the several other major theorists who could easily have been central to the project I pursue is Michel Foucault. I trust that anyone familiar with his work who reads this book will recognize the impact his thought has had on my questions and arguments, and my subsequent chapters periodically indicate the generally unacknowledged affinities that can be found between his work and that of both Tocqueville and Arendt.

11. My argument here benefits greatly from William Connolly's comments on an earlier version of the manuscript.

12. On this point see Wendy Brown, "Feminist Hesitations, Postmodern Exposures," *differences* 3, no. 1 (1991): 80. Other useful arguments on this need for an unprecedented diversity and mobility of spaces are offered in Nancy Fraser, "Rethinking the Public Sphere," in *Phantom Public*, ed. Robbins; Laclau and Mouffe, *Hegemony and Socialist Strategy*; and Bernice Johnson Reagon, "Coalition Politics: Turning the Century," in *Home Girls: A Black Feminist Anthology*, ed. Barbara Smith (New York: Kitchen Table/Women of Color Press, 1983), pp. 356–368.

13. James Boyd White, *When Words Lose Their Meanings: Constitutions and Reconstitutions of Language, Character, and Community* (Chicago: University of Chicago Press, 1984), p. 192. On the disadvantages of stipulative definitions for theoretical reflection on the political, see also Lefort's essay "The Question of Democracy" in *Democracy and Political Theory*, pp. 9–20.

14. I use "imaginary" in the sense common to many strands of recent and contemporary French social theory, but not with the specific technical inflections that the term is given in Lacanian psychoanalysis. In this broad sense, "imaginary" means something like a comprehensive archive of a society, culture, or tradition's constitutive imaginations, a terrain of collective hopes, desires, and structures of thought

and feeling. One can thus speak of the "American political imaginary" as a way of encompassing the contending discourses and visions that shape political struggles in this country.

15. Arendt, *Men in Dark Times* (New York: Harcourt Brace Jovanovich, 1968), pp. 205–206.

16. Communitarianism has not been a merely an academic enterprise, and the call back to community has resonated with a much broader reading and voting public. *Habits of the Heart* (Berkeley: University of California Press, 1985), Robert Bellah et al.'s explicitly Tocquevillian critique of contemporary American individualism, was a best-seller in the mid-eighties. More recently, candidate Clinton placed much emphasis on "service" and "responsibility," using language and policy ideas drawn from the work of contemporary communitarian writers. Several of these writers obtained roles (political theorist William Galston, for example) or influence (e.g., *Tikkun* editor Michael Lerner) in the Clinton White House.

17. Representative writings would thus include the following: Amitai Etzioni, *The Spirit of Community* (New York: Crown, 1993); Bellah et al., *Habits;* Alasdair MacIntyre, *After Virtue* (Notre Dame, Ind.: Notre Dame University Press, 1981); Michael Sandel, *Liberalism and the Limits of Justice* (New York: Cambridge University Press, 1982); Charles Taylor, *Philosophy and the Human Sciences* (New York: Cambridge University Press, 1985). The first two texts reveal strong Tocquevillian influence. MacIntyre has, in some moments of his work, been strongly informed by Marx (though one could argue about the ways that influence does or does not persist in his more recent work). Taylor's work quite obviously reflects the influence of all three thinkers.

18. They range across the conventional left-right spectrum, have quite different agendas on questions of cultural difference, and place differing degrees of emphasis on the practices of politics.

19. For a recent example, see the essays collected in Nancy Rosenblum's edited volume, *Liberalism and the Moral Life* (Cambridge: Harvard University Press, 1989). I argue at more length for the sterility of the liberal-communitarian debate in my review essay "Look Who's Talking," *Political Theory* 23, no. 4 (1995): 689–719.

20. Etzioni, *The Spirit of Community*, p. 26.

21. Among those critics of communitarianism who largely stand outside the liberal-communitarian debate, William Connolly and Michael Shapiro have brought the communitarians' ontological commitments into particularly sharp focus. See, for example, Connolly's *Identity\Difference* and Shapiro's *The Postmodern Polity* (Minneapolis: Minnesota University Press, 1992). Their work informs my arguments here.

22. This ideal/material dichotomy is rather crude and inflexible, of course. I argue against it in Chapter 4, where I find in Marx's rhetoric a more supple approach that emphasizes the discursive characteristics of institutions and the materiality and institutional dimensions of discourse. But such an approach is not a significant presence in communitarian literature, and I believe the simple ideal/material opposition is adequate to my task here.

23. In making this claim, I do not wish to be tendentious in my flattening of complexities and nuances. I readily acknowledge, for instance, that Charles Taylor

has long displayed a concern for problems of cultural diversity and his recent work has given a qualified endorsement to multiculturalism. But for reasons too complex and peripheral to elaborate here, I also think that even the most sympathetic communitarian works on difference, such as Taylor's *Multiculturalism and the Politics of Recognition* (Princeton: Princeton University Press, 1992), remain bound within the problematic framework that I am sketching here, and that even a more patient and shaded critique would result in more or less the same conclusion. Such a critique can be found in Tom Dumm's essay exploring the excessive limits Taylor's book places on efforts to analyze and respond to the contemporary entanglement of politics and cultures, privileged identities and marginalized differences. See Dumm, "Strangers and Liberals," *Political Theory* 22, no. 1 (1994): 167–175.

24. See, for example, Taylor's essay "Atomism" in *Philosophy and the Human Sciences: Philosophical Papers*, vol. 2 (New York: Cambridge University Press, 1985), pp. 187–210.

25. For representative samples, see the following essays from *The Responsive Community*: Etzioni, "A Moral Reawakening without Puritanism," 1, no. 4 (1991): 30–35; William Galston, "Rights Do Not Equal Rightness," 1, no. 4 (1991): 7–9; Etzioni, "Laudable and Troubling Communitarian Acts in L.A.," 2, no. 3 (1992): 4–5; Roger L. Conner and Robert Teir, "A Very Dubious Right: Pederasty in the Public Library," 2, no. 3 (1992): 9–12. If the journal deliberately skirts the complexities of sustained philosophical argument, it remains a useful example that is by no means disconnected from the world of academic political theory. It not only shows how some of the more abstract propositions about community life translate into quotidian struggles, but reflects the work of intellectuals who are prominent within the academic world as well. Among those involved in the journal, for example, are Benjamin Barber, Etzioni, Galston, and Mary Ann Glendon.

26. Homophobic conceptions of and rhetoric about "the general public" have been an explicit target of AIDS activists from the beginning, as I discuss in Chapter 5, but perhaps the most astute analysis of such rhetoric is one not centrally preoccupied with AIDS, Michael Warner's "The Mass Public and the Mass Subject," in *Phantom Public*, ed. Robbins, pp. 234–256. For the notion of imagined communities, see Benedict Anderson, *Imagined Communities: Reflections on the Origin and Spread of Nationalism*, 2d ed. (New York: Verso, 1991).

27. For a discussion of this point and of issues related to my concerns here, see J. Peter Euben, *The Tragedy of Political Theory* (Princeton: Princeton University Press, 1990), pp. 12–13.

28. Homi K. Bhabha, *The Location of Culture* (New York: Routledge, 1994), pp. 3, 9. Unhomeliness is thus not homelessness, the literal deprivation of a sheltered living space. Though the latter condition is also a sign of our times, I am, of course, by no means suggesting that it should be affirmed or taken as the inevitable accompaniment to politics in the present: to argue against the political effort to resurrect a familiar culture in which "we" were all, putatively, "at home" is not to argue against the just and urgent fight to assure all individuals a decent place to live.

29. "My point is not that everything is bad, but that everything is dangerous, which is not exactly the same as bad. If everything is dangerous, then we always have

something to do. So my position leads not to apathy but to a hyper- and pessimistic activism." Michel Foucault, "On the Genealogy of Ethics," in *Michel Foucault: Beyond Structuralism and Hermeneutics*, ed. Hubert Dreyfus and Paul Rabinow, 2d ed. (Chicago: University of Chicago Press, 1983), pp. 231–232.

2. Disturbing *Democracy:* Reading (in) the Gaps between Tocqueville's America and Ours

1. For a more detailed survey of academic writings on Tocqueville, and a discussion of how such readings tend to reflect the liberalism or conservatism of his interpreters, see Roger Boesche, *The Strange Liberalism of Alexis de Tocqueville* (Ithaca: Cornell University Press, 1987), pp. 15–17. Stephen Schneck notes the recent rise of republican readings and their departures from liberal accounts in "New Readings of Tocqueville's *America:* Lessons for Democracy," *Polity* 25, no. 2 (1992). Probably the most widely known and influential work that used Tocqueville in order to affirm existing American politics is Louis Hartz's *The Liberal Tradition in America* (New York: Harcourt, Brace and World, 1955). Although they sometimes took issue with him, the "pluralist" political scientists of the 1950s and early 1960s also drew on Tocqueville in pursuing their affirmative account of American power and governance. Later in the chapter, I will discuss how even critics of contemporary America can use Tocqueville to reinscribe conventional political categories. My understanding of Tocqueville's role in taming radical criticism has profited from Schneck's characterization of *Democracy in America* as a "regime of truth" for American political discussion, and from George Shulman's critique of the "pastoralism" of many contemporary radical democrats. See Schneck, "Habits of the Head: Tocqueville's America and Jazz," *Political Theory* 17, no. 4 (1989): 640 and passim, and Shulman, "The Pastoral Idyl of *democracy*," *democracy* 3, no. 4 (1983): 47 and passim.

2. This effort to disturb democracy and *Democracy* is neither unique nor unaided. My comments about the familiarity of *Democracy in America* and the ease with which it is appropriated for soothing purposes are not intended to disparage the large body of serious Tocqueville scholarship or to suggest that my own work has not drawn great benefits from some of that work. Despite my substantially different sense of the political uses of Tocqueville's work, I have learned much from Boesche's fine and thorough scholarship and from Jack Lively's exemplary liberal interpretation, in *The Social and Political Thought of Alexis de Tocqueville* (Oxford: Clarendon Press, 1962). More fundamentally, my sense of the political stakes in reading Tocqueville, and my own interpretation of him, have been worked out in conversation with the works of several theorists who *do* use Tocqueville to undermine established certainties. See William Connolly, "Tocqueville, Territory, and Violence," *Theory, Culture, and Society* 11 (1994): 19–41; Claude Lefort, *Democracy and Political Theory* (Minneapolis: University of Minnesota Press, 1988); Schneck, "Habits of the Head" and "New Readings"; and Sheldon Wolin, *The Presence of the Past* (Baltimore: Johns Hopkins University Press, 1989). My borrowings from and disagreements with those works will be addressed in more detail below, especially in Chapter 3.

3. This line, and hence the arguments of this paragraph, a recurring figure employed throughout the chapter, and the title of the chapter itself, were suggested to me by William Connolly's discussion of "a democratic politics of disturbance" in his "Democracy and Territoriality," *Millennium: Journal of International Studies* 20, no. 3 (1991): 463–484. Disturbance is also an important idea linked to democratic politics throughout his *Identity\Difference*. It is not clear to me, however, that my use of disturbance is altogether in keeping with his.

4. I quote the first two definitions listed by my *Webster's New World Dictionary* (New York: World Publishing Company, 1959).

5. In noting this Tocquevillian tension between two attitudes toward that which unsettles, it is worth remembering that one primary meaning of "to settle" is "to colonize." As we will see in Chapter 3, Tocqueville's response to the European colonization of America is one of the crucial ways in which his response to disturbance gets worked out.

6. Boesche, *Strange Liberalism*, p. 15.

7. Ibid., pp. 15–17.

8. Interesting reflections on the politics of cartography can be found in Fredric Jameson, *Postmodernism* (Durham: Duke University Press, 1991), chaps. 1 and 10, and Michel de Certeau, *The Practice of Everyday Life* (Berkeley: University of California Press, 1984), pt. 3.

9. *Democracy in America*, ed. J. P. Mayer and trans. George Lawrence (New York: Doubleday, 1969), p. 9. Unless otherwise indicated, citations are to the Lawrence translation.

10. See ibid., p. 12.

11. Ibid., p. 243.

12. Ibid., p. 177.

13. The argument that Tocqueville is the founding and crucial text for American exceptionalism is explored at some length by Rogers Smith in "Beyond Tocqueville, Myrdal, Hartz: The Multiple Traditions in America," *American Political Science Review* 87, no. 3 (1993): 549–566.

14. The most notable and interesting work in this vein, along with the obvious but arguable case of Arendt (who was concerned with public space and public freedom, but whose commitment to democracy was, as we will see, debatable), is that of Sheldon Wolin and the authors he gathered together in the journal *democracy*. Readers familiar with this work will recognize both its loud echoes in my own arguments and my ultimate departures from some of its key premises. Again, Shulman's "Pastoral Idyll" clarifies some of the problems with the journal's Tocquevillian strain, thereby suggesting some of the reasons why departures are necessary.

15. Shapiro, *The Postmodern Polity* (Minneapolis: University of Minnesota Press, 1992), pp. 77–78. My brief remarks lean heavily on his substantial and incisive critique of *Habits*. The chapter in which that critique is developed also serves, by extension, as one of the sharpest existing diagnoses of the limits of contemporary "communitarianism."

16. This interpretation displays considerably less charity toward *Habits* than I show toward Tocqueville's work. Surely *Habits* is also a text of conflicting tendencies,

of countervailing impulses? It does, after all, contain the beginnings of a critique of late-modern forms of corporate despotism. Why not "take liberties" with this text, too, turning it toward different ends and reading its democratic moments against its moralistic foreclosure of democracy? I do not rule out the possibility of a successful reading along such lines, but I leave that work for others: I have found Tocqueville's work rich and multi-layered enough to justify extensive hermeneutic labors in willful appropriation, while *Habits* strikes me most for its high-minded disparagements of the people who, on its own account, ought to rule.

17. Rather than mourning a lost unity, Wolin is more inclined to worry about the loss of an openness to diversity, a care for plurality, that he locates in past practices and premodern sensibilities.

18. See, for example, the critique of *Democracy* pursued by Sean Wilentz's "Many Democracies: On Tocqueville and Jacksonian America," in *Reconsidering Tocqueville's "Democracy in America,"* ed. Abraham S. Eisenstadt (New Brunswick: Rutgers University Press, 1988). See also Irving Zeitlin, *Liberty, Equality, and Revolution in Alexis de Tocqueville* (Boston: Little, Brown, 1971), pp. 50–60; Schneck, "Habits of the Head"; and, though it is far less critical, the discussion of *Democracy's* obscuring of religious differences in Dorris Goldstein's *The Trial of Faith: Religion and Politics in Tocqueville's Thought* (New York: Elsevier Scientific Publishing, 1975), pp. 15–31.

19. Wilentz, "Many Democracies," p. 226.

20. The most ambitious and provocative exploration of this problem is Connolly's "Tocqueville, Territory, and Violence." My framing of the problem here bears the stamp of Connolly's argument, and my reading of Tocqueville is, in part, an attempt to respond to his challenge.

21. Ibid., p. 12. Another memorable characterization of the limits of existing knowledge comes from the Conclusion: "The past sheds no light on the future and the spirit of man walks through the night" (p. 703).

22. Unlike, say, Thomas Hobbes or Jeremy Bentham, Tocqueville did not try to use the epistemological authority of science to justify his political program and shield important assumptions from political criticism. Indeed, Tocqueville could be an acute critic of the scientization of political thought. So while the appeal for a new science is a useful index of the seriousness of Tocqueville's commitment to thinking the new world in a new way, it is not fruitfully taken as a clue to a methodological program. Saguiv Hadari offers a contrary, though to my mind unpersuasive, view on this matter. His *Theory in Practice* (Stanford: Stanford University Press, 1989) sees Tocqueville as seeking, and largely succeeding in establishing, a formal method of social scientific inquiry.

23. On this, see Lefort's helpful commentary in *Democracy and Political Theory*, p. 170, and Wolin's argument in *Presence of the Past*, chap. 4 (especially pp. 68–69), though my sense of Tocqueville's project and uses differs from both of their accounts.

24. *Democracy*, p. 240. Tocqueville also uses "art" in the first epigraph to this chapter, and in a number of other passages in *Democracy*. I take the liberty of reading his "art" in light of the ways that Foucault and Certeau have written of the shrewd and mobile arts of struggle and resistance. Or is it that Tocqueville is an underacknowledged figure in the genealogy of Foucaultian studies of the arts and prac-

tices of micro-politics? We have heard much of the Nietzschean and Heideggerian currents that run through Foucault's work; it is time to attend to the Tocquevillian resonances of his analyses of discipline, biopower, governmentality, and struggle. Though its argument differs from mine, George Kateb's recent essay on individualism and docility suggests a fruitful point from which to record these resonances. See *The Inner Ocean: Individualism and Democratic Culture* (Ithaca: Cornell University Press, 1992), pp. 232–234.

25. Harvey Mitchell hints at this (though he does not pursue that hint very far) when he writes that Tocqueville "linked what may be called *virtuosity* and freedom." Mitchell, "The Changing Conditions of Freedom: Tocqueville in the Light of Rousseau," *History of Political Thought* 9, no. 3 (1988): 450. Freedom as a performing art, an activity for virtuosity, is among the most important ideas shared by Tocqueville and Arendt, as Chapter 5 will show.

26. The problems are explored over the course of this book, but I begin with these terms because, for all of their flaws, there are no obvious replacements. For example, Isaiah Berlin's well-known discussion of "positive" and "negative" freedom is of considerably less use. Much of what goes under the heading of public liberty, and much of what is most interesting in Tocqueville's notion of "art" falls through the gap between Berlin's two categories, because the latter's construction of positive freedom conflates ideas of freedom-as-action with conceptions of "objective reason" and the "true self." The public/private dichotomy is one that can be employed and, through its employment, challenged and complicated; the positive/negative framework simply renders significant strands in my authors' works, and significant topics of my concern, invisible.

27. This comparative framework is ideal-typical at best, and relies on the flattening out of nuance and particularity that marks such modes of comparison. But it may not do too much violence to their complexities to say that Hobbes is a particularly pure theorist of private liberty while Rousseau is the archetypal modern theorist of public liberty. However "pure" and privatizing his theory, though, Hobbes is hardly known as one who gives enormous scope to individual freedom; and so the Mill of *On Liberty* may be a more relevant example—for liberal societies and for comparisons to Tocqueville—of the theory of private liberty. Mill's separation between democracy and liberty, and his primary focus on defining the scope of conduct free from interference, fit neatly within the terms of this public/private typology. Whether his emphasis on the need for regular contestations over customs and truthclaims is usefully subsumed under the "private" category is another matter, one that already begins to suggest the trouble with the public/private dichotomy as a device for theorizing freedom.

28. This is Tocqueville at his best: my account here draws on one strand or voice in his conflictual text, privileging the voice that most values disturbance. This is the voice heard, for example, in his critique of tutelary power and the meditation on the problem of public opinion (both of which I discuss below). Listening for that voice is necessary to elaborating a reading of Tocqueville that is at once affirmative and provocative. But the voice that drowns out dissonance is a loud and (perhaps more)

important one. Chapter 3 explores that voice, and its place in the larger, contradictory ensemble of *Democracy*.

29. Robert Nisbet, "Tocqueville's Ideal Types," in *Reconsidering Tocqueville's "Democracy,"* ed. Eisenstadt, p. 189.

30. I draw here on ibid., pp. 188–189.

31. *Democracy*, p. 11. This story of equality and democracy is already enough to suggest that Tocqueville sometimes runs "equality" and "democracy" together. Here, too, we are dealing with terms that carry multiple meanings in Tocqueville's texts. By "equality" Tocqueville can mean formal equality before the law, the breakdown of class barriers and fixed hierarchies, real material equality of persons, or the predominance of egalitarian principles and sentiments. He uses "democracy," variously, to mean rule in the name or the alleged interests of the people, actual rule by a majority, a government and/or political life rich in spaces for participation, a culture in which many different kinds of people have a hand, a leveling of social power, and the suppression of difference. I will return to the many shades of "democracy" in *Democracy* later, exploring the politics of the different concepts at work in the text. Here, as an initial clarification, it may be useful to say that I hold, first, that when Tocqueville warns of the dangers of democracy he is most often and most significantly afraid of the effects of the leveling of difference and the single-minded pursuit of absolute material equality; and, secondly, that he sees political democracy-as-robust-participation as the best way of overcoming those democratic/egalitarian dangers. For two excellent, more elaborate, and somewhat different discussions of these questions, see Lively, *Social and Political Thought*, pp. 49–51, and François Furet, *In the Workshop of History* (Chicago: University of Chicago Press, 1984), pp. 186–188.

32. *Democracy*, p. 514.

33. Lefort is one of the few critics to understand the full importance of this affirmative view within Tocqueville's account of modern individuality. See for example *Democracy and Political Theory*, p. 15.

34. Perhaps the most intriguing of Tocqueville's claims for the enabling character of bonds is his comparison of authority to grammar, *Democracy*, p. 72. On this account, like grammar, authority at once restrains us and allows us to do things we could not otherwise do. Where the analogy either breaks down or gets more complicated is when we ask this democratic question: what *kind* of authority is fit for a democracy? The discussion of association that follows offers one kind of Tocquevillian answer; the discussion of religion in Chapter 3 suggests another. Those differences lead readers into the core ambivalence in his thought.

35. Ibid., p. 514.

36. Ibid., p. 667.

37. Nisbet's work is perhaps the most learned and interesting of such readings.

38. See, for example, *Democracy*, p. 243.

39. Ibid., p. 245.

40. Ibid., p. 69. As Tocqueville acknowledges, it is not "America" but New England that is the subject of his discussion of public freedom and localism. But despite his explicit acknowledgments of regional differences, the New England township

tends to function as a synechdoche for American democracy. This narrowing of focus is revealing: it is bound up with problems in the way *Democracy* construes the relationship between democratic institutions, on the one hand, and social structure and cultural practices, on the other—as I will show in Chapter 3.

41. Ibid., pp. 68-69.

42. Ibid., p. 68. Both this quote and much of my discussion above are drawn from the section on "The Spirit of the Township."

43. Ibid., p. 243.

44. Ibid., p. 63.

45. Might this institutionalization work, at the same time, as a kind of confinement? I address this in the next chapter.

46. Ibid., p. 62.

47. Connolly, "Democracy and Territoriality," p. 465.

48. *Democracy*, p. 62.

49. Ibid., p. 44.

50. Is this answer too easy? Certainly. As Connolly goes on to note in his discussion of paradox, the open acknowledgment of violence is not the only—or even the common—path taken by theorists caught up in the dilemma of turning cause into effect and effect into cause: "the legacy of violence in the founding must be concealed" ("Democracy and Territoriality," p. 465). Might something like that concealment be going on in the passages from *Democracy* I have been summarizing? In his "Tocqueville, Territory, and Violence," Connolly accuses *Democracy* of seeking to at least dull us to such violence (though he judges Tocqueville more open about the role of violence than many other democratic theorists). I take up the question in Chapter 3, but it is worth acknowledging here the tactical masking performed by my own discussion: crucial to *Democracy*'s history of free mores is its account of religion, an account that reveals both what Tocqueville's democracy excludes and what it imposes upon the citizenry. I also glide over, here, the (related) question of who was already on the land when the planters of "English liberties" arrived.

51. *Democracy*, p. 190.

52. Ibid., p. 190.

53. Ibid., p. 513.

54. Boesche, *Strange Liberalism*, p. 126. Boesche notes that Tocqueville's frequent use of the verb *s'accocier* has roots in the usages of Rousseau and Montesquieu, and the medieval understanding of friendship. My discussion here is indebted to Boesche's insight.

55. *Democracy*, p. 522.

56. Ibid., p. 517.

57. Ibid., p. 190. Emphasis added. Tocqueville's own words are: "Il n'y a rien que la volonté humaine désespère d'atteindre par l'action libre de la puissance collective des individus." *Oeuvres complètes: Oeuvres, papiers, et correspondances*, ed. J. P. Mayer (Paris: Gallimard, 1951-95), 1: 195.

58. Tocqueville develops his account of democratic struggle, of the correct use of association, by contrasting it to the European (mis)use of association as an instrument of class warfare. He suggests that the more martial European use of association

produces not only a drive to dominate those outside of the association but a hierarchical and intolerant internal associational life as well (see *Democracy*, pp. 193-195). My account of the salutary effects of association not only abstracts from Tocqueville's particular examples but highlights his happiest conclusions on an issue that troubled and perplexed him deeply. The contrast between European and American association offers contending explanations of the difference, and these explanations diverge in their political implications. At times, *Democracy* suggests that the American achievement is primarily a matter of political culture and political art, thus implying that a project of cultural transformation might produce a more benign European practice. At other times, the suggestion seems to be that the decisive differences are those of class structure, and that no amount of art could navigate the kinds of cleavages that divide European polities. The ambiguity on this point haunts *Democracy*, as I will show in Chapter 3. For the purposes of this chapter, however, it is more important to bring out the most ambitious claims made on behalf of association and political art.

59. For an account of the parallels, see Bernard Brown, "Tocqueville and Publius," in *Reconsidering Tocqueville's "Democracy,"* ed. Eisenstadt, pp. 43-76, and James T. Schleiffer, *The Making of Tocqueville's "Democracy in America"* (Chapel Hill: University of North Carolina Press, 1980), chap. 7. On the other hand, the importance assigned to local political life, and the account of the effects of association, depart substantially from both the analytic framework and normative political goals pursued by the Federalsits. Two readers who have recognized this with particular clarity are Sheldon Wolin, "Archaism, Modernity, and *Democracy in America,"* p. 73, and Richard Krouse, " 'Classical' Images of Democracy in America: Madison and Tocqueville," in *Democratic Theory and Practice*, ed. Graeme Duncan (New York: Cambridge University Press, 1983), pp. 58-78.

60. *Democracy*, p. 201.

61. Brown has even suggested that Tocqueville harbored resentment against the Americans for not taking this idea seriously. See "Tocqueville and Publius," pp. 59-65.

62. *Democracy*, p. 198.

63. Ibid., p. 198, 57.

64. Ibid., p. 57.

65. It is often hard to judge (and easy to overestimate) the effects of a theoretical text on everyday political discourse, but *Democracy* is a staple of op-ed pronouncements and other forms of journalistic punditry, and it also had a decisive influence on works such as John Stuart Mill's *On Liberty*, discussed below.

66. *Democracy*, p. 435.

67. The arguments and citations are all drawn from *Democracy*, pp. 506-508.

68. Ibid., p. 509.

69. Ibid., p. 510.

70. At least not all of the time: as in my earlier discussions of dissonance in political orders/subjects and of association, I turn to the most appealing and complex of Tocqueville's approaches. On this matter, too, he speakes in other, more confining ways. These will be taken up later.

71. Thus he maintains that there may have to be limits on association, in some contexts (though these remain unspecified); he acknowledges that this abridgement of freedom has very serious costs, but believes these costs must sometimes be paid (*Democracy*, p. 524). Even while resisting his endorsement of the need for limitations, I find instructive and inspiring his ability to place such profound hopes in associations while also finding them dangerous.

72. Some readers have found a fundamental inconsistency between the two volumes because they differ in their account of the greatest threats to democracy. I think it is a mistake to overdraw the distinction between the two volumes, to overlook the ambiguities and ambivalences that run through each of them. Of course the volumes differ, but Volume Two's analysis of the role of politicization in transforming the threat of individualism echoes many of Volume One's discussions of the virtues of political space and practice; and it is hard to see that the fear of excess, of wildness, disappears in the later volume. But this is an old debate: for some time, Tocqueville scholars have disagreed over the relationship between volumes. A classic source on the issue is Seymour Drescher's "Tocqueville's Two *Démocraties*," *Journal of the History of Ideas* 25 (1964): 201–216, and readers interested in a brief introduction to the recent literature are referred to his "More than America: Comparison and Synthesis in *Democracy in America*," in *Reconsidering Tocqueville's "Democracy,"* ed. Eisenstadt, pp. 77–93. I have not taken up that literature in this book. Given given my themes, my ultimate purposes, and my way of reading, the quarrel over the relationship between volumes is, most of the time, no more than a distracting detour—and so I touch on tensions between the volumes only when they raise questions that are directly relevant to my concerns.

73. *Democracy*, p. 511. Here, I use "freedom" for "*liberté*," where Lawrence has "liberty," because it is important to capture the participatory and political connotations of Tocqueville's comment.

74. Ibid., p. 503. This passage is another of the important moments in Tocqueville that Lefort stands out for recognizing. His discussion of it, however, takes it in a rather different (more metaphysical) direction than mine. See *Democracy and Political Theory*, pp. 192–195.

75. *Democracy*, p. 504.

76. One of Tocqueville's most powerful statements on this theme comes in his "praise" of equality "for the intractability it inspires." This praise is is a response to the way that intractability "insinuates deep into the heart and mind of every man some vague notion and instinctive inclination toward political freedom, thereby preparing the antidote for the ill it has produced." Ibid., pp. 667–668.

77. Ibid., p. 636.

78. Ibid., p. 538.

79. I trust that, even without my earlier remarks about Tocqueville's cartography, the evasions in this characterization of Jacksonian America would be obvious. It is essential to come to terms with the politics of these evasions, but I defer that encounter until Chapter 3. For the moment, I will accept his presentation as if it were simply true.

80. *Democracy*, pp. 583–584.

81. Ibid., pp. 557–558.

82. Jack Lively, *The Social and Political Thought of Alexis de Tocqueville* (Oxford: Clarendon Press, 1962), p. 272.

83. *Democracy*, p. 691.

84. Ibid., p. 692. Here, I am slightly modifying Lawrence's translation, which has "protective power" instead of "tutelary power." Yet Tocqueville writes of *un pouvoir immense et tutélaire* (*Oeuvres complètes*, 2: 324). I believe that "tutelary," a less common word with a narrower range of meanings, more exactly captures the aspect of modern institutions that most distresses Tocqueville. Such a translation also brings out the affinities between Tocqueville's analysis of modern power and the analysis of tutelary power that Foucault undertook in his writings on "governmentality." On the latter, see especially *The Foucault Effect*, ed. Graham Burchell et al. (Chicago: University of Chicago Press, 1991). My subsequent comments on *Democracy* make use of these affinities to sharpen certain Tocquevillian points, but, to reiterate, they can do so only because Tocqueville is such a significant (though underacknowledged) figure in the genealogy of the contemporary critique of tutelary power. This genealogy is revealed more clearly in *L'ancien Régime*, especially in its critique of the ideas and policies of the Economists, but is evident in *Democracy* as well. See, for example, *The Old Regime and the French Revolution*, trans. Stuart Gilbert (Garden City, N.Y.: Doubleday, 1955), pp. 158–163.

85. Ibid., pp. 692–693.

86. This act of translation follows one performed by Tocqueville himself: as Thomas L. Dumm has argued, *Democracy*'s characterization of democratic despotism borrowed heavily from Tocqueville and Beaumont's prior analysis of the micropractices of American prisons. See Dumm, *Democracy and Punishment: Disciplinary Origins of the United States* (Madison: University of Wisconsin Press, 1987), pp. 128–140.

87. It would be utterly misleading to suggest that our workplaces are monolithic regimes of inescapable domination. For many people, of course, the workplace is a primary source of pleasure and fulfillment. Being employed also seems to be a prerequisite for full public dignity and citizenship, in the dominant American understanding of what citizenship means, as Judith Shklar recently reminded us in her *American Citizenship* (Cambridge: Harvard University Press, 1991). Because of this understanding, and because of the meager level of public assistance available in the American welfare state, millions of Americans at the bottom of our social order experience the *absence* of a stable job as their fundamental personal and economic problem. Those Americans dependent upon state agencies during months, years, or lifetimes spent out of the workforce are subject to forms of discipline, surveillance, and control beyond anything experienced in the workplace. Finally, to treat the experience of work in strictly negative terms is to ignore the complexity of the social and political currents unleashed by that experience. Our work lives give us a wide range of desires and expectations—and it is at least arguable that some of these push against the limits of the existing regime and fuel demands for transformation. None of this should be ignored, yet none of it should be used to dismiss the insidious control large corporations exert within and without their organizational hierarchies.

88. Here again it is fruitful to acknowledge the Tocquevillian resonances in Foucault's thought. Foucault can sharpen this line of analysis with his account of the

way in which the economic techniques that enabled capital accumulation paralleled and helped produce a "political take-off," an intensification and increasing sophistication of tutelary powers through the modern elaboration of the techniques of discipline. Discipline, in Foucault's terms, "is the unitary technique by which the body is reduced as a 'political' force and maximized as a useful force." *Discipline and Punish* (New York: Vintage, 1979), p. 221. Foucault's analyses of discipline enable considerable refinement in the charting of these refashionings of bodies; Tocqueville's analyses of democratic action enables a considerably more substantive account of the forms of power that differ from, and can work as counters to, tutelary techniques and regimes.

89. Connolly, *Identity\Difference*, p. 24. Connolly's reflections on globalism have helped me to frame the problem *Democracy* puts to contemporary readers, as the subsequent paragraphs indicate.

90. Michael Sorkin, ed., *Variations on a Theme Park: The New American City and the End of Public Space* (New York: Hill and Wang, 1992), p. xiii. For a more elaborate development of this kind of claim, see Paul Virilio, *The Lost Dimension* (New York: Semiotext(e), 1991). I take up globalizing forces and their spatial transformations in more depth in "Republican Virtuality," a paper presented at the annual meeting of the American Political Science Association, 1993.

91. That desire is by no means limited to nostalgic theorists. It circulates through the polity at large, animating political movements and governments, underwriting programs and policies. Wolin is instructive on this point: he closes his genealogy of late-modernity by asserting that localism is the "state-sponsored Potemkin village" of our time (*Presence of the Past*, p. 179), an assertion that condenses his account of the political logic of Reaganism. As Wolin understands, Reaganism used the state both to advance the interests of international capital and to impose various disciplines on (racially, economically, culturally) marginal sectors of the population—and often justified this corporate-disciplinary enterprise through rhetorical appeals to "local control," to an evocation of the virtues of an earlier America. But if local*ism* has often functioned as a kind of duplicitous demonstration-project in public rhetoric and policy, the Tocquevillian local*ity*, the self-governing New England town, has become more like a theme park. I live in a small Massachusetts town that still conducts much of its political business in town meetings. It is no accident that the two main engines driving our local economy are a wealthy residential liberal arts college and tourism. As I write these words, our streets are clogged with out-of-state visitors here to admire the fall foliage and our village setting. Like the leaves and the church steeples, local self-government is just one more piece of the distinctive New England charm—and thus the town's commercial appeal. Self-government in our "Village Beautiful" (the official slogan of local boosterism) occurs under the sign of Disney, not Potemkin.

3. (Con)Founding Democracy: Containment, Evasion, Appropriation

1. Many writers have made this point. My summary of Tocqueville's omissions borrows particularly heavily from Sean Wilentz, "Many Democracies: On Tocque-

ville and Jacksonian America," in *Reconsidering Tocqueville's "Democracy in America,"* ed. Abraham S. Eisenstadt (New Brunswick: Rutgers University Press, 1988), pp. 207–228, which develops an account that is as astute as it is concise.

2. William Connolly, "Tocqueville, Territory, and Violence," *Theory, Culture, and Society* 11 (1994): 19–41; Stephen Schneck, "Habits of the Head: Tocqueville's America and Jazz," *Political Theory* 17, no. 4 (1989): 638–662, and "New Readings of Tocqueville's *America*: Lessons for Democracy," *Polity* 25, no. 2 (1992): 283–298. These works explore many of the themes pursued below, and my own reading—in both its agreements and disagreements—has been fundamentally affected by them. Connolly's arguments about the extermination of the Indian and the construction of the "civi-territorial complex" have, in particular, pushed this chapter into its current shape.

3. Schneck, "Habits of the Head," p. 644.

4. The major studies of Tocqueville tend not to connect the problems in *Democracy*'s analysis of slavery to his way of conceptualizing democracy. Indeed most of these works scarcely acknowledge the problems or even discuss the book's analysis of slavery at length. Race and slavery receive no serious analysis in, for instance, Roger Boesche, *The Strange Liberalism of Alexis de Tocqueville* (Ithaca: Cornell University Press, 1987); Jean-Claude Lamberti, *Tocqueville and the Two Democracies* (Cambridge: Harvard University Press, 1989); Jack Lively, *The Social and Political Thought of Alexis de Tocqueville* (Oxford: Clarendon Press, 1962); and Marvin Zetterbaum, *Tocqueville and the Problem of Democracy* (Stanford: Stanford University Press, 1967).

5. "The conduct of the United States Americans toward the natives was inspired by the most chaste affection for legal formalities. . . . The Spaniards, by unparalleled atrocities which brand them with indelible shame, did not succeed in exterminating the Indian race and could not even prevent them from sharing their rights; the United States Americans have attained both these results with wonderful ease, quietly, legally, and philanthropically, without spilling blood and without violating a single one of the great principles of morality in the eyes of the world. It is impossible to destroy men with more respect to the laws of humanity." *Democracy*, p. 339.

6. Ibid., pp. 361–362.

7. Ibid., p. 375.

8. Ibid., p. 342.

9. Ibid., p. 343.

10. Ibid., p. 355.

11. Ibid., p. 342.

12. Ibid., p. 359.

13. Ibid., p. 358.

14. Andrew Hacker closes *Two Nations: Black and White, Separate, Hostile, Unequal* (New York: Scribners, 1992) by celebrating the continuing power and relevance of Tocqueville's analysis and providing substantial excerpts from the "Three Races" chapter. These excerpted passages, Hacker suggests, "might have been written today" (p. 214). I think this comment is more double-edged than Hacker intends, for the most familiar and contemporary moments of Tocqueville's analysis are those where he avoids the political implications or consequences of his reporting.

15. *Democracy*, pp. 360, 363.

16. Connolly notes a parallel problem in Tocqueville's account of the extermination of the indigenous population, arguing that *Democracy* employs a "slippery
language of regret without moral indictment" and offers "recognition of undeserved
suffering without a plan to curtail it in the future" ("Tocqueville, Territory, and
Violence," p. 27). My thinking about Tocqueville's response to slavery has benefited
from this observation, though I think that the problem is less a refusal to indict injustice than a paralysis and duplicity induced by his simultaneously being moved to
name injustice and required to thwart the conclusions such a naming ought to provoke. Tocqueville's language *is* moralized, but his analysis is evasively depoliticizing
nonetheless.

17. We learn nothing from *Democracy* of those Americans, black or white, who
are fighting slavery—although, for instance, Nat Turner's rebellion, trial, and execution occurred during Tocqueville's and Beaumont's travels. Beaumont, of course,
made much use of these conversations in his novel about American racial struggle,
Marie; without the burden of accounting for the successful workings of democratic
politics, Beaumont was able to discuss much that Tocqueville kept out of his study.
What makes this all the more notable is that Tocqueville played a role in the abolition of slavery in the French colonies, writing two public reports that both argued for
abolition on principled grounds and considered the mechanisms of emancipation.
These reports show that his personal objections to slavery could underwrite a politics of abolition in a very different context. It is the context of American slavery—
especially the magnitude of the cleavage between free and slave states, and proslavery
and antislavery forces—that, in conjunction with the textual strategies inherent in
the project of *Democracy*, rendered Tocqueville incapable of presenting that politics. Only *both* pressures together account for the text's evasions, for Tocqueville was
able to remark privately to Beaumont that the evils that would follow emancipation
should be viewed as a necessary price for eliminating slavery once and for all. These
remarks are discussed in Boesche, *Strange Liberalism*, p. 121. Tocqueville's public proposals for abolition are available in English as "Report on Abolition," and "On the
Emancipation of Slaves" in *Tocqueville and Beaumont on Social Reform*, ed. and trans.
Seymour Drescher (New York: Harper and Row, 1968), pp. 98–173.

18. Smith argued that the "only stain" upon Tocqueville's "great work" was that
the book simply repeated Jefferson's arguments about the differences between black
and white and the barrier these differences pose to the emancipation and democratic enfranchisement of black people: *Democracy* "gives Mr. Jefferson's views as if
they were de Tocqueville's views . . . thus not only committing unpardonable pla-
giarism, but also adding the apparently independent and calm opinion of a foreign
observer in favor of the perpetuation of American slavery." James McCune Smith,
"On the Fourteenth Query of Thomas Jefferson's *Notes on Virginia*," in *The Voice of
Black America: Major Speeches by Negroes in the United States, 1797–1971*, ed. Philip S.
Foner (New York: Simon and Schuster, 1972), p. 217.

19. For examples of these characterizations see, respectively, *Democracy*, pp. 342,
317, 318, and 363.

20. Schneck, "Habits of the Head," p. 647.

21. Ibid.

22. The term "science" perhaps suggests more systematicity and settled conviction than are demonstrated by Tocqueville's rhetorical distancing and complex ambivalence (after all, whatever his own prejudices, the depth of American prejudice appalls him). It is also worth noting that Tocqueville emerged later as a critic of nascent European scientific racism. Examples of that criticism can be found in translation in *The European Revolution and Correspondence with Gobineau*, trans. and ed. John Lukacs (Gloucester, Mass.: Peter Smith, 1968); see, e.g., pp. 221-232, 290-295, 303-308. James Schleiffer argues that Tocqueville's quarrel with doctrines of racial destiny dates back to the period of his writing of *Democracy*. Schleiffer notes that drafts of Volume Two had several passages critical of racialist ideologies, including the following remarks: "Idea of races. I do not believe that there are races destined to freedom and others to servitude; the ones to happiness and enlightenment, the others to misfortunes and ignorance. These are cowardly doctrines." James T. Schleiffer, *The Making of Tocqueville's "Democracy in America"* (Chapel Hill: University of North Carolina Press, 1980), p. 68. But, as Schleiffer also points out, the remarks did not make it into the final version. Even had they done so, they would not have unwritten Volume One's already published "Three Races" chapter. Nor does anything in Schleiffer's discussion work to reduce the rhetorical problem that the cultural diversity and violent tensions of America posed to Tocqueville. And if one *were* to use information about Tocqueville's own political career to guide one's appropriation of *Democracy*—an approach counter to my enterprise in this book— one would have to confront the sordid spectacle of his dealings with Algeria.

23. *Democracy*, p. 316.

24. Wilentz, "Many Democracies," p. 222.

25. For outstanding treatments of the uses of race in the construction of white American identity, see Rogin, *Ronald Reagan the Movie, and Other Episodes in Political Demonology* (Berkeley: University of California Press, 1987); Morrison, *Playing in the Dark: Whiteness and the Literary Imagination* (Cambridge: Harvard University Press, 1992); and the essays collected in Frederick Dolan and Thomas Dumm, eds., *Rhetorical Republic: Governing Representations in American Politics* (Amherst: University of Massachusetts Press, 1993). On the role of slavery and racism in shaping the meaning of American citizenship, in particular, see Kenneth L. Karst, *Belonging to America: Equal Citizenship and the Constitution* (New Haven: Yale University Press, 1989), particularly chap. 8, and Shklar, *American Citizenship* (Cambridge: Harvard University Press, 1991), pp. 47-57, 92-99, and passim.

26. This is the point missed by Rogers Smith in his influential "Beyond Tocqueville, Myrdal, Hartz: The Multiple Traditions in America," *American Political Science Review* 87, no. 3 (1993): 549-566. Smith argues, persuasively, that the popular acceptance of ascriptive hierarchies is less an exceptional lapse than an enduring and powerful tradition in American political culture, and that the "Tocquevillian thesis" elaborated by American exceptionalists has failed to recognize this tradition and, consequently, has persistently slighted the importance of inequalities of race, gender, and ethnicity. Smith finds *Democracy* more attentive to the role of inequalities than were Tocqueville's followers, but he, too, faults Tocqueville for treating race as a "tangent" (pp. 552-553). Yet Smith never offers a serious account of *why* the

topic was segregated from the rest of *Democracy*. The importance of having such an account is revealed by the political consequences of his failure to develop one, for Smith misses the connections between conceptions of democracy and forms of subordination. When he shows that the Tocquevillian thesis overemphasizes the liberal and democratic features of American history and culture by neglecting the "ascriptive Americanist elements," he concludes that he has thereby absolved liberal democracy of the charge of complicity with these ascriptions; for Smith, the liberal democratic and the ascriptive are simply two of America's separable "multiple traditions" (p. 558). Claiming that no one has ever demonstrated a structural intellectual link between American liberal democracy and American cultural hegemonies, he summarily dismisses "postmodernist" work that traces the patterns of their mutual imbrication (pp. 556–557). In the name of moving beyond Tocqueville and coming to terms with the diverse and sometimes oppressive traditions shaping American history, Smith thus blunts the critical edge of recent radical scholarship on cultural power in liberal democratic societies. Acceptance of his argument would allow for a more critical historiography of American ethnicity than was offered by the exceptionalist paradigm, but it would still block critical inquiry into American democracy. The irony is that the central touchstone of Smith's argument, *Democracy in America*, demonstrates the very connections he would deny: as I have been arguing, Tocqueville's approach to matters of race and (as we will see) gender is shaped by the pressures *intrinsic to* his conceptualization of democracy. Smith could not acknowledge such constitutive relationships without rethinking his historiographical narrative and, hence, confronting political questions he would rather avoid.

27. "Everything which has a bearing on the status of women, their habits, and their thoughts is, in my view, of great political importance" (*Democracy*, p. 590).

28. Ibid., p. 591.

29. Ibid., p. 592.

30. Ibid., p. 601.

31. Ibid., p. 603.

32. Mary Ryan has documented the ways in which early and mid-nineteenth-century women created a rich political culture amidst an institutionally dense network of alternative public spaces. These spaces cannot be found in Tocqueville's America. See her "Gender and Public Access: Women's Politics in Nineteenth-Century America," in *Habermas and the Public Sphere*, ed. Craig Calhoun (Cambridge: MIT Press, 1992), pp. 259–288. Both Sean Wilentz and Nancy Cott note how the cult of domesticity that Tocqueville treats as monolithic and freely accepted was resisted by large numbers of women. Wilentz, "Many Democracies," p. 211; Cott, *The Bonds of Womanhood: "Woman's Sphere" in New England, 1780–1835* (New Haven: Yale University Press, 1977).

33. Delba Winthrop, "Tocqueville's American Woman and 'The True Conception of Democratic Progress,'" *Political Theory* 14, no. 2 (1986): 242. Winthrop overstates the case, for there are a number of references to differences of nature (men are more lustful, deserving of authority, etc.), and Tocqueville seems to take these differences seriously. But Winthrop's point remains useful because the rhetoric of natural difference does not play a decisive role in anchoring *Democracy*'s argument; that

Tocqueville underplays this rhetoric is indeed significant. I am indebted to her on this issue, even though I fundamentally reject her larger argument that Tocqueville's enthusiastic treatment of the American domesticity is part of a "devastating critique" of politics and public life in America and modernity ("American Woman," p. 240).

34. *Democracy*, p. 691.

35. Schneck discusses this point ably in his "New Readings," p. 293, although he sees Tocqueville's advocacy of women's moral role as part of a larger struggle against democracy, rather than as a discipline advanced in the name of democracy itself (a point to which I return below). Recognizing the constitutive role of women's labor of moral reproduction shows, again, the connection overlooked in Smith's account of the "Tocquevillian thesis."

36. Winthrop claims that, "in Tocqueville's presentation it seems to matter less which sex remains at home than that one sex does remain there." Though this claim could not be sustained for the whole of Tocqueville's work, which tends to present the politically active woman as a kind of terrible and dangerous absurdity (cf. *Recollections*, ed. J. P. Mayer and A. P. Kerr, trans. George Lawrence [Garden City, N.Y.: Doubleday, 1971], p. 137), it makes basic sense of the structure of *Democracy*'s arguments: the key thing, in the analysis of America, is simply that there be some kind of public/private split in the division of labor in order to provide the moral education democracy requires. For Winthrop, however, the Tocquevillian imperative for the gendered division of labor is the need to assure that at least some members of a democracy will be insulated from the banality and mediocrity of democratic politics. Her Tocqueville is primarily concerned with pointing out that democracy fails to improve people or to fulfill their deeper needs. Again, this misses the crucial point.

37. *Democracy*, pp. 291–292.

38. Ibid., p. 291.

39. Ibid., p. 603.

40. From the vast and edifying feminist literature on this topic, see, for instance Carole Pateman, *The Disorder of Women: Democracy, Feminism, and Political Theory* (Stanford: Stanford University Press, 1989), and Linda Zerilli, *Signifying Woman: Culture and Chaos in Rousseau, Burke, and Mill* (Ithaca: Cornell University Press, 1994).

41. *Democracy*, p. 62. See also his claim that, "in the United States, society had no infancy, being born adult," p. 303.

42. Ibid., p. 31.

43. Sanford Kessler is among the few Tocqueville scholars to pay sustained attention to *Democracy*'s emphasis on the Puritans' role as America's founders. Kessler does not, however, connect this emphasis on religious founding with any of the problems of homogenization, masking, or violence I am tracing here. Indeed he seems not to think these problems afflict Tocqueville's America. Though the analysis of Puritanism is much briefer than Kessler's, Connolly's emphasis on religion's role in the "civi-territorial complex" cuts much deeper into these problems. See Kessler, "Tocqueville's Puritans: Christianity and the American Founding," *Journal of Politics* 54, no. 3 (1992): 776–792, and Connolly, "Tocqueville, Territory, and Violence."

44. *Democracy*, p. 47.

45. Ibid., p. 291.

46. Ibid., p. 47.

47. Ibid.

48. Ibid., p. 292.

49. Ibid., p. 290. It is not that Tocqueville thinks that there are no interesting differences within Christianity. He suggests, for instance, that citizens of democracies who retain their faith will ultimately turn to Catholicism, and that this is beginning to happen in the United States. But this argument occupies a different level of his analysis; it does not fundamentally affect either his sense of the practical political ecumenicism of Christianity in America or his account of why untroubled foundations are necessary to democracy.

50. Ibid.

51. Ibid., p. 290.

52. Ibid., p. 291.

53. Ibid., p. 435; see also, e.g., p. 643.

54. Ibid., p. 434.

55. Ibid., p. 444.

56. Ibid.

57. James Davison Hunter's *Culture Wars: The Struggle to Define America* (New York: Basic Books, 1992) is a recent exemplification of this point: Hunter smuggles a Tocquevillian and essentially theological argument for homogeneity into an analysis that ostensibly accepts the inevitability of moral and cultural pluralism.

58. Lefort, *Democracy and Political Theory*, p. 179. Lefort seems to find inexplicable Tocqueville's refusal fully to come to terms with this adventure in uncertainty. I have offered the beginnings of an explanation already; I extend and refine the account below.

59. Connolly, "Tocqueville, Territory," p. 8. The quote here comes from a discussion of Rousseau, but characterizes Connolly's Tocqueville as well. See, e.g., ibid., pp. 24–25.

60. *Democracy*, p. 12.

61. Connolly, "Tocqueville, Territory," p. 24.

62. Ibid., p. 8. Once more, I cite a discussion of Rousseau that applies, quite straightforwardly, to Connolly's Tocqueville as well.

63. For instance, Stephen Schneck's Tocqueville is haunted by the "ambiguity of a politics without essences or ends, conducted in a forum of undirected popular desire," opposing such a politics not for the consequences it might have, but as, itself, the worst of all possible consequences ("Habits of the Head," p. 652). Schneck sees *Democracy*'s sympathetic discussions of democracy as part of a complex "ruse," an attempt to give a democratic appearance to what was, in fact, a work designed to preserve "aristocratic rule" ("New Readings," p. 295). Tocqueville, on this account, construed his book as a way of giving "the choicer spirits a technology for subduing and controlling the lifeworld," thereby keeping democracy at bay. Through the elite control of mores and cultural institutions, popular sovereignty is deliberately—but subtly, almost invisibly—thwarted. Although Schneck's bracing reading succeeds admirably in making the policy of containment central to *Democracy*, I think he also

errs in treating the text as too controlled and coherent an expression of Tocqueville's undivided will. If this book is a tool for elite control, it is not nearly efficient enough to accomplish the task Schneck assigns to it: *Democracy* is too complex and inconsistent for that. (*Democracy*'s escape from unitary intention and interpretation is the main reason that I have not used Tocqueville's own frankly counterrevolutionary political career, and the recounting of it offered in his *Souvenirs*, to guide my reading here.) The more important problem with Schneck's reading, however, is that, by taking the form of a conspiracy theory, his strongest criticisms work to obscure still more troubling possibilities. If the key instance of containment comes when Tocqueville slyly shows specific individuals how to seize control of crucial cultural institutions and technologies, then *Democracy*'s fundamental problem is one of political allegiance rather than political imagination. If, instead, containment structures even Tocqueville's genuinely sympathetic imagination of democracy, then—though he becomes a more personally appealing figure to democrats—it is more difficult to appropriate his thought for radical purposes.

64. Connolly, "Tocqueville, Territory," p. 27.

65. The key alternatives drawn on in Connolly's essay are Thoreau, Nietzsche, and Deleuze/Guattari.

66. As Connolly knows: he explicitly argues that there is no opportunity simply to escape the problem of sovereignty.

67. "Will" is not a term to which Tocqueville resorts with great frequency and is not a central category of *Democracy*'s analyses (a comparison with, say, *The Social Contract* is instructive on this point). When the quest for unity is linked to the category of will, there is very little room for difference; the comparatively minor role of will in Tocqueville's thought is one reason there is play in his work, room to push his thoughts toward other contexts and conclusions.

68. *Democracy*, p. 244. It is this interest in democracy as the source and result of restless social energy that makes Tocqueville's work more susceptible to redeployment than Connolly's critique suggests.

69. As Tocqueville wrote in an appendix to *Democracy*, "To force all men to march in step toward the same goal—that is a human idea. To encourage endless variety of actions but to bring them about so that in a thousand different ways all tend toward the fulfillment of one great design—that is a God-given design" (p. 735). In general, Tocqueville's care for difference is expressed more powerfully in his indictments of homogenization, especially the accounts of the tyranny of the majority and tutelary power, than in his affirmative statements. The best account of Tocqueville's care for difference is provided in Sheldon Wolin, *The Presence of the Past* (Baltimore: Johns Hopkins University Press, 1989), chap. 4.

70. Although this is a theme I have sounded repeatedly, the following remark is useful as a direct reminder: "Thus in the immense complication of human laws it sometimes comes about that extreme freedom corrects the abuse of freedom and extreme democracy forestalls the dangers of democracy" (*Democracy*, p. 195).

71. *Democracy*'s most explicit discussion of struggle is the comparison between the European and American approaches to association. In divided Europe, associations practice a kind of political warfare, promoting intolerance and tyranny both

202 Notes to Pages 85–86

within and without the organization. American associations leave far more room for independence and difference. Tocqueville summarizes the lesson of this contrast with these words: "So the exercise of the right of association becomes dangerous when great parties see no possibility of becoming the majority. In a country like the United States, where differences of view are only matters of nuance, the right of association can remain, so to say, without limits" (*Democracy*, p. 194). The connection with tutelary power comes out in the closing chapters of Volume Two, which are more about European dangers than American ones. There, Tocqueville links the new despotism to the sensibilities and social restructuring born of the French Revolution and, especially, to the abolition of intermediary powers (see, e.g., p. 688). But, though the argument I am characterizing here shapes *Democracy* profoundly, it is elaborated much more precisely and explicitly in his *L'ancien Régime*. Tocqueville's critique of the Revolution turns on his account of it as a disastrously homogenizing movement that intensified despotism through its attempts to smash social hierarchy. If anything, Tocqueville's valorization of difference is stronger in that later work and, as I noted in Chapter 2, the account of tutelary power is particularly rich as well. Because my focus here is on appropriating *Democracy*, I have resisted the temptation to draw more on Tocqueville's study of France, but it is worth noting that much of the anxiety specific to the later text came from his growing conviction that the modern destiny was not a naturally egalitarian democracy of the type invoked at the opening of *Democracy*, but revolutionary struggle against entrenched inequality. For further accounts of Tocqueville's analysis of the problem of difference and its relationship to revolution, and the relevance of this analysis to *Democracy*, see Wolin, *Presence*, especially pp. 67–68, and also pp. 97–131 of my dissertation, "The Art of Being Free: An Essay on the Theory and Practice of Public Liberty" (University of California, Santa Cruz, 1991).

72. For a brilliant essay on this problem of foreclosure that enriches and would be enriched by Tocqueville's work, see Judith Butler, "Arguing with the Real," in *Bodies That Matter*, ed. Butler (New York: Routledge, 1993), pp. 187–222.

73. Despite its insight and power, Sheldon Wolin's recent work shows the costs of failing to undertake this transposition: in his reading of our America through the lens provided by *Democracy*, he repeats some of Tocqueville's own policies of containment. Constructing Tocqueville's politics as a search for feudal remnants that can restrain the modern assault on difference, Wolin reads democracy today as an anachronistic holdover that is out of place in postmodern culture. Like his Tocqueville, then, albeit with a less ambivalent relationship to democracy, Wolin presents a politics centered on the self-conscious pursuit of archaism. Because Wolin constructs democracy as archaic, he aligns it with various fundamentalisms, suggesting that there is a deep historical and temperamental affinity between certain homogeneous and anti-cosmopolitan cultures and the democratic tradition in America, and arguing that those fostering the revival of democracy must therefore be willing to accept the growing power of such essentially reactionary movements against modernity (see *Presence*, pp. 74, 79). As in Tocqueville's work, then, a deep care for difference underwrites complacency in the face of certain forms of subjugation—precisely because Wolin does not transpose Tocquevillian democracy from one reg-

ister to the other. A notion of democracy this tolerant of such subjugations is one that has not sufficiently radicalized the problem of democratic (b)orders.

74. The relationship of the Bosnian carnage to the homogenizing policies of postwar Yugoslavia are an instructive example.

4. Reading Freedom, Writing Marx: From the Politics of Production to the Production of Politics

1. See Frank E. Manuel, "A Requiem for Karl Marx," *Daedalus* 121, no. 2 (1992): 1–20. Since my writing of this chapter, several ex-Soviet bloc states have witnessed the electoral triumphs of former communists and reconstructed communist parties. I do not think, however, that this amounts to anything like a revival of "Marxism."

2. By noting that post-Marxism is understood by both its advocates and its orthodox critics as a move away from Marx himself, and by observing that the cultural tendencies and incentive structures of contemporary academic life suggest that there will probably soon be movement still further away, I am *not* seeking to question the power or relevance of post-Marxist analysis. Indeed, the germinal post-Marxist work of Ernesto Laclau and Chantal Mouffe and (though he might resist this classification) Stuart Hall informs many of the arguments of this book.

3. Throughout this chapter, I shall refer to the author of the works I am discussing as "Marx," even though a number of "Marxist" doctrines and texts are the work of Friedrich Engels or of a Marx-Engels collaboration. I use this convenient shorthand largely because Marx was the sole author of two of the three texts that will stand at the center of my analysis. I will simply sidestep the ongoing quarrel over Engels' true role in the elaboration of Marxist theory: for my purposes, it seems unnecessary to enter this (ultimately rather theological) debate.

4. Among the works that reveal the republican roots of the young Marx's political thinking, the following are particularly helpful: Shlomo Avineri, *The Social and Political Thought of Karl Marx* (New York: Cambridge University Press, 1968); Alan Gilbert, *Marx's Politics: Communists and Citizens* (New Brunswick, N.J.: Rutgers University Press, 1981); Horst Mewes, "On the Concept of Politics in the Early Thought of Karl Marx," *Social Research* 43 (1976): 276–294; Nancy Schwartz, "Distinction between Public and Private Life: Marx on the *zoon politikon*," *Political Theory* 7, no. 2 (1979): 245–266. Although all of these sources give some account of Marx's effort to transform or transcend his early influences, the severity and seriousness of his critique of republicanism are brought out with particular clarity in Jeffrey Isaac, "The Lion's Skin of Politics: Marx on Republicanism," *Polity* 22, no. 3 (1990): 461–488, and Robert Meister, *Political Identity: Thinking Through Marx* (Cambridge, Eng.: Basil Blackwell, 1991). I take up the issue in considerably more depth below, but I wish to note from the outset that, though I depart from its readings and politics in many fundamental ways, I have found Meister's text to be an invaluable source to think with and against in elaborating my argument.

5. The main works here are: "A Contribution to the Critique of Hegel's Phi-

losophy of Right: Introduction"; *The Critique of Hegel's "Philosophy of Right"; Economic and Philosophical Manuscripts;* and "On the Jewish Question."

6. One might date these insights from *The German Ideology.*

7. All of the previous citations come from the *Manifesto.* See Robert C. Tucker, ed., *The Marx-Engels Reader,* 2d ed. (New York: Norton, 1978), pp. 476, 477, 500, 491. All subsequent citations to the *Manifesto* are to this version of the text.

8. The growing complexity of Marx's understanding of global economic power can be seen by comparing the vivid but brief and simple descriptions of the *Manifesto* to the massive cartography worked out in *Capital.* On Marx's own activist career and his internationalist commitments, Gilbert's treatment in *Marx's Politics* is particularly helpful (though the theoretical conclusions Gilbert draws on the basis of that practical record are often ones I would contest).

9. For a commentary with a lucid and especially illuminating exploration of this theme, see William James Booth, "Gone Fishing: Making Sense of Marx's Concept of Communism," *Political Theory* 17, no. 2 (1989): 205–222. Also helpful is his "The New Household Economy," *American Political Science Review* 85, no. 1 (1991): 59–74. Another striking, and rather different, reading of the role of unfettered individual development in Marx's thinking is elaborated in Marshall Berman's *All That Is Solid Melts into Air: The Experience of Modernity* (New York: Penguin, 1988).

10. In *Marx-Engels Reader,* p. 197.

11. This case is argued most assertively—though ineffectually—by Philip J. Kain in his "Marx and Pluralism," *Praxis International* 11, no. 4 (1992): 465–486. A more balanced and successful assessment that still emphasizes Marx's concern for difference is provided by Booth in "Gone Fishing." And a rather different, and quite powerful, case for the complexity and relevance of Marx's conception of difference is developed by Peter Stallybrass in "Marx and Heterogeneity: Thinking the Lumpenproletariat," *Representations* 31 (1991): 69–95.

12. Louis Althusser's arguments for an "epistemological break" in the 1840s provide a particularly—but not singularly—strong example of this claim. See Althusser, *For Marx* (London: Verso, 1979).

13. For examples of these constructions of the Marxist enterprise see, respectively: Bertell Ollman, *Alienation: Marx's Conception of Man in Capitalist Society* (New York: Cambridge University Press, 1986); Althusser, *For Marx;* John Elster, *Making Sense of Marx* (London: Cambridge University Press, 1985); and Gerald A. Cohen, *Karl Marx's Theory of History: A Defence* (Princeton: Princeton University Press, 1978).

14. This body of work suggests the need to qualify my rhetorically useful but overly broad earlier remarks on the contemporary state of Marxist studies: though the last few years *have* seen an epochal political turning away from Marxism, and a displacement of the Marxist problematic to the margins of radical academic analysis, there remain not only scholarly subdisciplines committed to Marx's insights but also the immense body of academic Marxology that has been generated over the past few decades.

15. "Transparency" has become a significant term in the critical vocabulary of political theorists influenced by post-structuralism's critique of the humanist subject.

In this critical work, many of the most problematic features of masculinist, colonial-
ist, and otherwise falsely (and hence oppressively) "universalist" publics or polities
have been linked to the fiction of a self that is purged of all internal opacity and that
is thus capable of being fully present to and available for others. Iris Young pursues
this theme at length in her *Justice and the Politics of Difference* (Princeton: Princeton
University Press, 1990). The ideal of transparency has been identified as an acute
problem within Marxist thought: see William Connolly, *Political Theory and Modernity* (London: Basil Blackwell, 1989) p. 129, Ernesto Laclau and Chantal Mouffe,
Hegemony and Socialist Strategy (London: Verso, 1985), p. 191, and Dominick La-
Capra, *Rethinking Intellectual History: Texts, Contexts, Language* (Ithaca: Cornell University Press, 1983). It is worth noting that Marx himself sometimes uses the language
of transparency to describe socialism's demystification of the processes of production and distribution. In a witty discussion in the first volume of *Capital*, for example,
he characterizes post-capitalist production as potentially transparent in just the way
that the labor of Robinson Crusoe (that stock figure from bourgeois political economy) is transparent. Just as Robinson knows what he has made and how he has made
it, so too will a free association of workers who hold the means of production in common. In such a group, "the social relations of the individual producers, both toward
their labor and the products of their labor are here *transparent* in their simplicity"
(emphasis added). Though Marx no doubt overstates the case for the achievements
of his collection of Crusoes, there is something appealing in the ideal of making the
structures and processes of labor more visible and legible to all participants. But, as
we will see, Marx often pushes this ideal of transparency much further, setting no
limits to the reach of interpersonal understanding and assuming that, with the abolition of structural exploitation, the work of understanding would be innocent of
power. In such moments, Marx has perhaps broken with Rousseau far less than he
thinks. For the specific discussion of transparency in production, see *Capital* (New
York: Vintage, 1977), pp. 171-172.

16. Consider, as an example of this messianic vision, a proclamation from the
Economic and Philosophical Manuscripts: "communism . . . is the genuine resolution
of the conflict between man and nature and between man and man—the true resolution of strife between existence and essence, between objectification and self-
confirmation, between freedom and necessity, between individual and the species.
Communism is the riddle of history solved, and it knows itself to be this solution"
(*Marx-Engels Reader,* p. 84). Remarks such as these show both the ambition of the
drive toward transcendence and also its essential link to the ideal of transparency. (A
particularly astringent treatment of Marx's messianic impulses is offered by Meister's *Political Identity*, especially chap. 5.)

17. The *locus classicus* of this vision is probably Engels' popular pamphlet, *Socialism: Utopian and Scientific.* See *Marx-Engels Reader,* p. 689. Among the most acute
critics of this Marxist impulse is Hannah Arendt. I have also found Mewes's discussions of Marx's attitudes toward politics particularly helpful. See "On the Concept
of Politics."

18. I am grateful to Tom Dumm for helping me find this way of characterizing
what (my) Marx is doing.

19. I take this terminology, and hence the subtitle of my chapter, from Stuart Hall's brilliant and (more or less) post-Marxist appreciation of Gramsci. Hall writes: "Where Gramsci departs from classical versions of Marxism is that he does not think that politics is an arena which simply reflects already unified collective political identities, already constituted forms of political struggle. Politics for him is not a dependent sphere. It is where forces and relations, in the economy, in society, in culture, have to be actively worked on to produce particular forms of power, particular forms of domination. This is the production of politics—politics as a production" (Hall, *The Hard Road to Renewal: Thatcherism and the Crisis of the Left* [London: Verso, 1988], p. 169).

20. Isaac's account is particularly helpful here. See "Lion's Skin," p. 473.

21. Of course this "all" is restricted: Marx is writing at a time when no polity had universal suffrage. Yet he seems not so much to be overlooking existing exclusions as to be suggesting that universal suffrage is the ultimate destination of the project of political emancipation. He is willing to grant that this time will come in order to explore the limits that would mark a society in which all can claim formal political rights. See "On the Jewish Question," p. 16. Here and in all subsequent citations, I use *Karl Marx: Early Writings*, ed. Quintin Hoare (New York: Vintage, 1975).

22. Ibid., p. 220.

23. Ibid., pp. 220, 231.

24. Ibid., pp. 220–221.

25. Ibid., p. 230.

26. Ibid., p. 229.

27. Ibid., p. 222.

28. Actually, this ends the first of the essay's two sections, but I believe that the passage brings Marx's central analysis of emancipation to its conclusion. The much briefer second section, which I have drawn on only in passing, adds a discussion of the alienation represented and produced by money (it also adds a blatant form of anti-Semitism, as I shall discuss below); but it is far less of an intellectual achievement.

29. "Jewish Question," p. 231, emphasis added. Throughout the "Jewish Question," Marx heaps sarcasm on the bourgeois state's claim to be a locus of political community. Of course, one cannot always take his moral language at face value, for one of his favorite rhetorical devices is to feign commitment to bourgeois principles in order to express wounded outrage at the way these principles are routinely and necessarily violated by bourgeois practice (this figure is used to particular effect in the *Manifesto*). But it is clear that in the "Jewish Question," Marx does not invoke the *ideal* of political community in bad faith. The outrage over the degradation of politics is not tactical: it expresses some of Marx's deepest yearnings and convictions.

30. In a letter written only a few months before the "Jewish Question," Marx expressed disdain for his contemporaries by noting that "a German Aristotle, who would derive his politics from our conditions, would start out by saying, 'Man is a social, but completely apolitical animal.'" Marx maintained that, in such conditions, it was essential to awaken the love of public freedom in the populace: "Only this feeling, which disappeared from the world with the Greeks and with Christianity vanished into the blue mist of heaven, can again transform society into a community

of men to achieve their highest purpose, a democratic state." See Loyd D. Easton and Kurt H. Guddat, eds., *Writings of the Young Marx on Philosophy and Society* (Garden City, N.Y.: Anchor, 1967), p. 206. By the time of the "Jewish Question," Marx was far less prone to identify the democratic state with the highest of human purposes, but this valorization of politics arguably remained at the core of his thinking. Both this quote and the case for reading Marx as continuing to adhere to a high estimation of politics are discussed in a useful way in Schwartz's "Public and Private Life," especially pp. 253–254. See also Mewes, "On the Concept of Politics."

31. Marx's argument about the material bases of certain illusions is most elaborately worked out in his claim that, like religion, the democratic state offers a "devious" emancipation, an imaginary resolution of actual social conflicts (see especially "Jewish Question," pp. 218–219). This argument, which is the core of his critique of Bauer's merely "theological" emancipation, is among the most provocative and significant features of "On the Jewish Question," and a crucial link between the essay and such vital works as the "Theses on Feuerbach." I underplay the argument in my account since it is something of a digression from my main purposes, not because I see it as without interest or as incidental to Marx's own intentions (and I return to the question of ideology and materialism, which is essentially what we are dealing with in these passages, in my discussion of *The Eighteenth Brumaire*). For fuller discussions of this dimension of "On the Jewish Question," see Meister, *Political Identity*, and Isaac, "Lion's Skin," especially pp. 474–477.

32. "Jewish Question," p. 222.

33. Schwartz argues that Marx often uses the term "social" to express his radical conception of politics because that term was more malleable, less limited by historical uses and associations hostile to his project than was "politics" itself. "Public and Private," p. 248. I have found this argument helpful, though Schwartz's gleanings from the *Grundrisse* lead her to undervalue the powerful lure of transcendence in Marx's thought.

34. "Jewish Question," p. 217.

35. It is here that *The Civil War in France*—though a "late" text—renders the vision of "On the Jewish Question" more concrete. Marx finds, in the federated structure of small participatory organs of self-government envisioned by the Communards, "a thoroughly expansive political form, while all previous forms of government had been emphatically repressive." This form would have "restored to the social body all of the forces hitherto absorbed by the State parasite feeding upon, and clogging the free movement of, society." Marx, *The Civil War in France*, in *Writings on the Paris Commune*, ed. Hal Draper (New York: Monthly Review Press, 1971), p. 75. I do not discuss *The Civil War* at length in this chapter because, despite its substantial merits, it neither alters the typologies of freedom found in "On the Jewish Question," nor gives readers the openings for resistant rereading of the type provided by the more rhetorically virtuosic *Manifesto* and *Eighteenth Brumaire*.

36. I place "Rousseauian" in scare quotes here in order to sidestep the question of whether Rousseau—himself a complex, canny, and highly ambivalent thinker—genuinely imagines the establishment of a politics without difference or dissonance. At the very least, however, there is a Jacobin current of political thought, informed by

the reading of Rousseau, that pursues these imaginings. I am content to invoke this current, here. Marx's lifelong attempt to exorcise this spirit from the body of radical movements is treated brilliantly in Meister, *Political Identity*. From my point of view, however, what the book fails to note is that it is precisely when Marx thinks he is moving farthest from his conceptual inheritance, when he critiques democracy as such as inadequate, that he is most possessed by that "Rousseauian" ghost: Marx's rejections of democracy are linked to one or another of his versions of transcendence.

37. Among the vast literature that treats Marx's theories of alienation, readers might consult Avineri, *Social and Political Thought*, and Ollman, *Alienation*, for lucid and sympathetic presentations. I skim quickly and lightly over the elaborate and complex arguments of the *Manuscripts*, here, because this is not the place for an extensive or subtle account of the alienation problematic. It suffices for my purposes to sketch a few basic points in order to show how they inform this early argument for transcendence. "Inform" but no more than that—if it is true that, by *The German Ideology* or, at the latest, by his critique of political economy, Marx leaves the alienation problematic behind (and I am sympathetic to the advocates of the "mature" Marx who make this claim), then the ideal of transcendence is not *dependent* upon alienation because that ideal persists through his late writings as well.

38. In the first *Manuscript*, Marx writes, "Man is a species being, not only because in practice and in theory he adopts the species as his object . . . but also because he treats himself as the actual, living species; because he treats himself as a *universal* and therefore a free being" (*Marx-Engels Reader*, p. 75).

39. See "Jewish Question," pp. 229–230.

40. Of course, Marx nowhere retracts his claim that the creation of rights was a historically progressive step. He considers alienation itself to be progressive, in the sense that the reunion that follows it will be of a higher and freer kind than the primordial unity of prehistorical humanity. Marx follows Hegel in this sense of alienation as progressive, though the latter was not (at least not in *his* "mature" political thought) so ambitious in his hopes for ultimate reconciliation.

41. "Jewish Question," p. 221.

42. The former phrase is Schwartz's ("Public and Private," p. 256). The latter perception is argued for in Kain's "Marx and Pluralism."

43. Kain's effort to save Marx as an unproblematic pluralist unwittingly reveals the ways the pursuit of transcendence has warped the Marxist imagination. Kain argues that Marx is advocating an abolition of political power but a retention of social power, of "the power which binds a community together." This is a power that "gives rise to a social coherence such that individuals can interact and have access to the objectifications of others, to the richness of a complex culture, so that they can appropriate it, can develop their own powers and capacities, and can contribute to further developing the powers and capacities of others. Moreover . . . this development implies difference, diversity, and pluralism" ("Marx and Pluralism," pp. 480, 481). All of this, on Kain's account, is possible without a residue of domination and struggle; the pursuit of one ideal or self will do no violence to others and will not make it more difficult for other selves or ideals to be pursued. And, though politics will have been transcended, all social relations will be "democratic." This happy fantasy would be

plausible only in the same alternative universe in which the following peculiar claim of Kain's could be true: "Marx's concept of the party, we must also see, is compatible with his emphasis on difference, diversity, and pluralism. The communist party does not stand above, dominate, or impose a set of its own totalistic views on the proletariat." Kain's faith that he resides in this universe seems to rest on Marx's own proclamation that the communist party "has no interests separate and apart from those of the proletariat as a whole" ("Marx and Pluralism," p. 478). How radical pluralism is compatible with the notion that "the proletariat as a whole" can be the coherent and uniform subject of interest is necessarily left unexplained in his account.

44. The issue of religion—central to Marx's essay but more or less unmentioned in my account of it—further illuminates this impulse in Marx's thought. Though the second section of "On the Jewish Question" makes Judaism a figure for the evils of commercial society, the question of anti-Semitism is, as Dennis Fischman points out, usually considered irrelevant to the "serious" issues raised by Marx. See Fischman, "The Jewish Question about Marx," *Polity* 21, no. 4 (1989): 755–775. Perhaps nothing is lost if we gloss over the casual anti-Semitism of his polemical asides (such polemics do not often appear in his work, and Marx never condoned anti-Semitic political practices), but surely we should pay attention to such considered philosophical assertions as, "The emancipation of the Jews is, in the last analysis, the emancipation of all mankind from Judaism" ("Jewish Question," p. 237). This is *not* a call to attack Jews, but it *is* a revealing claim about the cultural consequences of Marx's proposed revolution in social relations. Marx cannot conceive of free Jews who are not "emancipated" from their Judaism, because he here seems unable to imagine that a life of freedom and equality could be pursued without treating all traditions as part of the structure of unfreedom: faith is a mystery to be explained by material problems, and the solution to those problems will bring the mystery to an end. This belief that all religion is merely a representation of our imaginary relationship to real conditions, the expression of our experiences in a divided and oppressive social order, is linked to the ideal of transcendence-transparency. Marx is sure that the abolition of exploitation will bring the end to many kinds of differences and obstacles to communion and communication, and he is therefore always in danger—despite his genuine commitment to the cultivation of individuality—of sliding over into the notion that difference and particularity *as such* must be overcome.

45. Shlomo Avineri, for example, can do no better than to inform us that Marx believes that "the dichotomy between state and civil society cannot be overcome by the politicization of civil society but only through a synthesis of particularism and universalism brought about by the recognition of the universality of the individual" (*Social and Political Thought*, p. 216). Well, yes. But does this reading bring concreteness or coherence to Marx's argument? ("Synthesize particularism and universalism" is hardly a slogan around which to rally those struggling for freedom.) Now Alan Gilbert reminds us that, despite his general philosophical lucidity, Avineri has a tendency to gloss over the practice-oriented, political dimensions of Marx's work. Might this be the problem here? I think not. Gilbert's own *Marx's Politics*, for all of its attention to Marx's tactical and strategic thinking about revolutionary activity, cannot give the reader any clearer sense of what human emancipation means here.

(See *Marx's Politics*, p. 164.) Nor do I know of an account of the overcoming of the state/society distinction and the abolition of politics that makes much more sense of this early work.

A defender of this dimension of Marx's thought could invoke the *Civil War in France*, since that essay replays essentially the same conceptual tensions. But if one were to examine that text in detail, one would run up against the same obstacles. Marx refers to the institutions of the Commune as "the political form at last discovered under which to work out the economic emancipation of labor. . . . a lever for uprooting the economical foundations on which rests the existence of classes" (*Civil War*, p. 76). All the tensions and ambiguities I have been discussing return in this phrasing. It can be taken as either as advocating a process of unending, dissonant politicization, or as making politics a tool that can be dispensed with once the foundations of oppression have been uprooted. On the latter reading, the institutions of the Commune would ultimately wither away—thus leaving us, once again, perplexed about what an emancipated social world looks like. It is no surprise, then, that *The Civil War in France* has been read, plausibly and with textual evidence, both as a celebration of socialist democratic politics and as an anti-political tract. For examples of these positions see, respectively, Julie Mostov, "Karl Marx as Democratic Theorist," *Polity* 22, no. 2 (1989): 206–207, and Mewes, "Politics in Marx," pp. 291–292.

46. For an anti-Marxist version of this claim, see Berlin's "Two Concepts of Liberty" in his *Four Essays on Liberty* (New York: Oxford University Press, 1969). For a critique from within Marxism, see Althusser's *For Marx*.

47. That is how Andrzej Walicki put it in a variation on Berlin's classic theme. See "Marx and Freedom," *New York Review of Books*, November 24, 1983, p. 502.

48. Consider, for instance, Richard Rorty's *Contingency, Irony, and Solidarity* (New York: Cambridge, 1989) which, though it mentions Marx only in passing, is centrally preoccupied with reversing his challenge to the liberal version of the public/private split.

49. Emancipate is rooted in the word "mancipate," an archaic term which meant to sell or transfer a slave. See Eric Partridge, *Origins: A Short Etymological Dictionary of Modern English* (New York: Greenwich House, 1983). It is true that Marx is not responsible for bringing the term to the context in question, for he takes up a contested slogan from a conflict underway at the time he was writing: as Fischman indicates, "emancipation" was the term selected by Jewish activists in order to indicate that they deserved equal rights within the German state ("Jewish Question about Marx," p. 770). But this example just further highlights the limitations of the term that—after all—Marx chose to apply to his own ultimate vision: what the Jewish activists were suggesting was that they should be released from their formally established, second-class status; once released, they would be free and their political difficulties would be resolved. In proposing a shift from the vocabulary of political emancipation to that of human emancipation, Marx radically expands the objectives that must be pursued but retains the hope of an ultimate and perfect resolution.

50. Unlike the other works central to this chapter, the *Manifesto* was coauthored by Engels (and the translation used here is Engels' own); as a matter of convenience, however, I refer to the author as "Marx." Though this chapter deliberately ignores

the question of Engels' place in Marxist theory, it is worth briefly noting that the *Manifesto* was not only coauthored, but was the product of an unusually public process of composition. The pamphlet originated in a commission from the Communist League (in which Marx and Engels were dominant figures). The League originally requested a revolutionary "catechism," and a draft was written by two other members. Engels rewrote their draft and submitted his version to the League's first congress. The congress debated the draft for ten days. At this point, Marx and Engels were instructed to write the final draft, taking account of the League's discussions. Engels proposed to Marx that the catechism should be replaced by a manifesto, and Marx then wrote the document that has achieved such notoriety. (This account is taken from Gilbert, *Marx's Politics*, pp. 125–126). Though the precise details of authorship may not matter much in themselves, the fact that the text was a public summons to public, collective action—in short, a "manifesto"—matters a great deal, as we shall see.

51. *Manifesto*, p. 473.

52. Ibid., pp. 473–474. There is some reason to think that the comprehensive philosophy so-condensed is not always Marx's. Whether, say, the *Grundrisse's* arguments about ancient economic formations can be shoehorned into this philosophy is a debatable question. It is not, however, a debate that need detain us here. Interesting reflections on these matters can be found in Booth, "The New Household Economy"; Schwartz, "Public and Private"; and Cornelius Castoriadus, *Crossroads in the Labyrinth* (Cambridge: MIT Press, 1984), pp. 260–339.

53. *Manifesto*, p. 474.

54. Ibid., p. 476.

55. Ibid., p. 482.

56. This form of argument is hardly without precedent, of course. Christianity always had its own varieties of universal history. Global, secular, progressivist narratives have been with us since the Enlightenment, and their wild proliferation is one of the distinguishing marks of the nineteenth-century historiographical imagination (after all, Tocqueville had a grand narrative about the forward march of equality). And Marx's particular debt to Hegel's historiography—that creative transformation of both the Enlightenment narrative and Christian metaphysics—is so obvious, and so widely discussed, that I need not take up the subject here. But both the character and the political deployment of Marx's global theory mark it off from its predecessors. More worldly than its (overtly) theological predecessors, more forward-looking than Hegel, more elaborate in its predictive mapping of the mechanisms of changes to come than most Enlightenment stories, Marx's work is intended as a tool for concrete struggle and a break with present values in a way and to an extent that have few if any earlier parallels. The use of history here is certainly different from Tocqueville's.

57. These terms were worked out in less popular texts such as *The German Ideology* and thus precede the *Manifesto* by several years, but the *Manifesto* is the first of the texts considered here that uses them. Obviously, the map offered in *Capital* is considerably more detailed and comprehensive.

58. Though it would be a mistake to overemphasize the precision of the explanation offered by the *Manifesto*—the swift, almost manic, polemical narration does

not pause to give a careful account of how these crucial terms are being employed—it would also be a mistake to treat this imprecision as peculiar to Marx's popular texts. Marx did not use these terms in a consistent way over the years, and those looking for the security of a direct methodological statement on "historical materialism" from the author are reduced to scavenging such unsatisfying scraps as can be found in the preface to the *Critique of Political Economy* and the like. There is a vast body of literature debating the precise meaning of this terminology and the broader structure of Marx's explanatory theory, a debate to which Cohen's *Marx's Theory of History* is the most prominent and ambitious recent contribution. I steer clear, however, of both the intricacies of the theory and the controversies surrounding it. My interest is in the problems Marx is able to resolve and the objectives he is able to advance by claiming to *have* such a theory, in what this claim allows him to *do* (how does it shape his account of the relationship between political action and political knowledge, for instance?). Furthermore, I will try to show how Marx's practice of *writing* history actually subverts the framework of his grand theory, and I argue that this textual practice is a much more fruitful source for contemporary political bricoleurs than any strictly Marxist propositions or doctrines.

59. *Manifesto*, p. 481.
60. Ibid., p. 484.
61. Ibid., pp. 497–498.
62. See ibid., p. 490.
63. Ibid., p. 470. This comment comes from a preface to a later edition of the text.
64. Ibid., p. 490.
65. Avineri has seen with particular clarity the ways in which Marx's faith in the mission of the proletariat precedes his development of any of the methods or analyses of "historical materialism." As Avineri notes, the privileged site for observing the imperatives that lead Marx to reach for the proletariat is the discussion of the need for a class with "radical chains" that concludes "A Contribution to the Critique of Hegel's Philosophy of Right: Introduction," in *Early Writings*, p. 256. See Avineri, *Social and Political Thought*, p. 34.
66. Lefort, *Democracy and Political Theory*, pp. 150, 151.
67. This is particularly the case in Anglo-American political theory. One of the few exceptions to this tendency is Michael Shapiro who, in a brief discussion of *The Eighteenth Brumaire*, illuminates the central importance of rhetoric and performance to the politics of Marx's writings on action. See *Reading the Postmodern Polity: Political Theory as Textual Practice* (Minneapolis: University of Minnesota Press, 1992), pp. 22–24. In general, however, political theorists tend to treat rhetoric as decorative, as something that can be stripped away in order to get at the "real structure" of the theory—which is then judged in relation to the methodological strictures of mainstream social science. In contrast, recent literary theorists and cultural critics have made questions of rhetoric central to their explorations of Marx's historical writings, with results that unsettle prevailing understandings of methodology. I discuss the best of these explorations in my account of *The Eighteenth Brumaire*. For representative samples of social scientific readings, see, for example, James Farr's "Science:

Realism, Criticism, History" and Terence Ball's "History: Critique and Irony," both in *The Cambridge Companion to Marx*, ed. Terrel Carver (New York: Cambridge University Press, 1991); see also the essays in Ball and Farr's edited volume, *After Marx* (New York: Cambridge University Press, 1984).

68. *Manifesto*, p. 478. For these meanings of manifesto, see the *Oxford English Dictionary* (London: Oxford University Press, 1971), pp. 1715–1716. Claude Lefort touches on this aspiration to make manifest or lay bare reality, but ignoring the performative enterprise on which it launches Marx, he presents the aspiration as the source of the text's oppressive inertness. See *Democracy and Political Theory*, pp. 153–154. I am indebted to Peter Euben and Paige Baty for helping me to think about the relationship between the etymology of the word and the rhetorical practices of Marx's text.

69. Berman, *All That Is Solid Melts into Air*, p. 91, emphasis added.

70. Ibid.

71. See, especially, ibid., pp. 109–114.

72. Stallybrass, "Marx and Heterogeneity," pp. 84–85. As he notes, this transvaluation was not *solely* the product of Marx's work, but "Marx had a crucial impact on the articulation of a concept within a political project."

73. Lefort notes the odd subject position the text offers readers, observing that "although the *Manifesto* is published in the face of the whole world, it is, despite appearances, addressed to no one. Its discourse is deployed in the pure element of generality" (*Democracy and Political Theory*, p. 154). I am trying to show that this ostensible "generality" is an attempt to construct a *particular* political identity (albeit one with universal significance), an identity that does not altogether exist prior to the work done by Marx's rhetoric. This is not to suggest that the rhetoric is itself a self-sufficient agent of world transformation; rather it is one significant moment in a process that necessarily proceeded through similar rhetorical work in a great variety of places and for diverse, even conflicting, purposes.

74. *Manifesto*, pp. 475–476. For the bourgeoisie as sorcerer and epidemic, see p. 478. For the concept of "hailing," see Louis Althusser's classic "Ideology and Ideological State Apparatuses," in his *Lenin and Philosophy and Other Essays*, trans. Ben Brewster (New York: Monthly Review Press, 1972).

75. *Hegemony*, p. 151, emphasis in the original. Laclau and Mouffe are specifically referring here to a situation diagnosed some decades ago by Arthur Rosenberg, but the larger context of their text makes it reasonable to read the "mutation" in question as the source of their own rethinking of the Marxist project.

76. *The Eighteenth Brumaire of Napoleon Bonaparte*, in *Surveys from Exile: Political Writings*, vol. 2, ed. David Fernbach (New York: Vintage, 1974), p. 154. All future references are to this edition.

77. Lefort notes this shift in complexity in *The Political Forms of Modern Society: Bureaucracy, Democracy, Totalitarianism* (Cambridge: MIT Press, 1986), p. 168. See also Meister, *Political Identity*, chaps. 5 and 6.

78. *Manifesto*, p. 490.

79. See, especially, *Eighteenth Brumaire*, pp. 142, 197.

80. Ibid., p. 174.

81. Ibid., p. 154. That Marx seeks to think problems of difference and the political production of class out of heterogeneous materials is a point made powerfully by Stallybrass, in "Marx and Heterogeneity"; see especially p. 70. In general, *The Eighteenth Brumaire*'s treatment of class as a contingent and unstable political production is one of those themes treated more instructively in the writings of cultural and literary critics than in works by Anglo-American political scientists. The most sophisticated readings, and those that have most informed this section, are provided by Stallybrass and by Sandy Petrey, "The Reality of Representation: Between Marx and Balzac," *Critical Inquiry* 14 (1988): 448–468. The analyses of Dominick LaCapra and Claude Lefort are also astute. See, respectively, *Rethinking Intellectual History*, pp. 268–290, and *Political Forms*, pp. 139–180. Though, to my mind, less persuasive, Jeffrey Mehlman's work helped open up this fruitful line of inquiry. See *Revolution and Repetition* (Berkeley: University of California Press, 1977), pp. 1–41. The most adventurous recent extension of this line is Jacques Derrida, *Spectres of Marx* (New York: Routledge, 1994). Derrida's text, which shares some of the central preoccupations of this chapter, was published too late for consideration here.

82. Marx's own famous words cannot be surpassed: "Men make their own history, but not of their own free will; not under circumstances they themselves have chosen but under the given and inherited circumstances with which they are directly confronted. The tradition of the dead generations weighs like a nightmare on the brains of the living" (*Eighteenth Brumaire*, p. 146). In Stephen Tifft's elegant formulation, Marx's argument in this essay is that our rhetorical inheritance, our "semiotic matrix," is among the circumstances that delimit the field of possible action. See "*Drôle de Guerre*: Renoir, Farce, and the Fall of France," *Representations* 38 (1992): 150–151. Marx's ability simultaneously to see the possibilities of plasticity—under the right circumstances, even iron can melt and bend—while recognizing limit and constraint, is a useful corrective to the tendency of orthodox Marxism to deny the former point and of post-Marxism to pursue that point so exuberantly that the latter caution is forgotten. Laclau and Mouffe, for example, sometimes leave no theoretical space for the weight of history, the constraints that a historically given discursive-institutional context places on political actors.

83. *Eighteenth Brumaire*, p. 214. Marx's metaphor of chemical decomposition at "high political temperature" inverts mine of forging while still illustrating my general point.

84. Ibid., p. 174.

85. Ibid., p. 175.

86. Ibid.

87. Ibid., pp. 186–190.

88. Ibid., pp. 215, 221.

89. Ibid., pp. 190, 223.

90. The answer matters a great deal. I return to the question later.

91. *Eighteenth Brumaire*, p. 197. How can one ignore problems of rhetoric in a thinker who writes this way?

92. "Marx and Heterogeneity," p. 88. My discussion is indebted to his account of the ways that the lumpen-proletariat, a "sartorial" category as much as an economic

one, "figures the political itself." Stallybrass's essay is also the best discussion of the extravagance of Marx's language for talking about this class.

93. This dimension of Marx's argument tends to be overlooked or underestimated by the critics who are so sensitive to political articulation and the rhetorical/performative aspects of the text. In contrast, Meister's reading brings great lucidity and analytical precision to the problems of strategic class analysis and Marx's critique of the democratic left. See *Political Identity*, especially Part 2.

94. *Eighteenth Brumaire*, p. 172.

95. Ibid., pp. 179–180.

96. Ibid., p. 179.

97. Ibid., p. 194.

98. Ibid., p. 150.

99. Marx writes this of History: "First of all it perfected the parliamentary power, in order to be able to overthrow it. Now, having attained this, it is perfecting the *executive power*, reducing it to its purest expression, isolating it, and pitting itself against it as the sole object of attack, in order to concentrate all of its forces of destruction against it" (ibid., p. 236). This language fits far more easily into the happy teleological categories of the *Manifesto*'s explicit theoretical structure than into the analytical problematic of forging.

100. *Eighteenth Brumaire*, p. 177.

101. Ibid., p. 123.

102. Sandy Petrey, "The Reality of Representation," p. 458.

103. I take the term from Stuart Hall, *Hard Road*, p. 261. Hall's work is among the most nuanced Left critiques of simplistic materialism, and if he is correct in identifying himself as a Marxist, it can only be in the sense that he picks up on the richest elements in works such as *The Eighteenth Brumaire*.

104. All citations here from *Eighteenth Brumaire*, pp. 238–239.

105. Ibid., p. 242.

106. Ibid., p. 239, emphasis added.

107. This point is made in: Lefort, *Political Forms*, pp. 176–177; Stallybrass, "Marx and Heterogeneity," p. 80; Mehlman, *Revolution and Repetition*.

108. *Eighteenth Brumaire*, p. 146.

109. LaCapra, *Rethinking Intellectual History*, p. 278.

110. Mehlman puts it in terms of the text's "systematic dispersion of the philosopheme of representation" (*Revolution and Repetition*, p. 21).

111. The words are Terry Eagleton's, as quoted in Petrey, "The Reality of Representation," p. 460. In this paragraph I lean on Petrey's brilliant analysis of the ways in which "class being becomes a historical fact by virtue of its successful representation" (p. 461).

112. *Eighteenth Brumaire*, p. 198. Stephen Tifft, who also cites this passage, organizes his discussion of the essay from the sensible assumption that it might be worth taking Marx seriously when he says he is recounting a "farce." See *"Drôle de Guerre,"* pp. 147–153. By paying precise attention to matters of genre, Tifft thus refines an insight elaborated by some of the best of earlier readings of the "textuality" of the world described in Marx's essay. These readings had already established that life in

that world is "lived as parody and hence textually," and that, even in criticizing duplicitous phrases, Marx shows that they are "an essential constituent, of the reality lived by France and its citizens." See, respectively, LaCapra, *Rethinking Intellectual History*, p. 282, and Petrey, "Reality of Representation," p. 455.

113. Shapiro is helpful here. See *Postmodern Polity*, pp. 22–24.

114. *Eighteenth Brumaire*, p. 163.

115. Ibid., p. 170.

116. Ibid., p. 171, emphasis added. Petrey remarks that, "Marx's identification of men and events as shadows without bodies in no way revokes the Marxist imperative to explain the world and events men produce. All that changes is the form explanation must take" ("Reality of Representation," p. 455). I think Petrey is right, but he may underestimate the formal changes required, for I think he understates both the conflicts between theory and rhetoric in Marx's text and the ambivalences constitutive of the political.

5. Acting (Up) in Publics: Mobile Spaces, Plural Worlds

1. "Regimes of the normal" is not an expression of Arendt's, but it has an Arendtian (as well as Foucaultian) resonance and even, arguably, an Arendtian provenance. I borrow it from Michael Warner, who uses it in his analysis of queer theory's mappings of and challenges to normative heterosexuality. I do not think it coincidental that Warner coins the phrase at the moment when his analysis draws on Arendt's critique of the social. See his introduction to *Fear of a Queer Planet: Queer Politics and Social Theory*, ed. Warner (Minneapolis: University of Minnesota Press, 1993), pp. xxvi–xxvii.

2. This has long been a subject of contention. The most powerful argument for taking her as an anti-democratic thinker is offered by Sheldon Wolin, "Hannah Arendt: Democracy and the Political," *Salmagundi* 60 (1983): 3–19. Among the arguments claiming the status of democrat for her, a particularly extensive and nuanced case is made by Jeffrey C. Isaac, "Oases in the Desert: Hannah Arendt on Democratic Politics," *American Political Science Review* 88, no. 1 (1994): 156–168.

3. "Mistaken" because, while there *are* elements of nostalgic mourning in her writing, they do not make the whole of her thought either an attempt to revive premodern politics or a denial of contemporary possibilities for action. Arendt's writings insist that we cannot return to the past. And while I think her reflection on the Greeks in *The Human Condition* (Chicago: University of Chicago Press, 1958) produced her most powerful idealization of public space and the political, her concern with the problem of space long precedes that work. Indeed, as Dagmar Barnouw has pointed out, the problem is crucial to and arises from the prior engagement with Jewish politics that launched her vocation as a political thinker. See Barnow, *Visible Spaces: Hannah Arendt and the German-Jewish Experience* (Baltimore: Johns Hopkins University Press, 1990), p. 77 and passim. The question of political spaces is important not only to the critique of totalitarianism that first made Arendt famous at the beginning of the 1950s but to her essays on Zionism and refugee politics from the

forties and her analysis of the salons of Berlin, written in the late twenties and early thirties. See, respectively, *The Origins of Totalitarianism* (New York: Meridian Books, 1958), *The Jew as Pariah: Jewish Identity and Politics in the Modern Age*, ed. Ron H. Feldman (New York: Grove Press, 1978), and *Rahel Varnhagen: The Life of a Jewish Woman* (New York: Harcourt Brace Jovanovich, 1974).

4. Arendt argued repeatedly that the entire canon of Western political theory is marked by a pernicious hostility to the political. The argument is central to her writing from the mid-fifties onward, but see especially the essays gathered in *Between Past and Future: Eight Exercises in Political Thought* (New York: Penguin, 1977).

5. See *On Revolution* (New York: Penguin, 1977) and "The Concept of History," in *Between Past and Future*, pp. 41–90. A still broader critique of Marx, centering on his understanding of labor, runs through *The Human Condition*.

6. Cf. *Human Condition*, pp. 10–11, 179–181.

7. By this I mean that the elements of performance in her work are explicitly argued for and do not run counter to her main theoretical propositions. Of course, for all of her use of theatrical terms and metaphors, "performative" itself is not a part of her vocabulary. This theoretical term has been imported into the literature on Arendt by Bonnie Honig, who has succeeded brilliantly in making J. L. Austin's performative/constative distinction into an interpretive key to the ambivalences and contradictions in Arendt's thought. See Honig, *Political Theory and the Displacement of Politics* (Ithaca: Cornell University Press, 1993), chap. 4, and "Toward an Agonistic Feminism: Hannah Arendt and the Politics of Identity," in *Feminists Theorize the Political*, ed. Judith Butler and Joan W. Scott (London: Routledge, 1992). My reading of Arendt owes a substantial debt to Honig's exemplary critical work. While I am in the business of acknowledging my debts, I would like to mention the other critical writings upon which I lean particularly hard over the course of this chapter: Margaret Canovan, "Politics as Culture: Hannah Arendt and the Public Realm," *History of Political Thought* 6, no. 3 (1985): 617–642; Suzanne Jacobitti, "Individualism and Political Community: Arendt and Tocqueville on the Current Debate in Liberalism," *Polity* 22, no. 4 (1991): 585–604; George Kateb, *Hannah Arendt: Politics, Conscience, Evil* (Totowa, N.J.: Rowman and Allanheld, 1983); Alan Keenan, "Promises, Promises: Hannah Arendt and the Abyss of Freedom," *Political Theory* 22, no. 2 (1994): 297–322; Melissa A. Orlie, "Thoughtless Assertion and Political Deliberation," *American Political Science Review* 88, no. 3 (1994): 684–695, and "Forgiving Trespasses, Promising Futures," in *Feminist Interpretations of Hannah Arendt*, ed. Bonnie Honig (University Park: Pennsylvania State University Press, 1995) pp. 337–356; Hanna Pitkin, "Justice: On Relating Public and Private," *Political Theory* 9, no. 3 (1981): 327–352, and "Conformism, Housekeeping, and the Attack of the Blob: Hannah Arendt's Concept of the Social," in *Feminist Interpretations*, ed. Honig, pp. 51–81.

8. Much recent writing on Arendt has debated whether or not Arendt's thought should be thought of as most fundamentally influenced by Aristotle, Heidegger, Kant, or Nietzsche. For useful overviews of the argument, see Dana Villa, "Beyond Good and Evil: Arendt, Nietzsche, and the Aestheticization of Political Action," *Political Theory* 20, no. 2 (1992): 274–308, and especially, "Postmodernism and the Public Sphere," *American Political Science Review* 86, no. 3 (1992): 712–721. Tocque-

ville's absence from this debate has, I suspect, more to do with his having less cachet among those now interested in continental philosophy than with the degree of his actual importance to Arendt: she not only borrowed from him in important ways but also tended to place him among the theorists least hostile to politics. A particularly direct expression of her enthusiasm for him comes in her essay, "Civil Disobedience" in *Crises of the Republic* (New York: Harcourt Brace Jovanovich, 1972), pp. 94–98 and passim. That said, I am not trying to replace any of the above thinkers with Tocqueville or to claim him as the central figure for Arendt's writings. She makes use of all of these theorists in creative and even idiosyncratic ways, and is very much an independent thinker. Furthermore, the debate over her intellectual genealogy is primarily—and, from my point of view, appropriately—not a historiographical problem but a struggle over how to align her in contemporary political and theoretical skirmishes. Of the recent readings, I find the Nietzschean alignments the most politically congenial and theoretically stimulating (moreso even than those responses that *have* stressed the Tocquevilliean dimension), but I think that the Nietzschean Arendt can be made considerably more responsive to the spaces of contemporary publicity by drawing out her conversation with Tocqueville and Marx. For works that recognize Tocqueville's contribution to Arendt's thought, see Seyla Benhabib, "Hannah Arendt and the Redemptive Power of Narrative," *Social Research* 57, no. 1 (1990): 167–196; Jacobitti, "Individualism and Political Community"; Wolin, "Hannah Arendt."

9. The person who has made this point most directly is Margaret Canovan, who distinguishes between "subjectivist" approaches to politics and Arendt's "world-centered" approach ("Politics as Culture," p. 637). See also Canovan's more complete, but less useful, *Hannah Arendt: A Reinterpretation of Her Political Thought* (New York: Cambridge University Press, 1992), especially pp. 106–116. I think Canovan is fundamentally mistaken in her dismissal of Arendt's significant and (for my purposes) very useful concern with the politics of subjectivity. But that concern is best appreciated from within a recognition of what Canovan correctly identifies as Arendt's emphasis on the worldly spaces between subjects. Canovan's excellent account of those spaces (see also "Politics as Culture," pp. 634–635) informs my own. I have also benefited from Suzanne Jacobitti's comparison between Arendt and Tocqueville, though my readings and political projects differ substantially from hers. Jacobitti does not use the specific terminology of subject and world, but more or less implies such a distinction in her praise of Arendt's refusal of Tocqueville's embrace of religious consensus and other "habits of the heart." See "Individualism and Political Community," especially pp. 596–598.

10. Arendt, *Human Condition*, p. 57. My own langauge here slips from "political" to "public," as I previously slid from freedom to democracy, but this time I follow Arendt's own move: she tends to link the public and the political so closely as to make them almost interchangeable.

11. Ibid., pp. 175, 7.

12. I am indebted to comments from William Connolly for help in clarifying my argument on this point.

13. This frustration is expressed so widely in the Arendt literature that it is hard to single out examples, but for a classic expression see Mary McCarthy's direct ques-

tions to Arendt at a conference on the latter's work, reprinted in *Hannah Arendt: The Recovery of the Public World*, ed. Melvin Hill (New York: St. Martin's, 1979), pp. 315–316; and Pitkin, "Justice," p. 336.

14. My remarks in this paragraph are informed by Alan Keenan's probing exploration of the ways in which violence and rule necessarily return to the political despite Arendt's efforts to purge them. Keenan, "Promises, Promises," especially pp. 299, 309, 316–318.

15. The words quoted are from *Human Condition*, p. 234, but my remarks here also paraphrase the argument of ibid., p. 222; "What Is Freedom?" pp. 163–165; and *On Revolution*, pp. 30–33, 76–77.

16. *On Revolution*'s last chapter, a sustained attempt to theorize the organs of government constituted through revolutionary action, displays this tension repeatedly; see, for instance, her discussion of the fundamental conflicts between action and representation, politics and administration, pp. 272–275. It is true that Arendt elsewhere complicates her evasion of rule when she suggests that a special form of sovereignty can achieve "a certain limited reality": this is a sovereignty based not on the unity of will but on the agreement of a political body bound by mutual promises to pursue a particular purpose. *Human Condition*, p. 245. Yet as Keenan argues, the moment the promise does become particular, then coercion necessarily reenters politics ("Promises, Promises," p. 309).

17. *Between Past and Future*, pp. 153, 146.

18. Honig, "Toward an Agonistic Feminism," pp. 216–220, 231, and *Political Theory and the Displacement of Politics*, pp. 78–82. She recognizes not only Arendt's identification of politics with performance but also many of the difficulties posed by the attempt to keep performance pure. I think, however, that Honig tends to capture the invention of selfhood in action while ignoring the expressivist elements suggested by Arendt's language of "revelation." Kateb's earlier work offers a helpful correction on this point, acknowledging both elements (though I am not persuaded by his argument that these elements form the bases of two separate and incompatible theories of action). See Kateb, *Hannah Arendt*, pp. 10, 43. For a key passage in which the indeterminacy of the expressivist and performative impulses can be seen, see *Human Condition*, p. 179.

19. *Human Condition*, pp. 176–177.

20. Particularly strong instances of Arendt's argument that politics is about the world not the self are offered in "Civil Disobedience," *Crises of the Republic*, p. 60; and "Freedom and Politics," in *Freedom and Serfdom*, ed. A. Hunold (Dordrecht, Holland: D. Reidel, 1961), p. 200. For other important examples of Arendt's insistence that worldly interests inform action, see *Human Condition*, p. 182; "On Humanity in Dark Times: Thoughts about Lessing" in *Men in Dark Times* (New York: Harcourt Brace Jovanovich, 1968), pp. 13–17; "The Crisis in Culture," *Between Past and Future*, p. 223.

21. *On Revolution*, pp. 48, 91.

22. *Human Condition*, p. 28.

23. This particular characterization is from *On Revolution*, p. 122, but concisely captures a main point of Arendt's argument in *Human Condition*.

24. *Human Condition*, p. 30.

25. Ibid., p. 41.
26. Ibid., p. 23.
27. Ibid., p. 28
28. Ibid., p. 46.
29. Ibid., p. 7.
30. Ibid., pp. 46, 126.
31. *Human Condition*, p. 39.
32. Ibid., pp. 214, 213.
33. Ibid., p. 40.
34. Ibid., p. 40. Arendt notes elsewhere in writing of bureaucracy that, traditionally, tyranny means "government that is not held to give an account of itself" (*Crisis of the Republic*, p. 137).
35. *Human Condition*, p. 43. See also *Between Past and Future*, p. 150. Arendt extends her argument about this connection between normalization and the rise of the social through comments on the development of behavioral social science. She sees that development as both an expression of and a contributor to the withering of politics: the social sciences have grown up in a symbiotic relationship to bureaucracy. Her rejection of behavioral social science is not based on its faulty epistemology but the fear that its epistemological premises may help advance the very transformations of politics she is questioning: "The trouble with modern theories of behaviorism is not that they are wrong but that they could become true, that they actually are the best possible conceptualization of certain obvious trends in modern society" (*Human Condition*, p. 322). The connection between normalization, statistics, and the growth of the administrative state is, of course, one of Foucault's great themes. Despite the underlying differences between the aims and approaches of the two theorists, Foucault's accounts of both "governmentality" and "biopower" have particularly strong affinities with Arendt's argument here. I bear these affinitites in mind, below, when I turn Arendt's critique of normalization against her purification of politics.
36. *On Revolution*, pp. 249, 257.
37. Ibid., p. 68. This assertion is what makes her utter refusal of rule all the more paradoxical and disabling.
38. Ibid., p. 48.
39. Ibid., pp. 94, 60, 114.
40. Ibid., p. 94.
41. See, for example, Ibid., p. 91. There are other important sources of Arendt's critique of the political consequences of the preoccupation with the social. Much of her early writing on the modern European Jewish experience suggests that the prevalent perception (among both Jews and gentiles) of "the Jewish question" as one of social oppression stunted the growth of a Jewish politics of freedom and helped to pave the way for the genocidal anti-Semitisms of this century. A full account of the historical unfolding of Arendt's thought would begin with this problem, but that is not my purpose here. Astute explorations of the social in Arendt's early writings can be found in Pitkin, "Conformism," and Morris Kaplan, "Refiguring the Jewish Question: Arendt, Proust, and the Politics of Sexuality," also in *Feminist Interpretations*, ed. Honig.

42. See "Reflections on Little Rock," *Dissent* 6, no. 1 (1959): 45–56. Arendt argues there that, though the desire to maintain segregated schools is despicable, compulsory desegregation violates parents' constitutional right to free association and mistakenly attempts to impose the *political* value of equality on "purely social" matters. The theorist of revelatory, world-transforming action here denies legitimacy even to a *democratic movement* struggling for social equality. It is hard not to wonder whether the blackness of the bodies struggling for change fundamentally shapes Arendt's response to this issue. Despite her own remark that, as a Jew, she trusted that her sympathies for blacks could be taken for granted (p. 46), Arendt's (brief and sporadic) writings on the deeds of black political actors are marked by a noticeable degree of condescension and/or suspicion. From her comments on colonialism in *The Origins of Totalitarianism* to her responses to Black Power in *Crises of the Republic,* Arendt seems disinclined to see such action as genuinely political. But whatever impulses lie behind her hostility, it is only because of the way she frames the problem of political and social that she is *able* to take the stand she does.

43. For a particularly clear instance of Arendt's claim that action defies the vocabulary of ends and means, see *Human Condition*, p. 207; for this sense of administration see *On Revolution*, pp. 272–274. Also helpful are Arendt's remarks in *Hannah Arendt: The Recovery of the Public World*, ed. Hill, p. 318, and Richard Bernstein's excellent discussion of them in his *Philosophical Profiles* (Philadelphia: University of Pennsylvania Press, 1986), pp. 251–253. I am indebted to that discussion.

44. See, for instance, *On Revolution*, p. 56.

45. Fraser, *Unruly Practices: Power, Discourse, and Gender in Contemporary Social Theory* (Minneapolis: University of Minnesota Press, 1989), pp. 162, 160.

46. Pitkin, "Justice," p. 333, and "Conformism," pp. 20–25 and passim. Like many others, I am in Pitkin's debt. Among those who make similar distinctions are Kateb, *Hannah Arendt*, p. 24, and Honig, *Political Theory and the Displacement of Politics*, p. 222.

47. For instance, her remarks that "Wherever the relevance of speech is at stake, matters become political by definition" and that "An organization . . . is always a political institution; where men organize, they intend to act and to acquire power" (*Human Condition*, pp. 3, 271).

48. Honig, "Toward an Agonistic Feminism," p. 226.

49. Honig, *Political Theory and the Displacement of Politics*, p. 124.

50. To be fair, Honig's argument about the performative/constative distinction is offered as a critique of any theory, Arendt's included, that celebrates the performative without recognizing the unavoidable role of the constative (thus she follows Derrida against Arendt on the problem of founding). But even her acknowledgment of the constative moment is offered in an account that equates politics with resistance to that moment. Alan Keenan briefly notes this problem in Honig's work, "Promises, Promises," p. 322, n. 10.

51. The argument that politics necessarily intermingles the Arendtian what and the Arendtian who because of the ways our bodies and locations impinge upon others runs throughout both Orlie's "Forgiving Trespasses" (see, especially, pp. 4–5, 17) and "Thoughtless Assertion." Another valuable treatment of the intertwining of the who and the what can be found in Susan Bickford, "In the Presence of Others: Arendt

and Anzaldúa on the Paradox of Appearance," in *Feminist Interpretations*, ed. Honig, pp. 320-326. My arguments here and in the next paragraph have profitted greatly from these works.

52. *Human Condition*, p. 199.

53. Patton, "Tremble, Hetero Swine!" in *Fear of a Queer Planet*, ed. Warner, p. 145.

54. *Jew as Pariah*, p. 68. Also instructive is her remark about her own experiences as a Jew in the fight against Nazism: "one can resist only in terms of the identity under attack" ("On Humanity in Dark Times," p. 18).

55. *Jew as Pariah*, p. 77. See also ibid., p. 122.

56. See Bickford, "In the Presence of Others"; Orlie, "Forgiving Trespasses, Promising Futures," and "Thoughtless Assertion"; and Lisa Jane Disch, *Hannah Arendt and the Limits of Philosophy* (Ithaca: Cornell University Press, 1994), especially pp. 182-184.

57. Bonnie Honig makes this point persuasively in "Agonistic Feminism," pp. 229-231. But see also Orlie's use of the pariah in the elaboration of her insights into the limits of Arendt's most problematic purifications.

58. Surprisingly, one of the most sustained of them comes in *On Revolution*'s initial framing of "the social question." Arendt begins by pausing on Marx's "place in the history of human freedom," offering a divided judgment. One half of her response is fully consonant with her critique of the revolutionary focus on social matters: Marx ultimately corrupted the spirit of revolution by making necessity the governing category of his political thinking. In his mature work, the point of revolution was not "to liberate men from the oppression of their fellow men, let alone to found freedom, but to liberate the life process of society from the fetters of scarcity so that it could swell into a stream of abundance." But Arendt also suggests that the young Marx made a genuine contribution to human freedom, a contribution obscured and abandoned, but not invalidated, by his later work. Initially, she finds, Marx took relationships widely perceived as necessary and redescribed them as resting on human violence. By arguing that "poverty itself is a political, not a natural phenomenon," he "summoned up a spirit of rebelliousness that can only come from being violated." He articulated the call to rebellion "in political terms, as an uprising, not for the sake of bread or wealth, but for the sake of freedom as well." The young Marx thus wrought a "transformation of the social question into a political force." (All of the quoted remarks come from pp. 62-64.) This emphasis on transformation points toward a reading of political possibilities at odds with the book's major conclusions about the revolutionary tradition, but Arendt soon drops the discussion and does not pursue the path it suggests.

59. "Civil Disobedience," p. 89.

60. *On Revolution*, p. 269.

61. "What Is Freedom?" p. 149; *On Revolution*, p. 33.

62. *Human Condition*, p. 200. On newness, see pp. 8-9, 177-178.

63. Ibid., pp. 180, 176.

64. Ibid., p. 182.

65. Ibid., p. 57.

66. "Truth and Politics," p. 241. But this thought is most powerfully expressed in *Eichmann in Jerusalem* (New York: Penguin Books, 1965). There, Arendt argues that Eichmann was able to do what he did largely because he had "an inability to *think*, namely to think from the standpoint of somebody else." Because of this, he was "surrounded by the most reliable of all safeguards against the words and the presence of others, and hence against reality as such" (p. 49). Her analysis makes this in part a matter of his mentality, and in part an artifact of the language and procedures of the Nazi bureaucracy; but it is also crucial to her analysis that the structure of that bureaucracy undermined the *spaces* necessary to such "representative thinking."

67. Emphasis added. The words quoted are from *Human Condition*, p. 198, but the basic argument runs throughout Arendt's treatment of action in that book, as well as her account of the revolutionary tradition in *On Revolution* and the essays on political struggle in *Crises of the Republic*.

68. *On Revolution*, p. 264.

69. Ibid., pp. 267, 277.

70. Ibid., p. 278.

71. Ibid., p. 267; on the conflict between this model, on the one hand, and party and nation-state on the other, see pp. 245–247.

72. *On Revolution*, p. 279.

73. "Civil Disobedience," p. 77. Arendt treats Tocqueville's writings on association as the crucial source for understanding the American traditions of civil disobedience, an egalitarian way of constituting power relations. She quotes Tocqueville in arguing that this manner of acting together brings "into one channel the efforts of *divergent* minds" and thus preserves the diversity-within-unity necessary to political community (ibid., p. 98).

74. *On Revolution*, p. 275.

75. See, for instance, ibid., pp. 30, 33, 120, 267, 270.

76. Wolin, "Hannah Arendt," p. 3.

77. A classic example is "The Crisis in Culture," *Between Past and Future*, pp. 197–226.

78. *Human Condition*, p. 55.

79. Bruce Robbins, introduction to *The Phantom Public Sphere*, ed. Robbins (Minneapolis: University of Minnesota Press, 1993), p. xix.

80. Wolin, "Hannah Arendt," p. 7.

81. See, especially, "Civil Disobedience."

82. *On Revolution*, p. 279. In "Oases in the Desert," Isaac makes much of this remark in developing his rich reading of Arendt as a theorist of "grass roots" democracy. This reading has significant parallels to my own, particularly in its emphasis on Arendtian spaces that can supplement or push against the institutions of more conventional electoral politics. Isaac is both serious and instructive about the pluralization of Arendtian political spaces, but he imposes all-too-Arendtian limitations on this project for he too is seduced by the quest for purity. He treats all of the mass-mediated forms of culture as intrinsically inauthentic, presenting Arendtian politics as a turning away from, a source of alternatives to, the impossible conformism of mass society rather than a project that engages that society on its own terrain. Re-

latedly, he characterizes Arendtian spaces as open to citizens from all identities and social locations, but he obscures the possibilities of and the need for politicizing those identities and locations.

83. Both the quote and my description of the event are taken from Douglas Crimp with Adam Rolston, *AIDS demo graphics* (Seattle: Bay Press, 1990), pp. 76–83. This exemplary book offers by far the most detailed narrative of ACT UP's internal dynamics, key demonstrations, and distinctive style, focusing primarily on the New York chapter. Though I draw heavily on their account, and thus most often base my reflections on that chapter, my analysis is not a political sociology or narrative history of one organization. My discussion therefore blurs the differences among the ACT UP chapters in different cities, and between ACT UP and related groups. This discussion also offers no new factual information, for I have done no original empirical study of AIDS politics. Rather, I am reflecting on certain features of the activism visible in the literature on it, in order both to illuminate the problems laid out in my prior discussions of Arendt and to show how a resistant reading of her work can interpret these features. I am, frankly, concerned that this approach to the struggle runs the risk of turning AIDS, one of the great tragedies of our time, into mere grist for the academic mill of textual commentary on canonical theorists. That ACT UP arose out of rage against insular responses to AIDS only heightens my concern. This concern about my own reading is in no way a generic suspicion of theorizing AIDS, for I think such work is vital. Perhaps the most obvious theoretical task is to make sense of the obscene indifference and inaction (not to mention the fear and violent homophobia) with which Federal and State governments, both political parties, and most members of the straight population have greeted the crisis. This chapter does not take up that task. But despite my worries about using the life and death struggle over AIDS in the context of this book, I am also persuaded, as I argue below, that it is politically important to think about the forms of publicity created by ACT UP and the way these opened spaces for democratic struggle against contemporary regimes of the normal. Whether or not it succeeds, my discussion is an attempt to capture how those spaces worked and, thus, to register certain political possibilities to which prevailing ways of thinking often blind us. In making that attempt I have drawn on three kinds of sources: recent work in queer theory; scholarly writings on ACT UP and the broader cultural politics of AIDS and AIDS activism; and journalistic coverage of activism in both the queer and "mainstream" press. I cite relevant sources whenever appropriate, but I here note a few works, in addition to Crimp and Rolston's book, that are particularly central to my account of ACT UP: Douglas Crimp, ed., *AIDS: Cultural Analysis, Cultural Activism* (Cambridge: MIT Press, 1988); Steven Epstein, "Democratic Science? AIDS Activism and the Contested Construction of Knowledge," *Socialist Review* 2 (1991): 35–64; Joshua Gamson, "Silence, Death, and the Invisible Enemy: AIDS Activism and Social Movement 'Newness,'" in *Ethnography Unbound: Power and Resistance in the Modern Metropolis*, ed. Michael Burawoy et al. (Berkeley: University of California Press, 1991); Cindy Patton, *Inventing AIDS* (London: Routledge, 1990); Paula Treichler, "How to Have Theory in an Epidemic," in *Technoculture*, ed. Constance Penley and Andrew Ross (Minneapolis: University of Minnesota

Press, 1991); Simon Watney and Erica Carter, eds., *Taking Liberties: AIDS and Cultural Politics* (London: Serpent's Tail, 1989); Warner, ed., *Fear of a Queer Planet*.

84. The words quoted, which are read before each of ACT UP New York's weekly Monday evening meetings, are cited in Crimp with Rolston, *AIDS demo*, p. 13. For information on the locations and size of ACT UP chapters, see ibid. and Gamson, "Silence, Death," p. 36. Though ACT UP chapters are largely autonomous, they were, at the time of the FDA protest federated in the Washington, D.C.-based ACT NOW.

85. Each of these events is described in Crimp with Rolston, *AIDS demo*.

86. I do not claim to offer a careful assessment of ACT UP's current status, and many of my comments are inaccurate as descriptions of present circumstances. The most instructive literature currently available focuses on this earlier period, and as my purpose in this theoretical reflection is not to conduct original research, I have confined myself largely to what the literature reveals. Still, it is worth noting that while a few ACT UP chapters remain active, the organization has largely atrophied and it no longer plays the central role in struggles over AIDS policy that it did at the time upon which I focus. My understanding is that the style of politics I describe here has expanded its presence in various broader forms of queer struggle while becoming less visible in AIDS activism. Of course, this suggests reasons for being cautious in drawing general conclusions from the initial period of AIDS insurgency; I address these reasons in my concluding remarks.

87. Many commentators and participants have written about the direct influence of poststructural theorists, particularly Foucault, as well as that of postmodern artists and art critics, on the formation of ACT UP. See, for instance, Crimp with Rolston, *AIDS demo*, pp. 18–19; Patton, *Inventing AIDS*, p. 162; Daniel Harris, "AIDS & Theory," *Lingua Franca* (June 1992): 18. But though, as I discuss below, Arendt's work has informed some recent theoretical writings on queer politics, it is not invoked in ACT UP discourse. True, in his *Reports from the Holocaust* (New York: St. Martin's Press, 1989), Larry Kramer, a pivotal figure in the founding of ACT UP, does invoke Arendt: he uses *Eichmann in Jerusalem* (New York: Penguin, 1977) in making his argument about the ways in which gay forms of consumption have drawn homophobic responses. But as Morris Kaplan argues, Kramer's commentary has little to do with Arendt's theoretical terms or project, and, I would add, this particular invocation of Arendt has still less to do with the Arendtian resonances in ACT UP's organizational life. See Kaplan, "Refiguring the Jewish Question," p. 111.

88. On love, see, for instance, *Human Condition*, pp. 50–52. The quoted words on life come from ibid., p. 37. They refer to attitudes in the polis, but clearly reflect Arendt's views as well.

89. That the councils were considerably more engaged with questions of economic power than Arendt acknowledged is a point that has been made many times. See, for instance, John F. Sitton, "Hannah Arendt's Argument for Council Democracy," in *Hannah Arendt: Critical Essays*, ed. Lewis P. Hinchman and Sandra K. Hinchman (Albany: State University of New York Press, 1994), pp. 322–323.

90. Throughout the chapter, I tend to use "queer" when speaking inclusively of

gay men, lesbians, and bisexuals. Currently, as I understand it, queer functions both as such a designator and as a term, forged in struggle, that names an alternative way of mapping sexuality and identity. My usage moves back and forth between those senses. Terminology of this kind is, of course, neither politically nor theoretically innocent, and no choice is an entirely happy one. One problem with using queer as an umbrella term for gays, bisexuals, and lesbians, in this context, is that some of the activists so named would not have identified themselves in this way. But no other choice would be unproblemmatical either, and using "queer" highlights AIDS activism's vital role in the political growth of anti-assimilationist sexual dissent. Provocative and nuanced discussions of the recent lexical shift to "queer," can be found in Donna Penn, "Queer: Theorizing Politics and History," *Radical History Review* 62 (1995): 39; R. Anthony Slagle, "In Defense of Queer Nation: From *Identity Politics* to a *Politics of Difference*," *Western Journal of Communication* 59 (1995): 85–102; Warner, introduction to *Fear of a Queer Planet*; Simon Watney, "Queer Epistemology: Activism, Outing, and the Politics of Sexual Identity," *Critical Quarterly* 36, no. 1 (1994): 13–27.

91. Treichler, "How to Have Theory," p. 75; Crimp with Rolston, *AIDS demo*, p. 37.

92. Treichler, "How to Have Theory," p. 57.

93. Ibid., p. 76.

94. Crimp with Rolston, *AIDS demo*, pp. 79–81.

95. On these changes, see ibid., pp. 81–83, and Treichler, "How to Have Theory," p. 91.

96. Treichler, "How to Have Theory," p. 69. Epstein's "Democratic Science?" is also helpful on this point. There is an oversimplification in speaking of ACT UP as an "it" in this context and, hence, in the sweep of my claim about the dismissal of science. Activists, of course, differ in their convictions and sensibilities. Certain more categorical "New Age" dismissals of "Western" medical practice are to be found among a few activists and more PWA's, just as among those with cancer—it is not surprising that an extremely dangerous virus (HIV) and a fatal syndrome (AIDS), for which conventional medicine has at least so far been unable to devise cures, occasion such responses. But I describe the predominant response within groups such as ACT UP. A good discussion of diverse attitudes can be found in "How to Have Theory," pp. 83–93.

97. On the importance of specialized knowledges acquired by queer communities and their uses in waging the struggle over the public meaning of AIDS, see Crimp, "How to Have Promiscuity in an Epidemic," in *AIDS: Cultural Analysis*, ed. Crimp, pp. 237–271.

98. The first quoted phrase is from Paula Treichler's "AIDS, Homophobia, and Biomedical Discourse: An Epidemic of Signification," in *AIDS: Cultural Analysis*, ed. Crimp. The second quotation is from Patton, *Inventing AIDS*, p. 129. The role of immunology in constituting the self-other boundary is explored by Donna Haraway in "The Biopolitics of Postmodern Bodies: Constitutions of Self in Immune System Discourse," in her *Simians, Cyborgs, and Women: The Reinvention of Nature*. Gamson emphasizes the importance to ACT UP of the fight against "stigmatization" by medicine, "Silence, Death," p. 47.

99. I have particularly benefited from accounts of the confrontation with normalization that are central to both Gamson, "Silence, Death" and the last chapter of Patton, *Inventing AIDS*.

100. Queer Nation was founded at an ACT UP New York meeting in April of 1990.

101. Duggan, "Making it Perfectly Queer," *Socialist Review* 22, no. 1: 11–31, p. 20. As Duggan points out, "queer" identities may align less clearly along lines of gender than do "gay" and "lesbian." It seems clear to me, to take just one example, that both political allegiances and sexual relationships among today's self-identified queer undergraduates differ fundamentally from the more rigid and gender-segregated ones of fifteen or twenty years ago.

102. Warner, introduction to *Fear of a Queer Planet*, ed. Warner, pp. xxvi–xxvii. Warner perhaps pushes into a kind of utopianism in implying that this politics points toward an escape from social norms as such, but his reflections have helped me to see the critical leverage provided by Arendt's account of the social.

103. *Human Condition*, p. 200. To put the point flippantly: if there were a contest to design an Arendtian bumpersticker, "ACT UP" would be an outstanding entry. Of course, among the Arendtian views rejected by ACT UP's challenges to (often technical) *structures* and *discourses* of normalizing power is her claim (made in the second half of the sentence from which my quote is drawn) that power "vanishes" as soon as actors "disperse." This exemplifies my earlier argument that it is possible to read Arendt's insights into the social against her too-tidy distinction between violence and power and, thus, to recognize the multiple forms of power as domination without abandoning her account of the spaces of empowerment.

104. Crimp with Rolston, *AIDS demo*, p. 34.

105. On affinity groups in ACT UP see ibid., p. 20, and Simon Watney, *Practices of Freedom: Selected Writings on HIV-AIDS* (Durham, N.C.: Duke University Press, 1994), pp. 154–159. In his discussion, Watney hails Arendt's vision of public plurality as a crucial resource for understanding the most radical possibilities of AIDS activism. I think, however, that this brief invocation of her is limited by Watney's embrace of her evasive conception of a politics wholly disconnected from the problem of sovereignty.

106. Borddowitz, "Picture a Coalition," in *AIDS: Cultural Analysis*, ed. Crimp, p. 195.

107. Crimp with Rolston, *AIDS demo*, p. 36. As they report, the symbol actually preceded ACT UP's formation by six months, but became the ubiquitous icon of the group's early actions.

108. These graphics reprinted or in ibid., pp. 90, 56, 64, 67.

109. The term is Warner's (*Fear of a Queer Planet*, ed. Warner, p. xxi).

110. Michael Cunningham offers this report of a Queer Nation "kiss-in" in a straight bar: "I ask a straight-looking guy in a crew neck sweater what he thought about all this. 'All *what?*' he asked. 'Those people over there,' I said. 'The ones who are kissing. The ones with the stickers that say "Queer." ' He looked calmly at a pair of tattooed men who were kissing passionately among a bevy of big-haired secretaries sipping margaritas. He shrugged. 'Guess it means they're queer.' " Cunningham, "If

You're Queer and You're Not Angry in 1992, You're Not Paying Attention," *Mother Jones* (May/June 1992), p. 62.

111. On the importance of using media against normalization, see Gamson, "Silence, Death," p. 47.

112. The quote is from an anonymous broadside distributed at Gay Pride parades in New York and Chicago in 1990, quoted in Lauren Berlant and Elizabeth Freeman, "Queer Nationality," in *Fear of a Queer Planet*, ed. Warner, p. 201, and usefully discussed pp. 200–202. Other useful discussions of the shift to an emphasis on publicity are provided by T. Geltmaker, "The Queer Nation Acts Up: Health Care, Politics, and Sexual Diversity in the County of Angels," *Environment and Planning D: Society and Space* 10 (1992): 609–615, and Duggan, "Making it Perfectly Queer."

113. The role of heterosexually coded general publics in facilitating government inaction and popular indifference to AIDS is discussed in many accounts, but particularly helpful is Jan Zita Grover, "AIDS: Keywords" in *AIDS: Cultural Analysis*, ed. Crimp, p. 23.

114. *Human Condition*, pp. 198–199.

115. Patton, *Inventing AIDS*, p. 131.

116. Arendtian thought, I am trying to say, is a valuable resource for thinking amidst these dilemmas, but is not itself a sufficient account of them. Nor, to say the least, is my reflection on her. Here, as earlier, I am marking a problem that I think crucial, but which I do not explore in a sustained way in this work. In addition to Connolly's "Democracy and Territoriality," and the other recent works on globalization cited in previous chapters, I call the reader's attention to Michael J. Shapiro and Hayward Alker, eds., *Challenging Boundaries: Global Flows, Territorial Identities* (Minneapolis: University of Minnesota Press, 1995), which gives these dilemmas the scrutiny they deserve.

117. The foregoing and other examples of cross-territorial demonstration are in Crimp with Rolston, *AIDS demo*. Reflections on the cultural differences separating American activism from that of Europeans can be found in Watney, "Queer Epistemology," and John Borneman, "AIDS in the Two Berlins," in *AIDS: Cultural Analysis*, ed. Crimp.

118. As this book goes to press, it is beginning to look as if this statement should be revised fundamentally: some very recent evaluations of the use of "protease inhibitors" in combination with AZT and other drugs have suggested that a life-sustaining revolution in treatment is, in fact, at hand. Other scientific evaluations have been more skeptical, however; and even if the new treatment proves to be a medical turning point, at present the cost—well over $10,000 per person per year—is sufficiently high that it may prove unaffordable to a substantial percentage of people with AIDS. The politics of AIDS treatment is hardly over, and many of the equity issues with which ACT UP began are likely to endure for a long time.

119. Gamson, "Silence, Death," pp. 39–42, 50; Crimp with Rolston, *AIDS demo*, p. 58.

120. See Douglas Crimp, "Right on Girlfriend," in *Fear of a Queer Planet*, ed. Warner, pp. 300–320.

Index

Action: administration and, 155; normalizing power and, 152; personhood and, 147; republicanism and, 166; space created by, 142, 161; worldliness and, 148
ACT UP (organization), 9, 17, 149, 159, 166–178
Administrative bureaucracy. *See* Bureaucracy
Affinity groups, 172, 173
African Americans. *See* Black Americans
Agricultural bourgeoisie, 127
Agricultural workers, 134–135, 136
AIDS activism, xiii, 149, 166–178
Althusser, Louis, 204n.12
American Indians, 27, 64, 195n.5
American Revolution, 37, 153
Ancient households, 150, 152
Anglo-American civilization, 73
Appadurai, Arjun, 3, 181n.3
Arendt, Hannah, x, xiii, 6–12, 16, 19, 142–178
— *The Human Condition*: on political spaces, 165; queer politics and, 172, 174–175; on social realm, 150, 154, 158; on worldly interests, 160
— Marx and. *See under* Marx, Karl
— *On Revolution*, 165; on action, 147; on councils, 153; on democracy, 160; on elementary republics, 166; on social realm, 150, 154
— Tocqueville and, 88, 143–145, 148, 149, 155; governance and, 164; inequalities and, 154
— "Walter Benjamin," 180n.8
Aristocracy, 24, 33, 34, 35. *See also* Monarchy
Aristotle, x, 217n.8

Associations, 39–40, 88
Athens, 37, 143, 152, 153
Austin, J. L., 217n.7
Authority, 75, 77, 78, 84, 85. *See also* Despotism; Enforcement measures; Hierarchies; Sovereignty
Avineri, Shlomo, 209n.45, 212n.65
AZT (drug), 167, 169

Barnouw, Dagmar, 216n.3
Baty, Paige, 179n.5
Baudrillard, Jean, 91
Bauer, Bruno, 99, 207n.31
Beaumont de la Bonninière, Gustave-Auguste de, 193n.86, 196n.17
Bellah, Robert, 12, 26, 183n.16
Bentham, Jeremy, 187n.22
Berlin, Isaiah, 188n.26
Berman, Marshall, 119
Bhabha, Homi K., 19, 90
Bickford, Susan, 221–222n.51
Black Americans, 4. *See also* Desegregation
Black slaves, 27, 63–66, 69, 70–71
Boesche, Roger, 22, 39, 190n.54
Bonaparte, Louis [Napoleon III], 123–138
Bonapartism, 123–138
Booth, William James, 204nn.9, 11
Bordowitz, Gregg, 173
Bourbon family, 127
Bourgeoisie: American, 26, 50, 60–61, 177; *Communist Manifesto* on, 93, 110, 111, 113, 120–121; *Eighteenth Brumaire* on, 126, 127, 128, 129, 133, 134–135, 136; "On the Jewish Question" on, 99–100, 106; rights of, 108. *See also* Petty bourgeoisie

229

CONTESTATIONS

CORNELL STUDIES IN POLITICAL THEORY

A series edited by
WILLIAM E. CONNOLLY

The Other Heidegger
  by Fred Dallmayr
Allegories of America: Narratives, Metaphysics, Politics
  by Frederick M. Dolan
united states
  by Thomas L. Dumm
Intimacy and Spectacle: Liberal Theory as Political Education
  by Stephen L. Esquith
Political Theory and the Displacement of Politics
  by Bonnie Honig
The Self at Liberty: Political Argument and the Arts of Government
  by Duncan Ivison
The Inner Ocean: Individualism and Democratic Culture
  by George Kateb
The Anxiety of Freedom: Imagination and Individuality in Locke's Political Thought
  by Uday Singh Mehta
The Art of Being Free: Taking Liberties with Tocqueville, Marx, and Arendt
  by Mark Reinhardt
Political Theory for Mortals: Shades of Justice, Images of Death
  by John E. Seery
Signifying Woman: Culture and Chaos in Rousseau, Burke, and Mill
  by Linda M. G. Zerilli